D1560096

COLONEL HAMILTON
AND COLONEL BURR

COLONEL HAMILTON AND COLONEL BURR

The Revolutionary War Lives of Alexander Hamilton and Aaron Burr

ARTHUR S. LEFKOWITZ

STACKPOLE BOOKS

Lanham • Boulder • New York • London

Published by Stackpole Books
An imprint of The Rowman & Littlefield Publishing Group, Inc.
4501 Forbes Blvd., Ste. 200
Lanham, MD 20706
www.rowman.com

Distributed by NATIONAL BOOK NETWORK

Maps by Melissa Baker

British Library Cataloguing in Publication Information available

Library of Congress Cataloging-in-Publication Data available

ISBN 978-0-8117-3857-6 (cloth: alk. paper)
ISBN 978-0-8117-6854-2 (electronic)

♾™ The paper used in this publication meets the minimum requirements of
American National Standard for Information Sciences—Permanence of Paper
for Printed Library Materials, ANSI/NISO Z39.48-1992.

Whoever looks upon them as an irregular mob,
will find himself much mistaken.
They have men amongst them who know very well what they are
about . . .

—British General Hugh Earl Percy in a letter
to a fellow officer in England sent from Boston
at the start of the American Revolution

This book is dedicated to my friend Dr. Richard Prouty, MD.

Doctor Prouty shared my interest in the American Revolution and joined me on many research trips. Dr. Prouty died before I began work on this book. However, some of his research was used in writing it and I am pleased to have this opportunity to honor him and acknowledge his help.

CONENTS

PREFACE

O ne would be hard-pressed to find a figure in American history more controversial than Aaron Burr. There are numerous biographies of his life that present him as either a victim of American politics or a treacherous schemer. Alexander Hamilton has been more kindly treated by his biographers. Clearly, between the two, Hamilton was the more important person. He made significant contributions to the adoption of the US Constitution and the policies of the early republic that continue today. What I find troubling about Hamilton is that he is frequently depicted incorrectly as an important advisor to George Washington during the American Revolution. And while Burr is often identified as *Colonel Burr*, there is rarely an explanation for how he attained his military title.

Hamilton and Burr have been recurring figures in my previous books about the American Revolution. I was first introduced to Burr's impressive military service in my book *Benedict Arnold's Army*, a narrative of the 1775 Arnold Expedition through what is now rural Maine to capture the walled city of Quebec. It took place at the start of the American Revolution and remains one of the most daring and audacious events in American military history. Burr was a conspicuous member of the expedition and managed to survive the harrowing ordeal. Burr returned as an important figure in my book *Benedict Arnold in the Company of Heroes*, which traced the lives of the survivors of the Arnold Expedition and its desperate attack on Quebec led by General Richard Montgomery.

My research into Hamilton's participation in the Revolutionary War began with my narrative of the American flight across New Jersey in late 1776, titled *The Long Retreat*. Hamilton commanded an artillery company during the Continental Army's extraordinary retreat through New Jersey with the British in hot pursuit. I resumed my Hamilton research for my book about Washington's Revolutionary War aides-de-camp entitled *George Washington's Indispensable Men*. It was published by Stackpole Books and is currently available from them in a second, softcover edition.

I also benefited from conversations over the years with a number of historians about Hamilton and Burr's Revolutionary War service. They include discussions about Hamilton with the eminent historian James Thomas Flexner who authored *The Young Hamilton*. Published in 1978, it remains an important biography of Hamilton's youth and military service in the American Revolution.

There were already numerous books about Hamilton by the time Flexner published his *Young Hamilton*. The earliest known Hamilton biography is *A Sketch of the Character of Alexander Hamilton* written by his political ally and friend Fisher Ames. It appeared as a pamphlet in 1804, just months after Hamilton's death. The first major Hamilton biography appeared in 1834. It was written by his son John Church Hamilton (1792–1882). John C. followed it with a massive seven volume biography of his father titled *Life of Alexander Hamilton* published between 1857 and 1864. John Hamilton was twelve years old when his father died and his Hamilton biographies, and every book about Hamilton that followed his work, is based primarily on the Hamilton papers currently housed in the Library of Congress.

Surprisingly, while there are creditable biographies of Aaron Burr, the earliest one is the most important. The reason is that it was based on extensive interviews, note taking, and text dictated by Burr. The book, titled *Memoirs of Aaron Burr*, is a collaboration between Burr and his political crony and confident Matthew L. Davis. Colonel Burr died in 1836 and the first volume of Davis's two volume biography was published later that year. The second volume was released in 1837. Unfortunately, Burr was as evasive and vague in describing the significant events in his life in preparing his *Memoirs* as he was during his lifetime. Adding to the problem was that a trunk containing his public papers and personal correspondence written prior to 1808 was lost at sea.

Burr was a flamboyant and secretive person and was in good company with his friend Matthew L. Davis. Probably best known as the Grand Sachem (chairman) of the notorious Tammany Hall political organization in the early 1800s, Davis was a sleazy newspaper correspondent and publisher who often hid behind pseudonyms for his inflammatory writing. Davis wanted to present Burr as a model citizen and burned all of his friend's licentious love letters to prevent them from ever being published. Davis also admitted to toning down Burr's attacks on George Washington's inept generalship during the American Revolution. But despite its shortcoming, *Memoirs of Aaron Burr* remains an important source of information about the man who is arguably the most debated and baffling character in American history to date.

Additional research for my new book was done at the New York Historical Society, the David Library of the American Revolution, and the Beinecke Rare Book and Manuscript Library at Yale University. I am also grateful to have the expert assistance of a number of Revolutionary War scholars in writing this book. They include Eric Schnitzer (park historian at Saratoga National Historic Park), Ray Andrews (independent researcher specializing in uniforms and artillery), Dr. David Martin (president of the Friends of Monmouth Battlefield), John Muller (director of the Fort Lee Historic Park), Charlie Dewey (historian/educator at the Fort Lee Historic Park), and Revolutionary War authors John Ferling, Stephen Case, and Stephen Brumwell.

It is usual that some interesting historical trivia turns up when writing a book of this scope. Here are a few of my favorites, which are irrelevant to this book but included here to keep them from being scrubbed by my publisher for being *off the subject*.

One story that I like is that Aaron Burr's daughter, Theodosia, and her husband, Joseph Alston, are believed to be the first couple to honeymoon at Niagara Falls. Another less plausible story concerns Anthony Merry, the British minister to the United States during the Jefferson administration. Merry was an extremely cautious man. It was said that when someone asked Merry what time it was, he replied, *I will write my government for instructions*.

In another instance while researching this book I encountered an interesting French Army officer named Charles Noël Romand de Lisle. He traveled from his native France to join the Patriot cause as a volunteer. Lisle was appointed a major of artillery in the Continental Army by Congress on November 12, 1776. Major Lisle served throughout the war including the command of the American artillery during the 1778 siege of Savannah. He married an American woman during the war named Letitia Ingram and they had three sons. Major Lisle's great-grandson, Charles Albert Lisle, founded the Lisle Corporation in Clarinda, Iowa, in 1903. The company's first product was a horse-powered water well drilling machine. The Lisle Corporation continues to operate today as a large and successful family-owned business manufacturing auto mechanic's tools. Its management includes Lisle family members who can trace their lineage back to Revolutionary War major Charles Noël Romand de Lisle.

This book explores the wartime relationship that Washington had with Burr and Hamilton. Despite working at Washington's headquarters, Burr was never appointed an aide-de-camp to Washington. Hamilton, however, served for four years as Washington's aide. The Revolutionary War lasted for eight years during which time Washington had thirty-two aides-de-camp. This raises the question: Was Hamilton General Washington's most important aide-de-camp if he only served at headquarters for part of the war? This subject will be explored in the pages that follow. Meanwhile, below is a list of Washington's Revolutionary War aides-de-camp to help my readers understand that there were a number of other men who worked alongside Washington at headquarters. I have included the dates that they joined the commander in chief's so-called military family. The list was compiled by Worthington Chauncey Ford in 1906. He was the chief of the Manuscripts Division of the Library of Congress at the time. Ford listed thirty-two men plus Martha Washington as aides-de-camp and military secretaries to George Washington. Martha's inclusion on the list is an honorary title to acknowledge that she worked at her husband's headquarters. Ford established excellent guidelines for inclusion on his list. His criteria were: (1) an appointment as Washington's aide in the General Orders of the Continental Army (2) a citation in the journals of the Continental Congress as having been appointed or serving as an aide to Washington, or (3) a definite statement from the commander in chief that a particular individual was his aide-de-camp.

Thomas Mifflin, July 4, 1775
Joseph Reed, July 4, 1775
John Trumbull, July 27, 1775
George Baylor, August 15, 1775
Edmund Randolph, August 15, 1775
Robert Hanson Harrison, November 5, 1775
Stephen Moylan, March 5, 1776
William Palfrey, March 6, 1775
Caleb Gibbs, May 16, 1776
George Lewis, May 16, 1776
Richard Cary, June 21, 1776
Samuel Blatchley Webb, June 21, 1776
Alexander Contee Hanson, June 21, 1776
William Grayson, June 21, 1776
Pierre Penet, October 14, 1776
John Fitzgerald, November 1776

George Johnston, January 20, 1777

John Walker, February 19, 1777

Alexander Hamilton, March 1, 1777

Richard Kidder Meade, March 12, 1777

Peter Presley Thornton, September 6, 1777

John Laurens, September 6, 1777

James McHenry, May 15, 1778

Tench Tilghman, June 21, 1780 (served as a volunteer aide from August 1776)

David Humphreys, June 23, 1780

Richard Varick, May 25, 1781

Jonathan Trumbull Jr., June 8, 1781

David Cobb, June 15, 1781

Peregrine Fitzhugh, July 2, 1781

William Stephens Smith, June 6, 1781

Benjamin Walker, January 25, 1782

Hodijah Baylies, May 14, 1782

Martha Washington

INTRODUCTION

In his play *King Richard III*, William Shakespeare portrayed King Richard as a depraved hunchback. Shakespeare's grotesque depiction was a lie created by the playwright to please Henry VII, who had seized power from King Richard. Alexander Hamilton used the same technique two hundred years later to discredit Aaron Burr by portraying him as an unprincipled tyrant. History has favored Hamilton whose smear campaign to disgrace Burr has become fact.

Hamilton's denunciation of Burr started during the Federalist Era in American history. The Federalist Era began in 1789 with the first states to ratify the Constitution and ended with the election of 1800 and inauguration of Thomas Jefferson as president. During this period political parties were just beginning, and civic ideas were associated with individuals such as Hamilton, Jefferson, and Burr. The result was that politics was personal, and malicious attacks on the integrity and morals of office-seekers was a common tactic used to debunk their political agendas. Their assaults were enthusiastically reported in the rabidly opinionated newspapers of the day. Hamilton in particular exceled at character assassinations but he was matched in his verbosity by Thomas Jefferson who used his acerbic pen to humiliate his competitors for high office.

By 1800, George Washington was dead, and John Adams had failed in his bid for a second term as president. The result was that Jefferson, Hamilton, and Burr were the most powerful statesmen in America. The difference in their political beliefs has been the subject of numerous books. However, there was another compelling difference between the three that is overlooked today but important to voters at the time. The distinction was that Hamilton and Burr were distinguished Revolutionary War veterans while Jefferson was a civilian with an embarrassing record as the wartime governor of Virginia.

Jefferson's critics eagerly pointed out his failure to prepare for Virginia's defense during the war. His alleged inept leadership left Virginia easy prey when the British invaded the state in 1781. Facing disorganized American resistance, the invaders easily advanced inland along the James River. They ransacked and burned Charlottesville while Jefferson narrowly escaped being captured at Monticello, his nearby mountaintop estate. Jefferson's running and hiding during the British rampage gave his political enemies a pretext to accuse him of being a coward along with their other bombastic condemnations.

Jefferson never fought during the war and seemed uncomfortable in the presence of Revolutionary War veterans. An example concerns his appointment in 1785 as an American representative to the French government.[1] At the urging of General Washington, Congress appointed Revolutionary War veteran Colonel David Humphreys to accompany Jefferson to Paris as his secretary. The colonel was a Yale graduate with a distinguished wartime record. Although Humphreys was well qualified for the position, Jefferson quickly replaced him with William Short, a lawyer with no military service.

The fact that Jefferson never fought for American independence was exploited by his political opponents. Their attacks included newspaper editorials such as one that appeared in the *Washington Federalist* praising Burr whose wartime exploits included participating in the American attack on British-held Quebec,

> Burr never penned a declaration of independence, I admit,—but he has done much more—he has engraved that declaration in capitals with the point of his sword: It is yet legible on the walls of Quebec. He fought for that independency, for which Mr. Jefferson only wrote. . . . He has been liberal of his blood, while Mr. Jefferson has only hazarded his ink.[2]

Aaron Burr's threat to Jefferson's political ambitions was due in part to Burr's impressive service during the American Revolution. Hamilton was also a celebrated war veteran. Both Burr and Hamilton fought in several major battles of the war. At times they fought in the same campaigns including the disastrous 1776 Patriot defense of New York and the daylong Battle of Monmouth in 1778. They both spent the miserable winter of 1777–1778 at Valley Forge where they joined in celebrating the entry of France into the war as America's ally. They were both on the march from Valley Forge to Monmouth and the celebration that followed in New Brunswick, New Jersey.

Both Hamilton and Burr also worked on the personal staff of General George Washington during the war. Their relationship with Washington had far-reaching implications for both men as the general's prestige and authority increased during the Revolution and into the Federalist Era.

Yet despite their impressive wartime service, Hamilton and Burr's subsequent political lives and their notorious duel in 1804 absorbs their biographers. In comparison, their wartime exploits are routinely glossed over. Hamilton's biographers tend to focus on his wartime association with George Washington with inaccurate references to his being General Washington's right-hand man, chief of staff, or military advisor. Burr's wartime record is similarly marginalized when his heroic participation in the 1775 Arnold Expedition and attack on Quebec were significant events in his life.

Another reason to describe their wartime experiences is that they both were in their early twenties during the war. In fact, Burr was nineteen years old when he joined the Patriot army. Their political ideas were shaped during their wartime service. Their experience in the Continental Army, with soldiers fighting together from all the colonies, made veterans like Hamilton and Burr think of the United States as one nation. Veterans also had firsthand experience with the shortcomings of a weak central government to provide even basic items like food for its army during the war. In comparison, when Jefferson referred to *my country* he meant Virginia.

Another marginalized topic that I will explore in my narrative is that both Burr and Hamilton were fluent in French. Fluency in French seems like a detail of little significance during the American Revolution. However, there were a number of French Army volunteers who joined the Continental Army. Many of them spoke little or no English.

Burr's skill in capitalizing on his career as a soldier included encouraging people to refer to him as Colonel Burr. It was an honorary reference to his eventually being appointed a lieutenant colonel during the Revolution. Hamilton also served as a lieutenant colonel during the war. However, Hamilton is frequently referred to as General Hamilton. Hamilton's military title is a fine point of history that I want to clarify at the outset.

The fact is that Hamilton was appointed a general long after the Revolution ended. His general's commission happened when he returned to the army in July 1798 to help organize America's preparation for a possible war with France. Hamilton was named a general during the short-lived emergency. Thus, identifying Hamilton as a general is misleading particularly when describing his participation in the American Revolution. I will there-fore refer to him as Colonel Hamilton (technically lieutenant colonel), the highest rank he achieved during the Revolutionary War. In addition, to maintain historical accuracy, I will identify all officers with the rank they held when describing a particular period of the war. For example, Burr entered the war as a volunteer on the 1775 Arnold Expedition and was promoted to the rank of captain later that year during the siege of Quebec.

Using the term "Royal Navy" instead of "British Navy" is common practice. However, preceding the name of a specific Royal Navy vessel with the letter HMS (His Majesty's Ship) has been scrubbed or replaced with HM (His Majesty's) by some Revolutionary War historians. A review of the scholarly *Naval Documents of the American Revolution* shows that HMS was widely used during the American Revolution to identify Royal Navy ships and I follow this precedent.

Correctly using the term "Royal" when writing about the American Revolution is a regal pain. The term "Royal" is honorary and granted by a monarch. The navy of Great Britain was so honored and called the Royal Navy. The British Marines were recognized by King George III in 1802 and became the Royal Marines. However, the British Army was not similarly venerated. The problem is that the British government hired thousands of German troops to supplement their small professional army during the American Revolution. The Germans began arriving in America in 1776 and fought alongside the British Army for the balance of the war. The dilemma is what to call this combined army of British and German soldiers. Identifying them as a Royal army is inaccurate. Calling them the Crown forces is one solution that I use in my text. Another remedy that I employed is to identify this mixed force as the British Army with the un-derstanding that, beginning in 1776, it may have included German troops.

Another more easily resolved issue is the difference between an artil-lery company and a gun battery. Hamilton began his military career in early 1776 as a captain of artillery. Because this narrative will include his exploits as an artillerist, I want my readers to be aware that the terms gun battery and artillery company had very different meanings during the Revolution-ary War. The *Universal Military Dictionary*, published in England in 1779, defines a gun battery as "a defense [a place] made of earth faced with green sod or fascines [bundles of wooden sticks]." According to the same source, an artillery company "means a small body of artillery [men], the number of which is never fixed, but generally from 45 to 110, commanded by a captain."[3] Based on these definitions, I do not refer to Hamilton as com-manding a gun battery. He commanded an artillery company.

After serving in the war, Hamilton and Burr turned to practicing law to make a living. However, they retained their martial appearance for the rest of their lives. They were described as looking lean, neatly dressed, and standing erect. In addition, despite their small stature, both Hamilton and Burr imparted a commanding presence from their days as army officers accustomed to giving orders.

Washington's years of dedicated public service culminated with his election as the first president of the United States. His influence on the careers of Hamilton and Burr continued during his eight years as president (April 30, 1789 to March 4, 1797). Hamilton's prestige soared as Washington's secretary of the treasury and principal advisor. During this same period Washington snubbed Burr, referring to him as "a brave and able officer, but the question is whether he has not equal talents at intrigue."[4]

The current trend is to admire Hamilton's wartime service while Burr's contributions to winning American independence are subjugated to the back waters of history. Hamilton's participation in the Revolution was exceptional, and I will recount it in detail in this narrative. However, Burr's wartime contributions were equally impressive.

The exploits of Hamilton and Burr during the American Revolution is the theme of this book. I particularly hope that my account of Burr's participation in the Revolutionary War will at least salvage that part of his life from the same fate of Shakespeare's *Richard III*.

1

YOUTH

Historians and playwrights are fond of saying that Hamilton and Burr were both orphans, implying that they had a lot in common. However, a comparison of their formative years reveals a very different story.

Aaron Burr was born on February 6, 1756, in Newark, New Jersey. He descended from the country's religious and intellectual elite and was probably the closest person in colonial America who could be regarded as an aristocrat. John Adams said that "he had never known, in any country, the prejudice in favor of birth, parentage, and descent more conspicuous than in the instance of Colonel Burr."[1]

Burr's father, Aaron Burr Sr., was a descendant of the earliest settlers and leaders of Connecticut. Burr Sr. attended Yale College (today's Yale University). Following his graduation in 1735, he became a minister and eventually the pastor of Newark's First Presbyterian Church. He was also interested in promoting higher education in America and was one of the founders of a small college, the College of New Jersey (today's Princeton University). Started in 1746, the college was housed a few miles south of Newark in Elizabethtown (today's Elizabeth), New Jersey.[2] The Reverend Burr was named president of the college shortly after its founding. He moved the school to Newark to make it more practical for him to run it and continue his ministry. Under Burr's leadership the college attracted many new students. He proudly boasted in a letter that the school's enrollment had grown in three years from "eight students when the care of the college was committed to me to between 40 and 50 now.[3]

In 1756, the college was relocated forty-two miles to the isolated village of Princeton. Reverend Burr's reasoning was that students should be removed from the distractions of cities and towns to a secluded seat of learning where they could focus on their education. Burr Sr. not only moved the college to Princeton but raised enough money to construct a magnificent building that same year, named Nassau Hall, to house the school. Nassau Hall was the largest academic building in the colonies on the eve of the American Revolution. Reverend Burr next resigned from his church in Newark and moved to Princeton with his family to devote his full time as the first president of the college.

Legend says that Burr Sr. worked tirelessly to raise the money to build Nassau Hall. He died on September 24, 1757, at the age of forty-one, from a fever caused by exhaustion. He left behind a wife, Esther, and a young daughter and son. The Reverend Burr's daughter, Sarah, is best known by her nickname, Sally. His son, Aaron Jr., was one and a half years old at the time of his father's death. Young Aaron grew up to be a Revolutionary War hero and one vote shy of being elected president of the United States.

Young Aaron Burr's mother also contributed to his being character-ized as an American aristocrat. She was the daughter of the noted theolo-gian and scholar Jonathan Edwards. Esther survived her husband by a little over six months. She died on April 7, 1758, from smallpox. An orphan by the age of two, Aaron and his older sister moved to Philadelphia where they lived with family friends until 1760 when their twenty-one-year-old uncle, Timothy Edwards, became their legal guardian. Uncle Timothy was a merchant living in Stockbridge, Massachusetts, at the time. However, he moved to Elizabethtown, New Jersey, with Sally and Aaron the following year. Living in urban Elizabethtown was more attractive to Timothy than rural Stockbridge. A description of the colonial town helps to explain its appeal to Uncle Timothy.

Colonial Elizabeth was a compact town of about eight hundred people living on five tree-lined streets surrounded by salt meadows and orchards. The Swedish botanist Peter Kalm visited Elizabeth and described it as "situ-ated in a garden, the ground hereabouts being even and well cultivated."[4] The town was located on the Kings Highway, the main road between New York and Philadelphia. An old stone bridge on the highway crossed the Elizabeth River, which flowed through the center of town before empty-ing into New York Bay. Nearby, Elizabethtown Point could accommodate ocean-going ships. Elizabeth's strategic location made it an ideal place for merchants, including Timothy Edwards, to establish their businesses where they purchased animal hides, farm produce (especially wheat), timber, and livestock from the surrounding farmers, which they then shipped in bulk to nearby New York City or transported to ready markets in the Carib-bean Islands.

Elizabeth's appeal included an outstanding school called Elizabeth-town Academy. The school's curriculum offered an elementary education for boys and girls and advanced studies to prepare boys planning to go to college. Young Sally and Aaron attended the academy whose headmaster at the time was a scholarly Princeton graduate named Tapping Reeve.[5] Uncle Timothy hired Reeve to give private lessons to his young wards. Reeve's frequent visits to the Edward's household led to his admiring Sally. In 1772, Reeve and Sally married. She was eighteen years old at the time. In 1773, Reeve and his young bride moved to Litchfield, Connecticut, where he established the first law school in America.[6]

Young Aaron also made an important lifetime friendship with Matthias (Matt) Ogden while growing up in Elizabeth. Matthias's father, Robert, was a successful lawyer and leading member of the New Jersey Assembly.[7] Matt Ogden and Aaron Burr bonded as fellow students at the academy. Their connection grew even stronger when Uncle Timothy married Matthias's sister Rhoda. Matt and Aaron enjoyed their idyllic surroundings especially learning how to handle small boats along the meandering Elizabeth River and the waters around nearby Staten Island. In his *Memoirs*, Burr called these experiences his "childhood aquatic excursions," which helped him launch his military career.[8]

While Aaron and Matt were boating on the Elizabeth River, Uncle Timothy was establishing himself as one of the town's leading merchants. He also skillfully managed the modest inheritance that young Burr had acquired from his parents. The money was used to educate Burr and buy a musket for him to fight the British.

It seemed only natural for Aaron to apply for admission to Princeton, the college closely associated with his father. However, he was denied entry despite his impressive academic qualifications. The problem was that he was only eleven years old when he applied. Burr spent the next two years studying the college curriculum on his own. He reapplied in 1769, proposing to be admitted as a junior. Burr was thirteen at the time and about four years younger than his fellow students. Burr did well enough on his entrance examination that he was allowed to enter Princeton as a sophomore.

Aaron Burr's college years were among the most productive and influential of his life. Princeton was headed at the time by John Witherspoon, a Presbyterian minister. Witherspoon altered studies at the college to provide a practical education for the young men enrolled there. As a result, Burr studied history, science, geography, English composition, and French. Apparently, Burr was fluent in French as evidenced by his ability to travel undetected in pro-British French Canada during the American Revolution disguised as a Catholic priest.

Burr developed many of his characteristic traits while at Princeton. From his reading of poetry and compositions, he called the "labored ornaments of language, false ornaments and pompous epithets" (descriptions) and that they were ineffective and "diverts the attention from the subject before us." He said, "A simple style, like simple food, preserves the appetite." Burr adopted what he called "an elegant simplicity of language" when writing or speaking.[9]

Another of Burr's lifelong character traits that began during his college years was corresponding in code. While still a student at Princeton, he exchanged letters with his sister written in cipher. This habit continued throughout his life and contributed to his reputation of being a devious man who wrote coded letters to hide his ruthless intrigues.[10]

Burr graduated from Princeton in September 1772 with enough money from his inheritance to contemplate his future before deciding on a career. He decided to remain in the village, near the college, where he continued to study independently along with visiting family and friends.[11] After several indolent months young Burr decided to follow in his distinguished father's footsteps and become a minister. Having made his decision, seventeen-year-old Burr enrolled in the Reverend Joseph Bellamy's school in Bethlehem, Connecticut, in 1773 to prepare for the ministry. However, while Aaron seems to have inherited his parent's intellect, he lacked their religious piety. He abandoned his idea of joining the ministry in 1774 in favor of studying law. Burr was fortunate in this regard as Tapping Reeve, his brother-in-law, had opened America's first law school in nearby Litchfield, Connecticut. Burr moved to Litchfield in May 1774 and began to study to be a lawyer. He took time from his studies to visit his cousin, Thaddeus Burr, who lived forty miles away in the town of Fairfield, Connecticut. According to legend he actually made the long trip to spend time with Dorothy Quincy who was a guest at Thaddeus's home. She was engaged at the time to John Hancock, a leader in the Boston Sons of Liberty. Miss Quincy temporarily moved from Boston to Fairfield for her safety following the occupation of Boston by British troops. Dorothy was described as young, beautiful, and intelligent. The story is that she had an affair with the "handsome young man from Litchfield" prior to her marriage to Hancock.

While the legitimacy of Miss Quincy's liaison with Aaron is questionable, it is evident that he pursued women throughout his life. At first appearance Aaron did not seem particularly appealing to women. His height, for example, was five feet, six inches tall, which was slightly below average for men at that time. He had a slender body with a large head and hazel eyes capped by heavy dark eyebrows. But despite his seemingly awkward appearance, Burr moved with grace and elegance. He was intelligent, charming, and interesting and dressed tastefully in well-tailored clothing.

There are a number of eyewitness accounts of Burr's appearance and speculation why women were attracted to him. However, the most interesting of them is attributed to Eliza B. Jumel, born Elizabeth Bowen, best known as Madame Jumel. She was married to Burr for a short time when she was fifty-eight and Burr was seventy-seven. But her attraction to Burr began when he was a young officer in the Revolutionary War. Recalling Burr years later, Madam Jumel wrote a fascinating description of him, which reads,

> Capt. Aaron Burr, in the hey-day of his youth, as he now was, appeared to me the perfection of manhood personified. He was beneath the common size of men, only five feet and a half high, but his figure and form had been fashioned in the models of the graces. Petite as he comparatively was, he had a martial appearance, and displayed in all his movements these accomplishments which are only acquired in the camp and embellished in the boudoir of the graces. In a word, he was a combined model of Mars and Apollo. His eye was of the deepest black, and sparkled with an incomprehensible brilliancy when he smiled; but if enraged, its power was absolutely terrific. Into whatever female society he changed, by the fortune of war or the vicissitudes of private life, to be cast, he conquered all hearts without an effort; and until he became deeply involved in the cares of State, and the vexations incident to the political arena, I do not believe a female capable of the gentle emotions of love ever looked upon him without loving him. Wherever he went he was petted and caressed by our sex, and hundreds vied with each other in a continuous struggle to offer him some testimonial of their adulation.[12]

In late 1774, at the age of nineteen, Burr's attention was turning from romance and the studying of law to the growing unrest between Britain and her American colonies. Rural Litchfield was a peaceful village and far from the riotous action taking place 130 miles southeast in Boston. By early 1775, Boston had emerged as the center of colonial defiance by the British government to enforce trade laws and tax the colonists. Those Americans who viewed the British legislation to "bind them to slavery" became known as Whigs. Opposing them were Americans who remained loyal to Britain and known as Loyalists, often called Tories.[13]

Within the Whig faction were a group of pugnacious radicals who organized themselves into a secret society called the Sons of Liberty. Boston's prominence in the events leading to the American Revolution was due in part to its being the home of several well-known members of the Sons of Liberty including John Hancock, Joseph Warren, and Samuel Adams. These three men were gifted organizers and orators who, for example, said that the appointed colonial bureaucrats of King George III (the British monarch) were "instigated by the Devil . . . and composed of . . . Pimps and Parasites who dared to advise their Master to detestable measures."[14] The king's ministers resorted to sending troops to Boston to regain control of the contentious city. The menacing soldiers only increased Whig resistance and violence. Complicating Britain's efforts to assert their power was that the Americans were "armed and numerous." This was a reference to the colonial militia system of self-defense. By early 1775, British Redcoats held Boston while the Massachusetts countryside was controlled by the defiant militia. The tense standoff between the Crown Forces and the Massachusetts militia was destined to explode.

Burr was studying law when news reached Litchfield that the Massachusetts militia had fought British troops in the countryside near Boston. The fighting took place on April 19 and was centered in the towns of Lexington and Concord. The action began when British Redcoats were observed leaving Boston and marching west toward Concord, where the radical militia had stockpiled weapons and equipment. The day-long running battle was being called the Lexington Alarm. It was followed by thousands of New England militiamen converging on British-held Boston.

Burr was an enthusiastic Whig who was following the news of the war, which included the militia of the four New England colonies surrounding Boston calling themselves the Army of Observation. Arron shared the war dispatches with his good friend Matthew Ogden, who was living in Elizabeth. Reports of the June 17 Battle of Bunker Hill surely stirred the two youths to action. Adding to their excitement was news that the Continental Congress had assumed control of the rebel forces encircling Boston. Reports were that Congress was raising a Continental Army recruited with volunteers from all thirteen colonies and appointed George Washington as the army's commander in chief. By the summer of 1775, America was swept by a military spirit, a martial euphoria, and the idea that their armed rebellion would be brief and end in a favorable treaty with the mother country. Excited by the Revolution, Aaron quit law school and rode to Elizabeth where he convinced Ogden that they did not have a "moment to spare" to get to Cambridge and join the army.[15] Ogden agreed and they set out for Cambridge to join the Continental Army. Burr expected to be promptly commissioned as an officer, a position fitting his education and high standing in colonial society.

Alexander Hamilton's childhood and expectations differed sharply from those of Aaron Burr. Hamilton was born on Nevis, the smallest island in the British Leeward Island chain. Understanding the economy of Nevis is important as it was an early influence on Hamilton's character and his life-long opposition to slavery.

Nevis is situated midway in the busy Caribbean shipping route that stretches from Puerto Rico in the north to Antigua in the south. Nevis's climate is ideal for growing sugarcane, which after being crushed and boiled produces sugar. In the seventeenth century, sugar was so profitable that it was called "white gold" and every plot of land on Nevis's thirty-six square miles was devoted to cultivating the plant. Laboring in the island's swelter-ing sugarcane plantations was grueling work, and thousands of black slaves provided the critical manpower for the small white population that ruled the island. The whites on the island lived in constant fear of a slave revolt. To maintain control, they whipped indolent blacks and any rebellious ones were quickly shackled, beaten, castrated, or hanged to prevent a slave insur-rection. Alexander Hamilton was born into this setting of natural beauty and human misery.

John Adams contradicted the romantic notions of Hamilton's tropical island birth when he called him "that bastard brat of a Scotch Peddler."[16] Adams was not far off the mark. Hamilton was the illegitimate offspring of a liaison between James Hamilton and Rachel Faucett.

There is no known record of the exact date and year of Alexander Hamilton's birth. The most persuasive evidence is that he was born on January 11, 1755. Although Hamilton was circumspect about his parents, scholars have pieced together information about them. The venerated historian James Thomas Flexner states that Alexander's father, James Ham-ilton, was born in Scotland, the fourth son of a minor nobleman. Appren-ticed to a merchant, James "revealed no skill or aptitude . . . and wandered incompetently among the garishly and brutally prosperous West Indian islands."[17] The consensus is that Alexander Hamilton's father spent his life drifting between working as a clerk and a threadbare merchant.

More is known about Alexander's mother. Her full name was Rachel Faucett Lavien. She was of French Huguenot descent born on Nevis. She married Johann Michael Lavien when she was sixteen. Lavien abandoned her after several years of marriage but never divorced her. She began liv-ing with James Hamilton out of economic necessity. Writing years later,

Hamilton said that his mother "became acquainted with my father and a marriage between them ensued, followed by many years cohabitation and several children."[18] The truth is that they never married, however they had two sons during their relationship. The oldest was James and the youngest was Alexander.

James abandoned Rachel and she raised her two sons alone. Rachel moved to the Danish West Indies island of St. Croix where she opened a small shop in Christiansted, the only town on the island. There, Rachael squeezed out a living for herself and her two sons. The children apparently had some basic education from a neighbor woman who taught them to read and write. The hot and humid Caribbean islands were infested with disease, the most prevalent of which were malaria and yellow fever. Rachel died of yellow fever on February 19, 1768. Alexander was thirteen years old at the time.

Alexander's brother, James, found employment with a local carpenter, while he went to work as an apprentice in the Christiansted office of a New York City-based merchant firm owned by Cornelius Kortright and Nicholas Cruger.[19] Alexander may have been introduced to Kortright and Cruger by Thomas Stevens, a merchant who knew Rachel and her sons in St. Croix. With branches strategically located throughout the Caribbean islands, the firm of Kortright and Cruger was a sophisticated company, even by today's standards. Their thriving business was based on the premise that the production of sugar in the islands was so profitable that it was cheaper to import food from the American colonies than to divert acreage to growing crops and pasturing livestock. Kortright and Cruger also exported sugar and molasses from the islands for sale in the thirteen colonies. They were also active in the lucrative business of importing slaves to sell to the sugarcane plantation owners.

Cruger headed the company's St. Croix operations. He worked from the firm's office and warehouse located on King Street across from the wharfs along Christiansted's waterfront. Young Alexander worked on the firm's second floor where he could look out at the large enclosed pen where newly arrived slaves from Africa were held in chains for auction. Alexander was shocked by the misery he witnessed and supported the abolishment of slavery later in his life. But, ironically, he owed the greatest opportunity of his life to the slave trade.

A significant opportunity in Hamilton's life came from his wealthy employers. They were impressed with their young apprentice's intelligence, honesty, and intrinsic understanding of finance and eventually allowed him to manage their Christiansted operation. Hamilton was also writing articles and poems for the local newspaper, which brought him to the attention of local influential residents and a visiting New York clergyman named Hugh Knox. The respected Reverend Knox convinced Cruger that his talented young employee should have the benefit of a formal education. Cruger agreed in the hope that Hamilton would study medicine in the American colonies and return to St. Croix as a doctor. Several other island patrons joined Cruger and established a subscription to pay for Hamilton's education.[20] Arrangements were also made to help pay for his education from a small percentage of the money earned from the sale of sugar sold in America. It is ironic that Hamilton, who became an ardent opponent to slavery, had his schooling paid for from the profits of slave labor.

Cruger arranged for Alexander to sail on one of his company-owned ships bound for Boston. After arriving there, Hamilton quickly went to New York City where both Cruger and Knox had dependable contacts waiting to help him.

Hamilton probably arrived in New York in late July 1773. He was eighteen years old and had never been away from the small provincial island of St. Croix before. He was met upon his arrival in New York by Hugh Mulligan, who was a junior partner in Cruger's business. Hugh arranged for Alexander to stay at his younger brother Hercules's house until arrangements could be made for the teenager's education.

Hercules Mulligan is a fascinating but obscure character in American history. Mulligan was born in 1740 in Ireland and immigrated to New York City with his family when he was six years old.[21] He worked in his father's periwig (wig) shop before opening his own successful haberdashery shop in Manhattan that catered to the city's rich and fashion-conscious men.[22] He was also a successful suiter and married the niece of a Royal Navy admiral.

Mulligan was a devoted Whig whose prewar activities included membership in the secret Sons of Liberty. His late-night political discussions in his home with Hamilton influenced the teenager to join the Whig protests against the callous enforcement of existing imperial laws and adding new direct taxes (e.g., the Stamp Act of 1765) without the colonist's consent.

Once the Revolution began, Mulligan became an undercover agent for the Patriots. He used his haberdashery shop to obtain valuable information about enemy plans. Hamilton is credited with recruiting his friend Mulligan as a wartime spy. Mulligan's technique for getting information was ingenious. Although he employed a staff of tailors, Mulligan, an engaging raconteur, liked to deal personally with his clients, particularly the British Army and Royal Navy officers who frequented his shop. He would engage the enemy officers in seemingly innocent conversation while he fitted them for clothing. He would ask, for example, why they were in such a hurry to get new shirt or pants. It worked, and the charming tailor obtained valuable military information that he passed along to Washington's headquarters from unsuspecting Crown officers. Hamilton and Mulligan remained lifelong friends. Their friendship extended to the grave; when Mulligan died in 1825, at the age of eighty, he was buried near Hamilton in New York City's Trinity Church cemetery.

Hugh and Hercules Mulligan are credited with arranging for Alexander to study at the Elizabethtown Academy, the same school that Burr had attended a few years earlier. The academy was selected because of its successful program to prepare teenage boys for college. Alexander's education at the academy was supervised by Francis Barber, who superseded Tapping Reeve as the school's headmaster. Barber was a 1767 Princeton graduate and a protégé of Tapping Reeve, who helped Barber secure the headmaster's job.

Hamilton attended the Elizabethtown Academy during the late summer of 1773 where he studied English, mathematics, geography, Latin, and Greek. Burr was known to have visited his uncle Timothy in Elizabeth at the same time that Hamilton was attending school there. Elizabeth was a small community and Burr probably socialized with Hamilton at summertime social gathering and visits to the academy.

Hamilton's support of the Whigs grew during his time in Elizabeth. Influencing his ideas were Barber, who was a Whig sympathizer.[23] Barber later became a distinguished officer in the Continental Army. Ironically, he served under Hamilton during the 1781 siege of Yorktown.

Besides Barber, Hamilton's political thinking was influenced by two ardent Whig lawyers residing in Elizabeth: Elias Boudinot and William Livingston. Hamilton was known to have socialized with both men while he attended the academy. Boudinot's Revolutionary War service included serving as a New Jersey delegate to the Continental Congress. Livingston was the governor of New Jersey during the war.

Hamilton prepared to apply to college with Barber's training. He applied to Princeton with the idea of pursing his own course of study, but his proposal was rejected by John Witherspoon, the college's president. Alexander next turned to King's College (today's Columbia University) in New York City. He was accepted and enrolled there in October 1773. Hamilton began his college education determined to leave his blighted childhood behind. He found a perfect outlet for his ambition in the growing controversy between the thirteen colonies and Britain.

As Hamilton would soon learn, New York City's population was divided between Whig and Tory factions. The serious trouble between these two factions began while Hamilton was a college student. It started in 1773 when Parliament renewed its efforts to tax tea imported to America. The Boston's Sons of Liberty responded by dumping a newly arrived cargo of taxed tea into the city's harbor on the night of December 16, 1773. The king's ministers retaliated by closing the port of Boston and abolishing representative government in Massachusetts. The colonists responded by boycotting British goods and creating the Continental Congress to meet in Philadelphia on September 5, 1774, to discuss united action. The New York chapter of the Sons of Liberty organized a rally to support the boycott and the Philadelphia meeting. The New York rally took place in a field just north of the city on July 6, 1774. It was presided over by Alexander McDougall, a charismatic New York ship owner and merchant.[24] Hamilton was one of the speakers at the rally, adding to his reputation as a a talented pro-Whig speaker and writer.

Hamilton took a more militant role prior to the start of the Revolution when he joined other radical King's College students in organizing a Patriot militia company called the Corsicans. The unit's name was later changed to the Hearts of Oak. They adopted distinctive uniforms that included short green coats and round leather hats on which were written the words *Liberty or Death*. The unit met near King's College early each morning in the graveyard of St. George's Church to drill. Lining up among the tombstones, the college students learned the manual of arms from their experienced drillmaster Thomas Fleming. He was a former captain in the British Army described as "ardently attached to the American cause."[25]

The news of fighting between the Massachusetts militia and British Army on April 19, 1775, reached New York City five days later, on April 24. The arrival of the news soon ended Hamilton's college career and his youthful ambitions as he turned to soldiering in support of the colonial rebellion.

Hamilton's Hearts of Oak militia company saw its first serious action on August 1775, four months after the start of the war. The incident took place on the night of August 23 when the Hearts of Oak joined other militiamen and residents siding with the radicals to seize cannons from a gun battery facing the harbor. Their brazen act was in response to a declaration by the rebellious colonial legislature of New York to construct forts to defend the lower Hudson River (also called the North River at the time).[26] Cannons were needed to arm the forts, and the New York City radicals, including Hamilton, decided to steal them. The cannons they needed were at a place called the Grand Battery, in lower Manhattan, facing New York's harbor. There were twenty-one guns in the Grand Battery. They were heavy cannons, also known as naval, or fort cannons, weighing more than a ton each mounted on small wheels characteristic of the big guns used on warships. Besides the problem of moving the heavy guns, the HMS *Asia*, a sixty-four gun Royal Navy frigate, was in the harbor watching for any unusual activity in the city. Guard boats from the *Asia* were alerted to the activity on shore as Hamilton and his fellow conspirators pulled and tugged at the ropes tied to the heavy cannons. Suddenly, and without warning, the *Asia* began firing its cannons at the shadowy figures on the shoreline. Ignoring the gunfire, the rebels managed to pilfer eleven cannons from the Grand Battery.

Looking back at the opening months of the American Revolution, Aaron Burr was on his way to Cambridge to join the Continental Army as an officer while Alexander Hamilton was gaining a good reputation among New York City's radical leaders through his political writings and active service as a common soldier in the Hearts of Oak.

2

YOUNG OFFICERS IN THE
AMERICAN REVOLUTION

Burr and Ogden arrived in Cambridge, Massachusetts, on August 1, 1775.[1] The village was the headquarters of the Patriot army that surrounded the British forces occupying Boston. The two eager teenagers arrived as big changes were underway in the organization of the rebel army. Included in the shake-up was that the Continental Congress had assumed control of the army from the New England colonies. As a result, the New England troops surrounding Boston were no longer called the Army of Observation. They were now part of the recently established Continental Army, a national force under the control of Congress. After unanimously electing their fellow delegate George Washington as commander in chief of their new army, Congress appointed four senior generals with the rank of major general for the army. One of them was Artemas Ward, a Massachusetts militia officer who resigned within a year. The other three would play a significant role in the lives of Burr and Hamilton. They were Charles Lee, Philip Schuyler, and Israel Putnam. A number of lower ranking brigadier generals were also appointed, including Richard Montgomery, a former British Army captain, who would later befriend Burr. Montgomery fought with the British Army in America as a young officer during the French and Indian War (1754–1763). The war was the American theater of a worldwide conflict between Britain and France called the Seven Years War in Europe. Washington also acquired his military experience as a youthful officer in the French and Indian War. Washington's combat experience during the war included commanding an independent Virginia regiment assigned to protect the colony's frontier against Indian attacks originating in French held Canada. He was a wealthy and imposing man who was courteously addressed during the American Revolution as His Excellency.

Washington arrived in Cambridge on July 2, 1775, and quickly discovered that the army he inherited was composed of independent-minded New England militiamen who resisted his efforts to organize or discipline them. Adding to his problems was the arrival of rowdy frontier riflemen from western Pennsylvania and Virginia. They came armed with their personal American long rifles and began randomly shooting at British soldiers in Boston or getting into fights with the New Englanders.

Burr and Ogden arrived in the midst of the chaotic situation in the rebel camp. They found the place littered with a hodgepodge of tents and huts housing the army. Most of the troops had no uniforms and were poorly armed. Sanitation in the camp was primitive even by eighteenth-century standards. Adding to the disorder was quarreling among the officers. Their discord must have been particularly alarming to Ogden and Burr who wanted to join their ranks. Writing in July 1775, shortly before the time that Ogden and Burr were seeking commissions, an American officer described the situation in Cambridge, "The laxity of the discipline which pervades the camp at Cambridge, the inexperience of the officers and the contests and petty squabbles about rank, all tended to excite great jealousy and discontent in the army."[2]

The two shocked youths made their way to His Excellency's headquarters where they intended to join the army as officers. They arrived with three impressive letters of recommendation to help them obtain commissions. One was from Elias Boudinot, who was a friend of the Ogden family and a member of the Continental Congress. His letter was addressed to his fellow Princeton graduate Joseph Reed who was on the commander in chief's staff. Boudinot's letter to Reed recommended Ogden for a commission and further stated that, "the young Gentleman that accompanies him [Aaron Burr] will be equally taken notice of by you, as the only Son of our old worthy Friend President [of Princeton] Burr."[3] Their second letter of recommendation was from John Hancock, dated "Philadelphia, 19 July 1775." Hancock wrote, "Mr Ogden and Mr Burr of the Jerseys.Visit the Camp not as Spectators, but with a View of Joining the Army and being Active during the Campaign."[4] Their third recommendation is dated July 18, 1775. It was from Lewis Morris, who was a wealthy landowner and a New York delegate to Congress. Morris wrote to Washington recommending Ogden and Burr for commissions as officers.[5] With his formidable family background, education, and letters of recommendation from influential people including Congressman Morris, Burr felt confident that he would be commissioned as an officer in the rebel army.

Ogden and Burr managed to get an interview with General Washington. However, he was unable to offer them commissions despite their impressive endorsements. Washington explained in a letter dated August 4, 1775, to Congressman Morris why he could not accommodate the two eager teenagers. His Excellency used the situation to describe what he considered to be an unrealistic policy regarding the appointment of officers. Washington explained to Morris that he was unable to "do justice to the merits of those gentlemen" (Ogden and Burr) as he had already used "the two or three appointments" (commissions) allocated to him by Congress and that "the appointment of all other officers is vested in the governments [colonies] in which the regiments were originally raised." Washington told Lewis that the commissioning of officers should be vested with Congress and not the individual colonies "during the continuance of these disturbances" (an indication that Washington anticipated a short war). Washington said that *"merit only, without regard to Country* [colony] *should entitle a man to preferment."*[6] Unwittingly, Ogden and Burr had become the example of a disagreement between Washington and government functionaries over who had the authority to commission officers. Meanwhile, the two youths decided to remain in Cambridge hoping that some suitable opportunity would arise that would allow them to join the fighting before the war ended. After dawdling in camp for a few weeks an opportunity occurred that gave Burr and Ogden a unique opportunity to get into the war.

Their opportunity came when Ogden learned that Colonel Benedict Arnold was recruiting 1,100 volunteers for a secret mission. The camp at Cambridge was abuzz with rumors of Arnold's objective. A martial spirit prevailed within the army and everyone was interested in joining Arnold's corps. They wanted the chance to fight the Redcoats before the war ended.

One exception to the excitement was young Burr. He lay in a camp bed afflicted with a fever. His illness seemed to be a characteristic he developed in response to bad news. His friend Ogden shook him from his vexation to tell him that volunteers were being recruited for a secret mission that was particularly interested in men experienced in handling small boats. It will be recalled that both Ogden and Burr were skilled boatmen from their youthful outings on the Elizabeth River. Shaken from his lethargy, Burr decided to join Ogden in volunteering to join Colonel Arnold's secret mission.

The objective of Arnold's enterprise was a closely guarded secret. Even its name gave no indication of its purpose. It was simply called The Arnold Expedition. While rumors abounded in camp about the mission, only Washington, Arnold, and a handful of trusted officers knew its objective was the walled city of Quebec: the commercial and government center of British-held Canada. But capturing Quebec would not be easy. Arnold was familiar with the formidable location and defenses of the city, having traveled there for business before the war. He knew that the main part of the city was located atop Cape Diamond, a massive solid rock jutting out from the surrounding countryside and straddling the St. Lawrence River. There were cannons mounted atop Cape Diamond that defended Quebec and controlled ship traffic on the strategic river. The city's land side was protected from attack by a formidable wall bristling with long range artillery.

Capturing and holding Quebec was a prize worth the risk. The thinking in the Patriot camp in 1775 was that the purpose of their rebellion was to address their "redress of grievances" with the mother country. The colonists believed that their insurrection would end quickly, and that the occupation of Quebec would be a valuable tool in negotiating favorable terms to end the war.

Washington organized the mission to capture Quebec and chose Benedict Arnold to lead over more seemingly qualified men. Arnold got the coveted independent command because Washington believed him to be a courageous leader who could improvise as his corps moved through the wilderness and neared Quebec. Surprise was critical to the success of the operation especially since Arnold's corps would have no artillery to intimate the small garrison they believed was guarding Quebec.

Arnold promptly began recruiting volunteers from the army for the campaign. His orders were to seize Quebec and hold it until a larger American army, commanded by General Philip Schuyler, reached the city.[7] Schuyler's troops were already advancing north into Canada along a well-established inland water route of rivers and lakes. His plan was to first capture Montreal and then advance up the St. Lawrence River to rendezvous with Arnold at Quebec. General Richard Montgomery, a former British Army captain, took over when Schuyler became too sick to accompany his troops.

Ogden and Burr applied to join Colonel Arnold's corps, which already had a full complement of officers. But they agreed to join the mission as gentlemen volunteers without pay and no formal rank. One young Patriot gentleman volunteer accurately described his status when he said, "I am neither an Officer nor a Soldier."[8] The position of gentleman volunteer was common at the time. Author Don Hagist explains that men joined the army as volunteers "with the explicit expectation of becoming officers and were commissioned as soon as an opportunity arose and the appropriate approvals were obtained."[9]

Burr outfitted himself at his own expense for the mission with practical clothing and accoutrements. Writing to his sister, Burr said that she would hardly be able to recognize him in the coarse functional clothing he was wearing for soldiering. In one of the best descriptions of clothing worn in the American Revolution, Burr told Sally that his outfit consisted of coarse woolen trousers that covered the tops of his boots and a short jacket of the same material. A rifleman on the expedition made him a present of a fringed linen shirt that he wore over his jacket. He explained that his headgear was "meant to help my deficiency in point of size." This was accomplished by cutting off the brim of a hat and decorating it with a tall feather and a fox tail. Completing his outfit was a blanket slung over his back "as that's a thing I never trust from me [did not want it stolen]" and a musket, bayonet, and tomahawk that he purchased at his own expense. Burr was not the only member of the expedition wearing his own clothing and armed with personal weapons. In fact, every one of the 1,100 men who trekked to Quebec with Arnold wore whatever they brought from home including their own weapons. At this early point in the Revolution, uniforms were rare and if anyone on the expedition had one, they probably saved wearing it for marching through the gates of Quebec. From Burr's description, he apparently had purchased a desirable large caliber British Army musket and bayonet. The majority of the men in Arnold's corps were armed with small caliber smooth bore muskets. The three backcountry rifle companies on the expedition were armed with their handmade personal rifled guns (called American long rifles during the Revolutionary War). Their rifles were considerably more accurate and able to fire a longer distance than smoothbore muskets. A musket could fire effectively up to one hundred yards, but a marksman (the correct term during the Revolutionary War) armed with a rifle could hit a target at four times that distance.

Burr had to keep his valuable musket nearby at all times. Not only was there the threat of an enemy ambush, but the brazen Pennsylvania and Virginia backcountry riflemen on the expedition were prone to steal personal articles from their more affluent comrades like Burr.

Effects were made to conceal the preparations and movement of Colonel Arnold's detachment from Cambridge from prying eyes. However, enemy spies quickly alerted General Sir Thomas Gage, who commanded the British troops in Boston, of the departure of Arnold's troops from the Patriot camp. They informed Gage that Arnold's men were marching in small detachments on different roads toward the rebel held coastal town of Newburyport in northeastern Massachusetts. Gage incorrectly decided that

Arnold's objective was to seize the important Royal Navy base at Halifax, Nova Scotia.

Today, the Arnold Expedition is an obscure chapter in American history, but the hardships of the campaign were well-known during Burr's lifetime. The men who survived the trek through Maine and attack on Quebec were admired for their bravery and resolution. Burr, one of the campaign's heroes, was respected for his courage and tenacity during the ordeal.

The expedition's route was north from Newburyport aboard a hastily assembled flotilla of eleven unarmed sloops and schooners. One member of Arnold's corps described them as "dirty coasters and fish boats."[10] The ships carried the expedition to the Kennebec River, which was then in the Maine District of Massachusetts. Maine was part of Massachusetts at the time. Maine became a state in 1820.

Washington and Arnold believed that there was an inland water route from the Kennebec River to the St. Lawrence River. The course followed up the Kennebec River across a series of inland lakes and streams in Maine that led to Lake Megantic in Canada. Lake Megantic was the source of the Chaudière River, which flowed north into the St. Lawrence River near the City of Quebec. The route was mostly through uncharted wilderness that would test the endurance of every man on the expedition.

Burr was nineteen years old at the time and appeared to be too frail for a rigorous military campaign. However, the first test of his fortitude was the march from Cambridge to Newburyport. Burr survived this leg with ease. He wrote a letter to his sister from Newburyport on September 18, 1775, proclaiming with elation, "I marched from Cambridge here in a day and a half, about 45 miles. This first attempt convinces me I am equal to the undertaking."[11]

The flotilla of ships carrying the Arnold Expedition sailed up the Kennebec to the boatyard of Reuben Colburn. Under contract from General Washington, Colburn built two hundred bateaux for the expedition.[12] Bateau are simple flat-bottomed boats with sharply pointed bows and sterns. They were commonly seen on the rivers of colonial America and Canada. Colburn, who was familiar with the rough, rock strewn waters of the Kennebec, built heavy bateaux with thick hulls. Canoes were not an option. They required too much time to build and could not carry all the food, gunpowder, tents, and other equipment that the expedition needed. Furthermore, heavily-laden canoes would be torn apart by the jagged rocks lurking below the surface of the river.

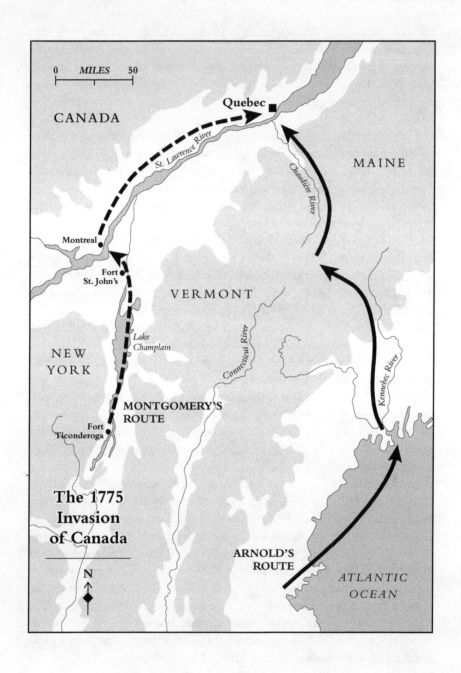

The 1775
Invasion
of Canada

The ships from Newburyport, accompanied by Colburn's bateaux, proceeded up the Kennebec River to Fort Western (today's Portland, Maine). The fort was at the height of navigation on the Kennebec (the highest point on a river that ships could sail). Once there, the 1,100 men on the expedition were divided into four divisions. The plan was for the divisions to be staggered a day or two apart in order to prevent bottlenecking at rapids or waterfalls where the boats had to be offloaded, portaged over the obstacle, and reloaded. Volunteers Burr and Ogden were assigned to the second division commanded by Lieutenant Colonel Christopher Greene.[13] Greene was a veteran of the Battle of Bunker Hill and a dedicated Patriot. He was also politically well-connected and married to a daughter of Samuel Ward who served three terms as the governor of Rhode Island before he was elected as a delegate to the Continental Congress. Greene was hacked to death by Loyalist troops later in the war when he was cornered and refused to surrender. Burr was fortunate to begin his military career in the service of this outstanding officer.

Based on the diary of Dr. Isaac Senter, the expedition's physician, Colonel Greene appointed Burr and Ogden as his aides-de-camp.[14] The origin of the term is French and literally means camp helper. They were and still are the military equivalent of administrative assistants. Only generals were authorized to have aides. The 1779 *Universal Military Dictionary* emphasizes that an aide is a paid position: "An aide-de-camp is an officer appointed to attend a general officer [army general]. . . . He receives and carries their orders, as occasion requires. He is seldom under the degree of a captain [draws captain's pay and allowances] and all aides have an additional daily allowance for their duties."[15] Lower ranking officers like Greene circumvented the rules by commandeering unpaid volunteers like Burr to serve as his aides. Greene used Burr and Ogden on the Arnold Expedition as messengers and to assist him in writing orders and keeping records.

Burr was an educated young man with an impressive family lineage which made him a minor celebrity on the expedition. His status got him an invitation to spend the night of September 23 at the home of Captain James Howard at Fort Western. After a hardy chicken dinner, Burr wrote his sister that he spent the night at the Howard residence "wallowing in a good feather bed."[16] It would be many months before Burr would sleep in a bed again.

As the expedition proceeded, Burr's good friend Ogden was identified as Major Ogden. The title is correct: Ogden was referred to on the trek as Major Ogden while Burr was addressed as Mr. Burr. To clarify this point, Ogden was not a major in the army but a brigade-major. He was appointed

to the post by Arnold. According to the 1779 *An University Military Dictionary*, "A Brigade-Major is an officer appointed by a brigadier [general], to
assist him in the management of his corps."[17] In the eighteenth century, the
terms "brigade" or "corps" meant a minimum of three regiments, usually
operating together, under the command of a brigadier general. Although
Arnold was a colonel at the time, his independent command of more than
one thousand men necessitated appointing a brigade-major to be responsible for issuing orders and maintaining records. Arnold decided to appoint
Ogden to the position instead of tapping one of his small cadre of officers
for the tedious job. Ogden's position as brigade-major was breveted meaning that it existed only while he held the job. As a military custom, Ogden
was referred to as Major Ogden as opposed to Brigade-Major Ogden.[18]

The Arnold Expedition officially began on the morning of September
25, 1775 when the first division left Fort Western. It was composed of the
three rifle companies totaling 350 men. Their titular commander was Captain
Daniel Morgan from Virginia. The riflemen were put in the vanguard to
clear the way for the three divisions that followed. The bateaux transported
the expedition's provisions, gun powder, tents, etc. The total was estimated
to be one hundred tons. The lightly equipped men walked along the shoreline carrying their weapons and personal gear. Beyond the sparsely settled
lower Kennebec, the corps would be travelling through uncharted wilderness with the constant threat of being ambushed by hostile Indians or British
troops. Despite the dangers, everyone was excited and ready for adventure.

Lieutenant Colonel. Greene's second division left Fort Western on
the morning of September 26. Three men were assigned to each of the
expedition's bateaux. As experienced boatmen from their youth, Burr and
Ogden were assigned to help man the boats. It was not easy work as the
boats were moving upstream, against the river flow. Two crewmen used
long iron tipped poles, called setting poles, to push their boat upstream.
The third man was in the stern steering the boat with a pole or an oar. In
a strong current, ropes were thrown to the shore and the boats were towed
against the current by teams of men, a technique called cordelling. When
the expedition got underway, the Kennebec River was at its lowest depth
and at times Burr had to get into the cold water to help pull the bateaux
over shallow water. One of the boatmen wrote an account of the work,
"We were often obliged to haul the boats after us through rock and shoals,
frequently up to our middle and over our heads in the water; and some of
us with difficulty escaped being drowned."[19]

Arnold sent a scouting party ahead that surveyed the expedition's
intended route. The scouting party's route ahead was known to include a

so-called Great Carry, a portage across three lakes to a tranquil tributary of the Kennebec called the Dead River. This waterway was believed to lead to a pass through the mountains that separated Maine from Canada. However, the fear of an Indian ambush discouraged the reconnaissance party from travelling beyond the Great Carry.

The expedition got its first inclination of hardship when it reached Ticonic Falls, a half-mile of rapids cascading over rock ledges. The site was eighteen miles up the Kennebec from Fort Western. Greene's division, which included Burr and Ogden, reached Ticonic Falls on September 28. They poled and dragged the boats as far as possible into the rapids. When they could advance the boats no further, they muscled them to the western bank of the river for portaging. The fully loaded bateaux were too heavy to drag ashore, so Burr, Ogden, and the others had to wade into the cold water and unload the boats. After the tons of cargo were brought to dry land it had to be carried around the rapids. Emptying, pulling, and dragging the boats out of the war was demanding. Once ashore, the boats, each weighing four hundred pounds, were turned over and carried on the shoulders of the men over the portage. This exhausting and time-consuming process was repeated as the expedition continued to make its way up the Kennebec River. Winter came early in Maine and the boat crews were constantly wet and freezing as the temperature began to drop. At the same time, the casks of provisions, especially the salted meat, got wet and began to rot.

The estimate of a 180-mile journey from Fort Western to Quebec turned out to be 280 miles and took two months to complete. General Washington had picked the right man to lead the mission. Arnold, the expedition's commander was a tenacious fighter who drove his men ceaselessly toward their goal. He was supported by the majority of his equally stalwart officers who included Christopher Greene, Daniel Morgan, and Henry Dearborn. They were ready to risk their own lives and those of their men to reach Quebec.

Not every officer on the expedition was as fanatical as Arnold. The most experienced American officer on the expedition was Lieutenant Colonel Roger Enos. He was a veteran of the French and Indian War and second in command of the Arnold Expedition. Enos was in charge of Arnold's fourth division, which was carrying the corps reserve food supply. Operating in the rear of the straggling column, he had lost contact with the other divisions. Enos was more prudent than Arnold and believed his first responsibility was to safeguard the lives of his troops. With his men cold and sick, running dangerously low on food, and far from Quebec, Enos decided on his own to turn back. He defected on the night of October 25, taking with him his three companies totaling about 250 men plus stragglers and invalids that joined him as he retreated back to Fort Western. Enos later claimed that there was no reserve food supply.[20]

Just after crossing into Canada, Arnold admitted in a report to Washington of the expedition's precarious situation. At the time, his little army was still more than one hundred miles from Quebec and on the verge of starvation. Arnold concluded his letter with the following words, "Our march has been attended with an amazing deal of fatigue. I have been much deceived in every account of our route which is longer, and has been attended with a thousand difficulties I never apprehended."[21]

Burr's recollection of the final horrific push to reach Quebec was still vivid many years after the event. He described how "every man was left to take care of himself, and make the best of his way through the woods. The sufferings of this detachment from wet, and cold, and hunger, were excessive."[22] The men were reduced to boiling leather and eating their pet dogs as they staggered along the shoreline of the Chaudière River. There was no big game to kill as the animals had bolted to safety at the sound of hundreds of men trekking through the underbrush. Slowly, and in small groups, they reached the French-Canadian settlements along the lower Chaudière River. Prudently, Arnold and his officers had hard currency to buy food from the peasant farmers. Those members of the Arnold Expedition who made it to the farms became known as the famine-proof veterans.

Of the 1,100 men who started out from Cambridge, only 650 of them ever got to see Quebec. It is estimated that at least twelve members of the expedition had starved to death. Others had turned back when they became too sick or terrified. Burr, who was looked upon as too frail to endure the campaign, was one of its strongest survivors. He claimed that he weathered the horrendous ordeal due to "his abstemious [moderate] habits in regard to eating."[23]

While the Arnold Expedition was struggling to reach Quebec, General Montgomery's advance toward Montreal was facing problems of its own. It was stalled by two British forts along the strategic Richelieu River (also called the Sorel or St. Johns River at the time), which flowed north from Lake Champlain and emptied into the St. Lawrence River at the village of Sorel. Fort St. John defended the approach to the Richelieu River from Lake Champlain. Fort Chambly was located twelve miles further downstream near Montreal. The British troops defending Fort St. Johns surrendered on November 2, 1775, after a fifty-five-day siege. Fort Chambly's small garrison capitulated earlier, on October 18. The seizing of the two forts cleared the way for Montgomery to advance to Montreal, which surrendered without a fight on November 13.

On November 14, a day after Montreal fell to Montgomery, Arnold's famine-proof veterans reached the Plains of Abraham, an expanse of pastureland and houses facing Quebec's walls. They expected to find the gates facing the plains open and a warm welcome from the city's civilian population. Instead, they found Quebec locked down with the perimeter walls manned by an assortment of Royal Navy sailors, British Redcoats, Marines, civilian militia, and merchant sailors. They were a mixed lot but well-armed with muskets and cannons. They mocked the ragtag army below them demanding their surrender. Warned of the approach of Arnold's so-called Kennebec Corps, a handful of determined government officials along with British Army and Royal Navy officers had scrapped together a defense force of 1,248 able-bodied men in the city.[24] Arnold needed cannons and mortars to force the city to surrender, but he had none.

After failing to capture Quebec, and fearing a sortie from inside the city, Arnold retreated eighteen miles "in a slovenly style" down the St. Lawrence River to the rambling village of Pointe-aux-Trembles (today's Neuville).[25] After arriving, the army was forced to spread out and occupy the farmhouses in the area. The locals were friendly and provided the Americans with the luxuries of warm fires and simple but plentiful food. Burr was especially fortunate because he spoke French and could converse with his hosts. The peasant's warm welcome was due largely to the news that General Montgomery had captured Montreal. But despite the good news, Burr wrote his uncle Timothy in distant Elizabethtown a pessimistic letter from the village. "I expected some weeks ago," Burr told his uncle, "to have had the satisfaction of writing you a letter from Quebec. When that time will be is now very uncertain."[26]

After retreating to Pointe-aux-Trembles, Arnold addressed a fretful letter to Montgomery telling him, "I am very anxious for your arrival." Arnold selected Burr to deliver the message to Montgomery's headquarters in Montreal, which was 144 miles away. Burr told the story to his friend Matthew Davis years later describing how he disguised himself as a Catholic priest for the mission. The French Canadians were devoted Catholics, which allowed Burr, dressed in clerical garb, "to be conducted in perfect safety from one religious family to another." Helping his masquerade succeed, in addition to speaking French, Burr said that he spoke some Latin, which he learned when he studied briefly for the priesthood after graduating from college. Burr claimed that at one point during his journey he hid in a convent for three days probably to avoid marauding pro-British

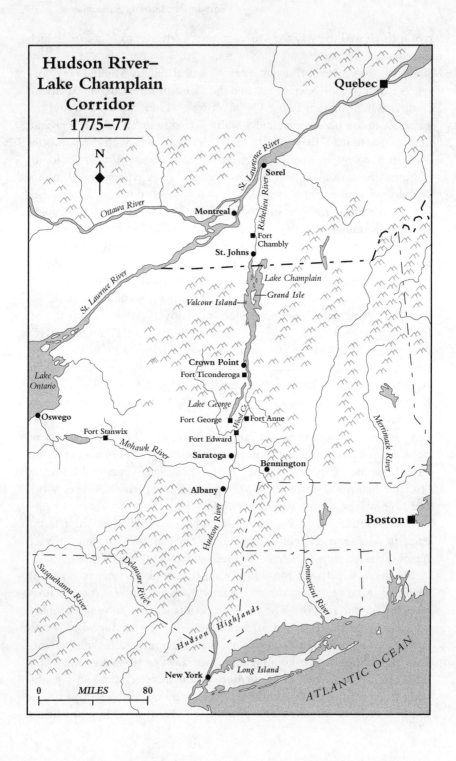

Hudson River–
Lake Champlain
Corridor
1775–77

N

Quebec

St. Lawrence River

Sorel

Ottawa River

Montreal

Richelieu River

Fort
Chambly

St. Johns

St. Lawrence River

Lake Champlain

Grand Isle

Valcour Island

Lake
Ontario

Crown Point

Fort Ticonderoga

Lake George

Oswego

Fort George   Fort Anne

Wood Cr.

Fort Stanwix

Mohawk River

Fort Edward

Merrimack River

Saratoga

Bennington

Albany

Boston

Hudson River

Susquehanna River

Delaware River

Connecticut River

Hudson Highlands

New York   Long Island

ATLANTIC OCEAN

0   MILES   80

sympathizers. "At the expiration of this period," Burr alleged that, "he again set off, and reached Montgomery without further detention or accident."[27] He delivered Arnold's letter along with a note to Montgomery from Arnold which read,

> This will be handed you by Mr. Burr, a volunteer in the army and son to the former president of New Jersey College [Princeton].
>
> He is a young gentleman of much life and activity, and has acted with great spirit and resolution on our fatiguing march. His conduct, I make no doubt, will be a sufficient recommendation to your favor.[28]

Montgomery acted on Arnold's recommendation and appointed Burr as his aide-de-camp with the breveted rank of captain. The appointment meant that Burr was now an officer working for one of the most experienced and promising generals in the Continental Army. Captain Burr was promptly introduced to John Macpherson, Montgomery's other aide. Macpherson was good company for Burr. He was twenty-one years old and a fellow Princeton graduate.[29]

The enlistments of many of Montgomery's troops expired following the capture of Montreal leaving him with only eight hundred men. Of his remaining troops, Montgomery assigned five hundred of them to garrison Montreal under the command of General David Wooster. This left only three hundred troops, all veteran New York soldiers, to rendezvous with Arnold at Quebec.

General Montgomery reached Point-aux-Trembles December 2, 1775, where he received a warm welcome from Colonel Arnold and his famine-proof veterans. Montgomery arrived with his troops aboard a flotilla of ships captured from the British at Montreal. His ships brought badly needed plunder from Montreal including muskets, field artillery, and warm clothing for Arnold's men. As the senior officer, Montgomery took command of Arnold's Kennebec Corps. Montgomery was impressed with Arnold's corps calling it "an exceeding fine one, inured to fatigue, and well accustomed to cannon shot. There is a style of discipline among them, much superior to what I have been used to see this campaign."[30]

Montgomery and Arnold's personalities complimented each other's, and they made an excellent team. Arnold's recklessness, hot temper, and raw courage was balanced by Montgomery's methodical planning, calm disposition, and organization. Together they returned to Quebec and plotted how to force its garrison into surrendering. The captured field artillery that Montgomery brought from Montreal proved to be too feeble to terrorize the city into capitulating. His cannons were manned by Captain John Lamb and forty artillery men who came to Quebec with Montgomery. Although a few hundred French Canadians joined the American Army giving Montgomery a force of 1,200 men, it was too small an army to attempt to storm Quebec. Instead, Montgomery and Arnold devised an unconventional plan. It called for a small group of men to stealthily scale Quebec's walls on ladders at night near one of the city's gates, overpower its defenders, and open the doors for the rest of the army to rush in. Feisty Captain Burr volunteered to lead this dangerous mission. He constructed wooden ladders and began training fifty men for the operation. The term in use at the time for a hazardous military enterprise like this was "forlorn hope," originating from the Dutch term *verloren hoop*, literally the "lost troop."

Burr's forlorn hope was planning to scale the walls of Quebec during a snowstorm on a dark night. Conditions were ideal for the operation during the early hours of December 26, 1775. But Montgomery called off the attack at the last minute when the sky cleared, and the moon began to shine. It was a providential decision as a deserter had informed Quebec's garrison of the Patriots plan.

Montgomery and Arnold then decided on an alternative plan based on information they learned from several residents who fled the city. Their new idea was to attack the lower section of the city from opposite directions at night during a snowstorm. Quebec's Lower Town was the city's commercial district comprised of wharves and warehouses located on narrow streets along the waterfront. This part of Quebec was open with no permanent fortifications to protect it. American lookouts peering through spy glasses from across the St. Lawrence River reported that the British had erected wooden barricades and positioned field artillery on several streets in the Lower Town. They also saw men guarding strategic points along the waterfront as well as buildings that were boarded-up to prevent the rebels from using them as firing positions. Montgomery believed that some of the derelict buildings had been converted into blockhouses with armed men and possibly artillery secreted inside.

The plan was for Montgomery to lead his three hundred New York troops along the riverbank from the south and Arnold and his Kennebec Corps to attack the Lower Town from the north. Arnold gathered a larger force for his assault. Joining him were five hundred men—every able-bodied soldier from his Kennebec Corps along with forty Canadians and Indians in addition to Lamb's Artillery Company. The artillery men were pulling a cannon mounted on a sled. After overwhelming resistance in Lower Town, Montgomery and Arnold planned to join forces and fight their way up the Cote de la Montagne, the only street that led to the strategic Upper Town where the Château St. Louis (the governor's place), barracks, and gun batteries were located. To confuse the enemy, a detachment of Montgomery's Canadians would create a diversion by trying to set fire to one of the gates on the opposite side of the city.

The snowstorm that Montgomery and Arnold waited for to conceal their movements began on the night of December 30, 1775. The British defenders were aware that the Americans would probably use the cover of a snowstorm to attack the city and they were watching that night for any suspicious movement.

The Americans reached their designated starting positions at 2:00 a.m. on December 31. Montgomery led his division accompanied by his two aides: Burr and Macpherson. Captain Jacob Chessman was also in the vanguard leading a detachment of pioneers armed with saws and axes. Chessman carried five gold coins in his coat pocket hoping that they would be used to pay for a proper burial if he were killed in the attack.

Montgomery's New Yorkers had to reach the edge of Lower Town along a narrow two mile-long path wedged between the base of Cape Diamond and the St. Lawrence River. Progress was slow as the snowstorm turned into a fierce, blinding blizzard. Men were slipping in the darkness along the icy trail that was covered with immense snow drifts and great slabs of ice pushed ashore from the river. Montgomery led the column accompanied by Captain Chessman, aides Macpherson and Burr, and a Canadian guide named Desmarais. At 4:00 a.m. two rockets illuminated the sky. They were a signal from the Canadian detachment that they were starting their diversion. Montgomery reached a fifteen-foot high picket fence that blocked their route into the Lower Town. His pioneers quickly made an opening in the fence and the advance party crawled through. About one hundred feet further along the column was stalled by a second barricade. This time Montgomery took an axe and pushed away the splintered wood with his bare hands. The pioneers behind him quickly enlarged the opening and the New Yorkers followed their commander into the Lower Town. Directly ahead of them they could see the outline of a house at the edge of a neighborhood in the Lower Town called Près de Ville. The building that attracted their attention was about fifty yards in front of them standing between two narrow openings just wide enough for a wagon to pass through. The house belonged to a businessman named Simon Fraser. Beyond the house was Champlain Street, which led to the Cote de la Montagne. Montgomery knew that the British had fortified several houses in the Lower Town, converting them into compact forts called blockhouses.

However, he did not know their location. There was no sign of life from the building and the only sounds they could hear were from the gale-force winds and the city's church bells ringing as the Canadians pressed their diversionary attack on the opposite side of the town. It was dawn when Montgomery and his advance party cautiously approached the silent building. They believed it was a blockhouse but wondered if its occupants had fled at their approach. In the chilling calm, Montgomery drew his sword and turning to Burr he said, "We shall be in the fort in two minutes."[31] Then he waved his sword in the air and shouted, "Push on, brave boys, Quebec is ours" and ran toward the silent building.[32] Chessman, Macpherson, and Burr were running beside him shoulder to shoulder followed by some of the New York troops.

Unknown to the racing Americans, there were forty-one armed men inside the two story blockhouse. They included thirty anxious French Canadians and Loyalists led by two inexperienced militia officers named Joseph Chabot and Alexandre Picard. There were also nine sailors commanded by a ship's master (navigation officer) named Adam Barnsfare. He shared the overall command of the blockhouse with John Coffin, a Loyalist. Coffin had immigrated to Quebec with his family from war-ravaged Boston earlier in the year seeking a peaceful place to live. Although Coffin and Barnsfare had no military experience, they remained calm and resolute. They could faintly see the rebels approaching through the drifting snow and dim light of early dawn. Without wavering, Coffin and Barnsfare ordered their men to quietly get their arsenal of weapons loaded and ready including their four small cannons. They waited until the rebels were within forty paces, when Barnsfare yelled, "Fire!" Loud explosions erupted from the bowels of the house as a shower of musket and cannon balls screamed through the air. Captain Chessman caught shards of metal through his midsection and fell to the ground. He tried to get up, motioning with his arm for his men to push forward, then he fell back to the ground a corpse. Montgomery was nearby, sprawled in the snow; killed instantly by the sudden enemy barrage that tore open his head. His young aide Macpherson lay dead beside to him. The British salvo also killed Desmarais and six soldiers. Miraculously, Burr stood untouched surrounded by his dead comrades. Burr later claimed that he was within ten feet of Montgomery when the shooting started.[33] Burr was joined by some veteran New Yorkers who soon arrived on the scene from the second fence and began exchanging shots with the men inside the building.

A determined American attack might have sent the men inside the house scurrying out the back door for safety. But Colonel Donald Campbell arrived on the scene. He was Montgomery's quartermaster and now in command. According to historian Justin Smith, Campbell "confabulates [talks] instead of charging, and presently he orders a retreat."[34] As the Americans withdrew, Burr struggled to lift the body of his dead commander and carry him away. But Montgomery was a big man and some eyewitnesses reported seeing the small captain carry the heavy, blood-soaked corpse a few feet before giving up the effort and retreating with the others.[35]

After returning to the Plains of Abraham, Campbell, Burr, and the rest of Montgomery's men listened for some sign that Benedict Arnold's troops had succeeded in their attack that was launched from the opposite end of Lower Town.

Unknown to them at the time, Arnold led his attack on schedule with a forlorn hope of thirty volunteers. Lamb's brass six pound field gun followed them, but it could not be dragged fast enough through the snow and it was abandoned. The alert garrison spotted Arnold's column and began firing at it from behind their barricades. Arnold was seriously wounded in the left leg early in the attack and carried off to the rebel's field hospital with his boot filled with blood.[36] His column continued their attack but was trapped in the narrow streets of Lower Town. Daniel Morgan led a heroic effort to break out, but with Montgomery's division gone, the British were able to concentrate on Arnold's Kennebec Corps. After being hopelessly surrounded, Arnold's famine-proof veterans surrendered. This was the tragic ending of the heroic but ill-fated Arnold Expedition.

The failed American attack on Quebec did not tarnish the reputations of Arnold or Burr, both of whom survived the disaster. But in retrospect, Montgomery's death was a significant blow to both men. Montgomery was a rising star in the Continental Army and destined to become one of its senior officers. Had he lived, Arnold and Burr would have benefited from their warm relationship with the capable and popular general. Burr wrote Montgomery's wife Janet a letter in which he praised the bravery and dedication of her husband. She replied to Burr saying, "You have awakened all my sensibility by the praise you bestowed on my unfortunate General. He was indeed an angel sent us for a moment."[37]

It is unfortunate that Burr is only remembered for his duel with Hamilton. Burr deserves recognition as a heroic survivor of the Arnold Expedition and the American attack on Quebec. We shall see as this narrative continues, that he risked his life on numerous occasions to help win American independence.

One week after the failed American attack to seize Quebec, and 150 miles to the south, a significant event in Alexander Hamilton's life was about to unfold. It began on January 6, 1776, when New York's Provincial Congress voted to create their own artillery company to help defend New York City. They insisted that it had to be commanded by a man with gunnery experience who be appointed the captain of the Artillery Company of the Colony of New York. Hamilton heard about the proposed detachment and leaped at the opportunity to command it. He had no gunnery experience such as the mathematical knowledge necessary to determine the elevation of a cannon to hit a target at a specific distance. To fill the void, Hamilton read artillery treatises such as the authoritative *Treatise of Artillery* published by John Muller in 1757.[38] He also studied gunnery with Robert Harpur, King's College's professor of mathematics.[39] At the same time, Hamilton lobbied for the captaincy with McDougall who, on February 23, recommended "Mr. Alexander Hamilton for Capt. Of a Company of Artillery."[40] Based on McDougall's recommendation, the Provincial Congress had Hamilton examined by Captain Stephen Badlam, a Massachusetts artillery officer who was in New York at the time. After receiving a good report from Badlam, the Provincial legislature voted on March 14, 1776, to commission Hamilton as a captain, with instructions to raise the New York Company of Artillery (today, the United States Army 1st Battalion, 5th Field Artillery) with instructions to safeguard New York City. The fact that Hamilton's company was created and funded by the colony of New York had important implications. Foremost, Hamilton's company took its orders from the provincial (New York) government. It was not part of the Continental Army. It was raised and funded to defend New York and expected to remain in the colony for the duration of the war.[41]

Hamilton was fortunate to get the coveted command. His appointment proved to be a major turning point in his life. As a youthful teenager in St. Croix he believed that the only way he could escape from his dreary life was as a soldier. He expressed this idea in his now famous lines, "I contemn [condemn] the groveling condition of a clerk . . . to which my Fortune condemns me and would willingly risk my life. . . . I wish there was a war."[42] Now he had the opportunity he had dreamed of. Hamilton left school to organize his artillery company. He never returned to college and has the distinction of being Colombia University's most famous dropout.

In accordance with the practice at the time, Captain Hamilton was expected to recruit the men for his company. He found the recruits he needed along New York's docks and waterfront warehouses. The war and the intimidating presence of the *HMS Asia* in the harbor had curtailed trade. Unemployed longshoremen and sailors signed on with Hamilton for the pay. An existing return (roster) from the period lists sixty-nine men in his company. Many of them were illiterate as evidenced that they signed their names with an "x."

While there are no known details of the quality of Hamilton's men, there are some observations about the men recruited from the laborers in the city who enlisted in the 1st New York Regiment early in the war. The unit was commanded by General Richard Montgomery who called its enlisted men "the sweepings of the New York streets."[43] Montgomery also had harsh words for the officers as well once referring to New York's Captain John Quackenbush as Captain "quakes-in-the-bush."[44]

Loading and firing the muzzle loading cannons of the period required discipline and coordination, particularly in a combat situation where rapid fire was essential. With no command experience, Captain Hamilton faced the challenging job of turning a capricious lot of laborers into proficient artillerymen. His approach was to impose strict discipline while instilling pride and showing concern for his men's well-being. To encourage his recruits, Hamilton advanced the money to purchase uniforms for them, which consisted of blue regimental coats with buff cuffs and facings (lapels). Their trousers were made of durable buckskin. He had a more elegant uniform made for himself of better materials and tailoring. His trousers, for example, were made of white fabric rather than coarse buckskin. Hamilton also arranged for his New York Provincial company to have their pay increased to match that being offered by the Continental Army. As for discipline, Robert Troup, his friend and former roommate at college, said that Hamilton "with indefatigable pains" drilled his company in "every branch of discipline and duty; and it was not long before it was esteemed the most beautiful model of discipline in the whole army."[45] Insubordination, stealing, and desertion were Hamilton's biggest discipline-related problems. In one instance he offered a reward for the return of Uriah Chamberlain, a deserter from his company. Chamberlain was found and stripped to the waist in front of the company and whipped. In another incident, five men in Hamilton's company were court-martialed for insubordination. They were reduced in rank or "stripped of their clothing [uniforms] and discharged from the Company."[46] In still another recorded occurrence, the General Orders for May 8, 1776, reported that John Reling of "Capt. Hamilton's Company in the New-york Artillery" had escaped from prison where he was being held for desertion. Reling was recaptured and "confin'd for six days upon bread and water."[47] Training was a problem as there was a shortage of gunpowder to actually load and fire their cannons. But Hamilton's artillery company made an impressive appearance when General Washington arrived in New York City with his army.

3

THE DEFENSE OF NEW YORK CITY

A series of events brought Washington's army to New York City and Hamilton's abilities to the attention of several influential officers in the Continental Army.

The episode began during the winter of 1775–1776 as Washington's army continued to surround British-held Boston. The besieged Redcoats, now commanded by General William Howe, lacked sufficient troops to attack the rebel positions and end the siege. At the same time, the Americans had no long range artillery to threaten the city and end the stalemate. Washington decided to act by implementing a daring plan to bring captured British artillery from Fort Ticonderoga in upstate New York to Cambridge. The fort was seized by the Patriots early in the war. His Excellency gave the difficult assignment to Henry Knox, a little known twenty-five-year-old Continental Army artillery officer.[1] Some background information about Knox is relevant as Hamilton would serve under Knox's command later in the war.

Like Hamilton, the American Revolution catapulted Knox from obscurity to fame and prominent social status. Knox's father abandoned his family in 1759 when Henry was nine years old. To help support his family, Henry went to work for a Boston bookseller and went on to open his own bookshop in 1771. Knox was an ardent supporter of opposition to British taxation. The growing hostility created a market for military treatises from enraged colonists who were ready to go to war if necessary to defend themselves against what they believed was "the most unprincipled government that ever disgraced humanity."[2] Besides reading the military treatises he sold in his shop, Knox joined a local militia artillery company and discussed military theory with bored British Army officers stationed in Boston.

Knox's knowledge of artillery became known to General Washington who gave him the extraordinary opportunity of transporting cannons captured at Fort Ticonderoga to Cambridge. Knox moved sixty-two tons of ordinance in the depth of winter using horse drawn sleds.[3] The journey took more than six weeks across three hundred miles of frozen rivers, mountains, and along roads that were nearly undetectable in the deep snow. But Knox persevered and delivered fifty-nine cannons to an elated General Washington.

General Howe's Boston garrison awoke the morning of March 5, 1776, to discover that the Americans had Knox's big guns aimed at the city. General Howe decided to evacuate Boston rather than fight. He wasn't interested in risking his limited resources to defend Boston. The city was isolated and located in a hotbed of rebel sympathizers. Besides, Howe and his civilian bosses in London were already contemplating evacuating Boston in favor of quashing the rebellion from New York City.

British possession of New York City made sense. It was located in a strategic location and directly on the Hudson River, which was navigable for 150 miles north to Albany. New York City was also only ninety miles overland from the rebel capital of Philadelphia. Another factor was the city's excellent deep-water harbor, which made the city an ideal naval base for Britain's warships to support army operations and launch devastating and demoralizing raids along the American coastline. King George III and his ministers also believed that the majority of the New York region's population were Loyalists (pro-British colonists) who would welcome the liberation of their city from the rebels. Adding to the Patriots belief that the British would attack New York were reports that New York City was the destination for the fleet of ships and thousands of troops being assembled in Britain to end the colonists upstart rebellion. Washington sent General Charles Lee to New York even while the siege of Boston continued in anticipation that New York would become the seat of the war. Washington instructed Lee on January 8, 1776, to travel to New York that winter and "put that City in the best posture of Defence which the Season & Circumstances will admit of."[4]

Lee was an eccentric man with slovenly habits, but he was also a former British Army officer with a quarter century of soldiering experience. His eccentricities were tolerated as he was considered the most experienced soldier in the Continental Army. Lee arrived in New York on February 14, 1776, and quickly realized that the region, with its network of waterways and islands, offered an almost endless combination of sea approaches and landing places. "What to do with the city puzzles me," Lee wrote to Washington on February 19 from New York. "It is so encircled with deep navigable water that whoever commands the sea must command the town."[5] The Americans had no navy but would be facing the most formidable naval power in the world. The rebels should have burned the city and moved inland beyond the reach of the Royal Navy, but Washington was determined to defend New York with the encouragement of the armchair generals in the Continental Congress.

The first detachments of Continental Army troops reached New York City from Boston on April 3, 1776.[6] Washington arrived ten days later establishing his headquarters in a house on Pearl Street in the heart of the city.[7] He later moved to a stately mansion called Richmond Hill. It sat on high ground north of the city with a beautiful view of the Hudson River. From his headquarters, Washington quickly took charge of New York's defenses. His orders included attaching all the artillery in the region to the Main Army (also called the "Grand Army").[8] He also appointed Colonel Henry Knox as the army's senior artillery officer. As a result of these changes, Hamilton's artillery company became part of the Main Army and reported to Knox. However, Hamilton's detachment would continue to be paid, fed, and equipped by the New York Provincial Congress. Knox must have been impressed with Hamilton since he assigned his company to the most important gun batteries defending the city. The following explanation of the American defenses of New York will show the importance of Hamilton's assignment.

Basic to understanding the city's defenses is that Knox commanded a total of ten Continental Army artillery companies plus Hamilton's New York Company. They manned 121 cannons and 19 mortars that Knox had available to defend New York.[9] This amount of ordinance seems substantial, however it was paltry in relation to the defensive needs of the city. The problem was that while New York was a compact city located on the southern end of Manhattan, the island itself was 12.5 miles long flanked on both sides by navigable rivers. The west side of Manhattan Island was bordered by the broad Hudson River and the east side was edged by a brackish estuary of New York harbor called the East River.[10] Directly across the East River from lower Manhattan was the western tip of Long Island (today's Brooklyn). The high ground in Brooklyn facing the East River was known as Columbia Heights. This high ground, known today as Brooklyn Heights, was heavily fortified by Knox whose well placed artillery prevented the Royal Navy from penetrating the East River. These same rebel cannons could fire across the East River and into New York

City if necessary. The Americans protected their gun batteries on Colombia Heights by constructing a chain of earthen forts fanning out into the interior of Brooklyn.

Knox placed the bulk of his heavy long range cannons at the tip of Manhattan Island to discourage the Royal Navy from attempting to approach the city from the harbor or trying to break through and sail their warships north on the Hudson River. Knox's big guns were positioned facing the harbor in fortifications built of stone walls, some of which dated back to the Dutch occupation (1624–1664) of New York. They consisted of the star-shaped Fort George and a lengthy stone wall called the Grand Battery. The entire defensive works facing the harbor was about one-third of a mile long and put under the command of Captain John Pierce, who was a Continental Army officer. Hamilton and two other artillery officers identified as [Henry] Burbeck and [Sabastian] Bauman reported to Pierce.

Artillery at the time was identified by the weight of the solid shot (cannon ball) it fired. Captain Pierce's arsenal consisted of 32 pound cannons as well as 24, 18 and 12 pounders. The 32 and 24 pound big guns were referred to as "smashers." They could fire a shot more than one mile. Knox put Hamilton in charge of the cannons in Fort George and in the portion of the Grand Battery facing the Hudson River. Hamilton's guns were in the best position to fire on any enemy warship that approached the waterfront or attempted to navigate the Hudson River. Hamilton was given tremendous fire power to protect the harbor consisting of four 32 pounders and two 12 pounders in Fort George and a number of additional cannons in the Grand Battery. The firepower in the Grand Battery was awesome. It consisted of thirteen 32 pounders, one 24 pounder, three 18 pounders, two 12 pounders, and an assortment of mortars that were designed to lob a ball high into the air at short range and drop with tremendous force.[11]

The Americans also constructed a defense line further north on the Hudson River. It proved to be a sanctuary later in the war for the American army. It was built at a place called Burdett's Landing, which was the narrowest point on the lower Hudson River. This complex consisted of Fort Washington on the Manhattan side of the river and Fort Lee on the New Jersey side. Barriers called Chevaux-de-Frise were sunk in the river between the forts to force ships to sail near the Manhattan shoreline where they could be fired upon by rebel artillery at point-blank range.

By mid-June 1776, the Americans were also feverishly constructing earthen forts and gun batteries along the entire 12.5-mile length of Manhattan Island. At the bottom of the island, New York City looked like a ghost town. May of its houses were shuttered, and its streets deserted. The great city's prewar population of twenty-five thousand had shrunk to about five thousand as residents fled into the country, especially woman and children. Leading the exodus were the Loyalists who ran off leaving their homes and shops to the mercy of looters and the army. Many of the city's magnificent elm trees were cut down to make barricades that blocked every street leading from the waterfront. The male residents who remained were put to work by the army building fortifications; blacks worked every day and whites every other day. The sight and sound of soldiers and civilians digging with shovels and pickaxes was everywhere in daily expectation of the enemy. However, the situation in New York was placid in comparison to the situation in Canada following General Montgomery's failed attack to capture Quebec.

4

AARON BURR'S EPIC JOURNEY

On the morning of January 1, 1776, one day after General Montgomery's failed attack on Quebec, Burr lie dazed and forlorn with the other survivors. Montgomery was dead and his demoralized men were huddled in their makeshift quarters on the Plains of Abraham facing the formidable ramparts of Quebec. They did not know the fate of Arnold's attack from the other side of Lower Town. However, the eerie silence made them expect the worst. It was bitter cold, and the landscape was bleak as the remaining Americans expected the British defenders of Quebec to sally forth and finish off what was left of Montgomery's command. Arnold was nearby, lying in Dr. Senter's hospital after being carried off early in the attack. He lay in a bed with two loaded pistols at his side, ready to shoot the first enemy troops that entered the hospital. Following Montgomery's death, Arnold was the senior American officer at Quebec. He awaited news from inside the city. Matthew Duncan, one of the volunteers on the expedition, received permission from Arnold to reconnoiter the Lower Town on the afternoon of December 31. Duncan never returned.[1]

On the morning of January 2, Major Jonathan Meigs, a captured member of Arnold's famine-proof corps, was temporarily released from confinement inside Quebec. Meigs had permission to visit the American camp outside the city. He arrived unarmed and told his comrades that he was allowed to leave Quebec briefly on his honor to return. Meigs confirmed the unthinkable: every officer and enlisted man from the Arnold Expedition who had attacked Quebec was either dead or a prisoner of war.

It took weeks for the news of the heroic but failed attack to reach every corner of the rebellious colonies. Initial reports said that General Montgomery was killed in the assault along with his aides-de-camp. Burr's family and friends knew that Burr was one of Montgomery's aides and feared that he was dead. A letter that Burr wrote to his sister from Canada following the failed American attack brought welcomed relief that he was alive.

Arnold doggedly resumed the siege of Quebec throughout the winter of 1776 from his hospital bed. Some reinforcements and supplies trickled in from distant Albany. It was a small consolation, but Congress promoted Arnold to a brigadier general. Arnold appointed Captain Burr as his brigade-major. According to one of Burr's earliest biographers, General Arnold recognized Captain Burr as "an officer of sleepless vigilance and of activity that nothing could tire."[2]

Burr's new position allowed him to see how irrational the invasion of Canada was from the outset. American resources were already hard-pressed trying to keep Washington's Main Army in the field when Congress voted to send a second force to seize Canada. Their decision also was inconsistent since they had declared that they were fighting a defensive war when they ordered an offensive campaign across the Canadian border. Congress also underestimated the loyalty of the one hundred thousand French Canadians when France ceded Canada to Britain in 1763. The Canadians were well treated by the English, including protecting the Catholic religion, which won British support of the colony's influential Catholic clergy. Recognizing these objections, Burr said Congress was "either drunk or crazy" for believing that they could annex Canada.[3] Burr's vexation was based on his sharing the miserable conditions under which Congress expected the American troops in Canada to fight. One Patriot writing from Montreal said he

> could not find words strong enough to describe our miserable situation: you will have a faint idea of it if you figure to yourself an Army broken and disheartened, . . . soldiers without pay, without discipline, and altogether reduced to live from hand to mouth, depending on the scanty and precarious supplies of a few half-starved cattle and trifling quantities of flour.[4]

Arnold and Burr struggled to isolate Quebec through the winter months of 1776. Adding to their problems, the French Canadians recruited early in the campaign lost their confidence in the Americans and were deserting. In addition, Congress' paper money was rapidly decreasing in value and merchants were demanding cash for food and supplies. To seize their stores would have further alienated the American's relationship with Canada's population.

Aware of the small size of Arnold's army, Governor Carleton kept his garrison nestled behind Quebec's formidable stone walls protected by artillery and stockpiles of food. It was during the frigid winter blockade of

1776 that Burr began to become cynical of Arnold. In one incident, Arnold ordered Burr to deliver a threatening demand for Carleton to surrender. Burr refused to carry out the absurd mission and the officer Arnold sent in his place was humiliated by the governor. In time, Burr would say that Arnold "is a perfect madman in the excitement of battle . . . but he is utterly unprincipled and . . . not to be trusted anywhere but under the eye of a superior.[5]

Arnold was fortunate that he did not have his badly wounded leg amputated following the failed attack to capture Quebec. However, his recovery was slow and prevented him from actively directing the ongoing siege. Arnold persistently wrote General Wooster during the winter begging him to come to Quebec to relieve him. On April 1, with the arrival of warmer weather, General Wooster suddenly arrived from Montreal to take charge at Quebec. Although both Wooster and Arnold were brigadier generals, the date of Wooster's commission proceeded Arnold's making Wooster the senior officer in Canada. Wearing an enormous periwig, the pompous sixty-year-old Wooster toured on horseback Arnold's twenty-six mile siege line surrounding Quebec. He criticized everything that Arnold had done during the winter claiming he was "the only competent judge of what is proper and what is not."[6] Arnold remained at Quebec until April 12 when Wooster ordered him to take command of Montreal. Burr accompanied Arnold and the two of them rode away from Quebec never to see the exasperating place again in their lives. They left behind the inept and arrogant Wooster who wasted precious artillery ammunition in useless bombardments of Quebec and marching his ragged army around its walls in pointless parades. Smallpox and other contagious diseases began to take a dreadful toll of Wooster's cold and dirty troops. As conditions worsened, his troops went home the moment their enlistments expired while others died from smallpox.[7]

Warmer weather brought additional American reinforcements to Canada along with a new and competent senior officer, General John Thomas, a prewar doctor and a favorite of General Washington. Thomas left Arnold in charge at Montreal and continued to Quebec. He arrived at Quebec on May 1 to find about one thousand American troops fit for duty. The others, amounting to more than three hundred, were suffering from smallpox.

Early on the morning of May 6, General Thomas and his small army could hear the rumbling of cannons from downriver. This was followed by the peeling of Quebec's church bells and the booming of cannons as a flotilla of British warships and transports came within view of the besieged city. The ships landed reinforcements that immediately went into action. After making a short stand, Thomas ordered a retreat. His panic-stricken corps quickly packed up whatever they could load into boats and steered upriver toward Montreal. Thomas's retreat was the pathetic conclusion to the siege of Quebec.

Burr was in Montreal with General Arnold when the news arrived of General Thomas's humiliating retreat from Quebec. The weeks that followed were tragic for General Thomas's army in Canada. The arrival of more troops during early May 1776 only added to the turmoil caused by a shortage of food, clothing, gunpowder, and medicine. Unable to hold back the British advance, the rebels retreated toward Montreal. An American officer described the scene, "[I] found not an army, but a mob, . . . ruined by sickness, fatigue and desertions and void of every idea of discipline or subordination.[8]

Burr had endured six months of privation, several near-death experiences, taking orders from the aged windbag Wooster, and dealing with Arnold's overbearing personality. As an officer, Burr could have resigned his commission at any time. He also had the right to leave as the enlistment of all the members of the Arnold Expedition expired at the end of 1775. According to Burr's memoirs, he decided to resign as General Arnold's brigade-major during a visit to the village of Sorel. Arnold was there with Burr to attend an urgent council of war on May 21 ordered by General Thomas. Following the meeting, Burr told Arnold that he was resigning to "visit his friends [a break from the war] and ascertain what was doing [visit Philadelphia and New York to explore opportunities for advancement], as he wished more active employment [an appointment as an officer in a combat regiment]."[9] Although Burr claimed that Arnold angrily objected, he could not stop him.

Burr probably left Sorel on the morning of May 23 in the company of two members of the Continental Congress who attended the council of war at Sorel.[10] The two congressmen were Charles Carroll and Samuel Chase who were in Canada on a fact-finding mission. Referred to as the commissioners, Carroll and Chase were given extraordinary powers by Congress, including the right to remove incompetent officers. The commissioners were well meaning but arrived in Canada with no military experience or hard cash. Congressman Carroll kept an official journal of their mission. He said that they started back to Philadelphia from the meeting in Sorel on the morning of May 23. The first leg of their journey was to Fort Chambly, a post south of Montreal on the inland water route to Albany. Their itinerary coincides with a letter that Burr wrote to his sister from Fort

Chambly on May 26, 1776. An additional clue that Burr accompanied the commissioners comes from a letter Matthias Ogden wrote to his friend Burr on June 5, 1776. The pertinent text of Ogden's letter reads, "I yesterday saw Mr. Price he informed me that you were on your way, in company with the commissioners." Ogden's reference to "Mr. Price" is James Price, a wealthy Canadian who sided with the Americans and loaned General Montgomery money. Apparently, Burr traveled with Chase and Carroll as far as Fort Ticonderoga in New York. The commissioners remained at the fort to confer with General Schuyler while Burr continued his journey south. It will be recalled that Ogden was Burr's childhood friend and fellow volunteer on the Arnold Expedition. Tracing Ogden's exploits in the spring of 1776 are valuable as he played an important role in the next chapter of Burr's life.

Ogden received a shoulder wound during the New Year's Eve attack on Quebec. He returned home to Elizabeth to recover. Regarded in New Jersey as a hero of the Arnold Expedition, Ogden was offered a commission in one of the regiments that the colony was recruiting for the Continental Army. Helping him was a recommendation to Congress by Arnold, which read in part, "I beg leave to recommend him [Ogden] as a gentleman who acted with great spirit and activity through our fatiguing march, and in the attack on Quebeck, in which he was wounded."[11] Ogden accepted the commission and was appointed a lieutenant colonel in the 1st New Jersey regiment on March 7, 1776. Ogden was twenty-two years old at the time of his appointment. Once formed, Ogden's regiment was ordered to Canada.[12]

Burr was in Albany, New York, when he received Ogden's June 5 letter. Besides mentioning his seeing "Mr. Price," Ogden's letter included the electrifying news that General Washington invited Burr to come to New York "and stay in his family." The term "family" in this instance meant Washington's personal staff, which he called his military family. The implication was clear: Washington was interested in appointing Burr as one of his aides-de-camp. An appointment as an aide to Washington was a coveted position sought by many young men eager to add to their prestige and social status. Besides its stature, Washington's aides held the brevet rank of lieutenant colonel. As previously mentioned, brevet means that an individual holds a military rank only while he is in a particular position. It is a temporary rank. But this situation was overlooked as a position in His Excellency's military family was prestigious and looked upon as leading to a desirable permanent commission as a senior officer in a Continental Army regiment.

Washington had no formal system for selecting his staff. He relied on his personal knowledge of potential candidates. If Washington did not know someone himself, he was guided by written or verbal recommendations from trustworthy army officers, reliable government officials, and friends. Washington emphasized the importance of letters of introduction (recommendations) in a December 1775 letter he wrote to his confident Lieutenant Colonel Joseph Reed, "Indeed no Gentleman that is not well known, ought to come here without Letters of Introduction."[13]

Ogden claimed that he was responsible for Washington's coveted invitation. Washington had a favorable opinion of young Ogden who he mentioned in a May 11 letter to John Hancock. His Excellency's letter was prompted when he learned that recruits in the newly organized 1st New Jersey Regiment were disobedient. Washington was impressed when Lieutenant Colonel Ogden arrived on the scene and "quelled a disagreeable spirit both of munity and desertion" in the regiment.[14] Ogden claimed that Washington later offered him a position in his military family but Ogden opted to lead his regiment into combat and recommended Captain Burr for the job. Washington agreed, and Ogden's June 5 letter extended His Excellency's invitation: "General Washington desired me to inform you that he will provide for you and that he expects you will come to him immediately, and stay in his family."[15] Note that while Burr was being addressed at the time as "Capt Burr," it was an honorary title. Burr was appointed a captain and aide-de-camp by General Montgomery. Burr's position ended with Montgomery's death. Technically, Burr was a volunteer without rank when Washington invited him to join his staff. If appointed, Burr would have immediately been commissioned as an aide-de-camp to Washington with the rank of lieutenant colonel, a huge jump from a volunteer.

Burr spent about two weeks in Elizabeth recuperating and recovering his health after his horrific six months in Canada before riding to Washington's headquarters in New York.

5

AARON BURR'S LOST
OPPORTUNITY

Burr reported to Washington's headquarters in New York on June 12, 1776. He arrived in the midst of the intense efforts to prepare New York City for the now certain attack by a large British force. Washington was an experienced administrator and he needed help at headquarters in organizing the city's defenses. He was short staffed, and Burr was probably put to work soon after he arrived. Burr worked for only a short time in Washington's military family, but the ramifications of this lost opportunity had a major impact on Burr's life. Just what happened during the short time that Burr worked at headquarters begins with understanding Washington's management style.

Fundamental to Washington's management system (the modern military term is "administrative control") was to have an impressive headquarters no matter how impoverished the army was. Washington learned the importance of a visible display of military precision from observing the British Army as a young colonial officer during the French and Indian War. He acknowledged that a dignified headquarters helped to maintain respect for the officer's corps, build morale, and maintain discipline. Burr met Washington's notion of the kind of officer he wanted at his headquarters. Besides being educated, Burr was judicious, well manned, took pride in his military bearing and appearance, and arrived at headquarters with combat experience.

Besides displaying an impressive headquarters staffed by impressive officers, another component of Washington's management style was frequent and persuasive written communications with anyone involved in the operation of the army. His regular correspondents included the members of the Continental Congress (his civilian bosses) and colonial governors and legislatures. It is estimated that Washington wrote twelve thousand letters, orders, and memorandums during the American Revolution. Some were several pages long. The finished letter that was dispatched to its recipient was called the "fair copy." Another copy, called the "docketed copy," was carefully filed at headquarters. Sometimes the same letter had to be produced in a number of fair copies. They were called "circular letters" and sent, for example, to the governor of each colony. Washington was a workaholic, but it was impossible for him to write all his often detailed letters and orders. Therefore, he assigned the work to his small headquarters staff.

As commander in chief of the Continental Army, Washington was authorized by Congress at the start of the war to select a personal staff consisting of a military secretary and three aides-de-camp. A military secretary's function was to write letters and orders and an aide-de-camp was the military equivalent of a personal assistant. But Washington made no distinction between his military secretary and his aides-de-camp. He called them all "penmen" because they were expected to be able to compose his correspondence from his verbal or written instructions. Writing to a fellow officer in February 1776 , Washington said "the multiplicity of business I am Involved In—the number of Letters, Orders, & Instruction's I have to write—with many others matters which call loudly for Aides that are ready Pen-men."[1]

Washington enlarged his staff during the war by successfully petitioning Congress to allow him to add additional paid secretaries and aides. He also used more judicious techniques to increase his workforce including recruiting volunteers or calling added personnel "acting, assistant, or temporary" secretaries or aides. Their major function was to prepare competent drafts for his review and then write the fair copies in legible and attractive handwriting. He was particularly fussy about the appearance of his correspondence with the enemy.

Washington controlled the writing process at his headquarters as evidenced that all his correspondence reads the same no matter which secretary or aide wrote them.[2] His insisted that his correspondence was clearly worded, to the point, respectful, and stated what action was required of its recipient. Washington's style was often an ominous description of a situation to spur his readers to action. A good example of his portentous prose appears in a letter that he wrote to Congress on December 23, 1777, soon after arriving at Valley Forge. Describing the plight of the army, Washington spurred Congress into action by warning them, "I am now convinced beyond a doubt, that . . . this Army must inevitably be reduced to one or other of these three things. Starve-dissolve-or disperse."[3]

Washington's aides-de-camp played an important role in the winning of American independence. Their contribution was essential in the day-to-day operation of the army that allowed the Americans to outlast the British. To explain, today's armies have staff officers who specialize in four major administrative functions: personnel, military intelligence, operations (planning), and logistics (supply, transportation, maintenance, and record keeping). However, the idea of a general staff did not exist at the time of the American Revolution. Its earliest use is debated but probably began during the French Revolution (1789–1799). The Continental Army did have some of the rudimentary elements of a professional staff, notable in copying the office of the adjutant general from the British. The adjutant's function at the time was to maintain records and distribute the commander in chief's orders. The Americans also copied the British Army by establishing various departments at the start of the Revolution. Practically everything that the army needed was purchased, transported, and distributed by a department. These departments included the quartermaster (responsible for procurement and distribution of supplies other than food) and the clothier and commissary departments. The head of each department was appointed by Congress and they were sometimes more of a burden than a source of help to General Washington. The problem was that a number of the department heads were inexperienced or incompetent. In addition, they were often overwhelmed by their own responsibilities. Adding to the troubles was that Congress suspected that the various departments were corrupt, which added suspicions of recommendations to reform them. As a result, Washington was forced to spend part of his working day involved with the routine operations of the army. He relied heavily on his aides-de-camp to help him keep the army functioning on a daily basis. He selected his aides carefully looking for dedicated, intelligent, hardworking men who were willing to spend long hours working with him to prepare his voluminous correspondence as well as assisting him in managing the army.

Washington's responsibilities increased following his arrival in New York as he added the defense of the city to his workload. One result was an increase in his correspondence, which required the need for additional penmen. Captain Burr seemed like a perfect candidate. As previously mentioned, Burr was educated, intelligent, and took pride in his appearance, which was important to the military flair that Washington sought in his aides. Also favoring Burr was his fluency in French, a skill that was important to Washington at the time as volunteer French Army officers were joining the Continental Army with little or no knowledge of English. In addition, Burr had laudable combat experience and had served as an aide-de-camp to the venerated General Richard Montgomery. Burr's prestigious family background also made him a desirable person to join Washington's staff. Burr's impressive record did not go unnoticed at the time. For example, Congressman Oliver Wolcott complimented Burr in a February 1777 letter saying "Young Mr. Burr is amongst the newspaper heroes. He behaved very bravely."[4] Delegate Richard Smith also commended him saying, "Mr. Burr, son of the late President of Princeton College behaved well, as they say, in the Affair at Quebec."[5]

Burr was not the civilian teenager that the general had briefly met at Cambridge the previous year, but a veteran of the Arnold Expedition with an impressive record as a tough and courageous combat officer. Also favoring Burr's appointment was that Washington was short staffed. Two members of his military family had recently left. They were aide William Palfrey who was appointed the paymaster general of the army and assistant aide Stephen Moylan who was named the army's quartermaster general. His remaining staff consisted of Robert Hanson Harrison (officially his military secretary) and aide-de-camp George Baylor. Harrison was Washington's principal lawyer before the war and involved in a number of the general's complicated prewar business transactions. Baylor was the son of His Excellency's friend Colonel John Baylor. Washington also pressed the two officers who commanded his bodyguard into service: Caleb Gibbs and George Lewis.

Despite Burr's impeccable credentials, Washington must have had some reservations about him as he put him to work at headquarters as a provisional aide. It was equivalent to Burr being on probation, or a trial basis, for the job. While there does not appear to be a formal trial period before Washington would appoint a man as his aide, there was a good example of a promising young man who worked at headquarters for a few months before being tactfully discouraged enough to leave. His name was Anthony Wilton White and he was employed at headquarters during the autumn of 1775, before Burr arrived. White was twenty-five years old at the time and the son of a wealthy New Jersey landowner. He was privately tutored at home, which was a common practice among the wealthy at the time. He was recommended to Washington by George Clinton, who was a New York delegate to the Continental Congress. Clinton recommended the young man in a letter to Washington dated July 4, 1775, stating that Anthony was "inspired with love for our much injured country he now visits your camp to offer his service as a volunteer."[6] White's family connections warranted His Excellency to treat him deferentially. His family included his mother, Elizabeth, who was the daughter of a colonial governor of New Jersey. His sister Euphemia was married to William Paterson, an eminent colonial statesman who later became the governor of New Jersey.

White arrived in Cambridge in late July 1775 and went to work at Washington's headquarters as a volunteer apparently to test his writing skills and commitment to the long and grueling workday. Washington's trepidation was justified as evidenced by a letter he wrote to his confident Lieutenant Colonel Joseph Reed. The colonel was in Philadelphia at the time. Dated January 23, 1776, Washington told Reed,

> At present, my time is so much taken up at my desk, that I am obliged to neglect many other essential parts of my duty; it is absolutely necessary therefore for me to have persons that can think for me, as well as execute orders—This it is that pains me [*sic*] when I think of Mr White's expectation of coming into my Family. . . . I can derive no earthly assistance from such a Man.[7]

Washington was too astute a politician to publicly disparage White. Instead, he sent flattering letters to White's father, which fell short of appointing his son as an aide. In one letter to White's father, Washington said "believe me sincere, when I assure you that it will give me pleasure to show any kind of Civility in my power to your Son, whose modest deportment richly entitles him to it."[8]

White finally departed headquarters on his own in late October 1775 to pursue a commission in one of the Continental regiments being raised in New Jersey. He succeeded and was appointed lieutenant colonel of the 3rd New Jersey Regiment on January 18, 1776. He served with some distinction mainly as a cavalry officer throughout the war.[9] Washington spoke of White many years later saying he was "never celebrated for anything . . . but frivolity and empty show."[10]

White's story is an example of Washington testing a man before appointing him as an aide-de-camp. Burr is another such example of Washington deciding to assess qualifications before officially adding another to his military family.

Burr began working for Washington on June 12, 1776, and left just ten days later, on June 22. Some scholars claim that Burr was bored with the routine lifestyle at headquarters and wanted to experience action. For example, Milton Lomask's landmark biography of Burr concludes, "To the romantic stripling, fresh from his moment of glory before Quebec, the company of the methodical, realistic, and apparently disapproving Virginia squire was less than stimulating."[11] Other Burr biographers, including Nathan Schachner, conclude that Burr served on Washington's staff until a permanent position could be found for him. Schacher said, "The appointment on Washington's staff had been a temporary one, a mere stopgap until a more satisfactory one could be found."[12] Historian William Ferrand Livingston has Burr biding his time with the commander in chief, "He [Burr] had been living at Washington's headquarters in New York, where he was invited to stay until a suitable appointment could be procured for him."[13]

However, a more likely explanation for Burr's brief service is that Washington quickly became dissatisfied with him. Something happened to cause Washington not only to dismiss Burr but to dislike him for the rest of his life. Burr would hold similar ill-will toward Washington. In his *Memoirs of Aaron Burr*, author Matthew Davis said that the life-long animosity between Burr and Washington began while Burr was working at headquarters. The pertinent text in *Memoirs* pertaining to Burr's working for the commander in chief reads, "His prejudices against General Washington were immoveable. They were formed in the summer of 1776, when he resides at headquarters."[14]

There is no known eyewitness account of what occurred during Burr's brief tenure at headquarters. Neither Washington nor Burr ever mentioned what transpired between them to cause their life-long animosity. Burr only included a brief reference in his 1834 pension application, "The declarant [Burr] forthwith . . . reported himself to General Washington, and was immediately thereafter appointed aid de camp to General Putnam."[15]

After Burr left Washington's headquarters, he was immediately appointed as an aide-de-camp to Major General Israel Putnam. This move has also attracted speculation by historians. Historian Milton Lomak decided that Burr wanted to work for Putnam instead of Washington, "His new boss [Putnam] was of a different stripe . . . his roaring ways comported with Burr's notions of how a great war should be conducted."[16] Burr biographer James Parton reached a similar conclusion that Burr was unhappy at Washington's headquarters and wanted to work for Putnam, "Burr," said Parton, "the born soldier, the most irrepressible of morals, found himself sinking into the condition of a clerk. The situation was intolerable to him."[17] Nancy Isenberg states in her Burr biography that his working at headquarters "was a temporary post." Isenberg concludes that Burr simply wanted a more active role in the war, "He wished to leave Washington's staff even before he met the general. Assigned to Putnam, Burr stood to exercise more influence. As Putnam's right-hand man, he would not have to compete for attention in the way he would have as one of several aides in Washington's large military family."[18]

Israel Putnam was one of four major generals commissioned by the Continental Congress at the start of the war. He was a charismatic combat veteran of the French and Indian War, adored by the people of Connecticut and throughout New England. Putnam was a poorly educated man often described as being almost illiterate. To clarify this point, here is a rare example of a wartime letter he wrote to General Washington in 1778,

Picskill [Peekskill], ye 24 Sept 1778

Dear Ginrol,—Last night I received a Leator [letter] from Collo Spencor [Spencer] informing me that the Enimy had Landed at the English Naborwhod [English Neighborhood]and ware on thar March to hackensack. I immedat called the ginrol ofesors [general officers] togather to consult what was beast to be don it was concluded to Exammin the mens gons [guns] and Cartridges&&and to have them ready for a March at the shortest notis.[19]

Written communication was important at the time and General Putnam obviously needed help with his letters and orders. The men who he could call upon to prepare his correspondence were his aides-de-camp. As a Continental Army general, Putnam was authorized by Congress to have two aides-de-camp. They were men of his own choosing. Putnam's original choices were stated in the General Orders of the army for July 22, 1775: "Capt. Israel Putnam and Lieut. Samuel Webb, being appointed Aids-de-Camp to Major General Putnam; they are to be obey'd as such."

"Capt. Putnam" was Israel Putnam Jr., the general's oldest son. Putnam Jr. served as one of his father's aides from 1775 to 1779 when he resigned from the army to return to his family and his Connecticut farm.[20] He was born in 1740 which made him thirty-five years old when his father appointed him as one of his aides. The captain grew up on his father's farm in Pomfret, Connecticut. His education was described as "similar to that of the sons of the surrounding yeomanry, equal to all the common concerns [reading, writing, and basic mathematics] of life."[21] His biographer described him as "a farmer, remarkable for his plain, common sense; abrupt and homely in his manner and address."[22] Based on what is known about him, Israel Putnam Jr. was a good soldier but lacked the education to write well crafted communications for his father. General Putnam made up for his son's deficiency in his choice of his other aide who was Lieutenant

Samuel Blatchley Webb. He was born in Wethersfield, Connecticut, on December 15, 1753. His father was Joseph Webb, a wealthy Wethersfield merchant who died in 1761. Samuel's mother remarried Silas Deane, another prominent Wethersfield merchant. Deane was a Yale College graduate who taught school and practiced law before becoming a businessman. Deane was also a Connecticut delegate to the First Continental Congress. Young Samuel was educated at home by his accomplished stepfather. Webb proved to be a ready penman, so much so that Washington wanted him as one of his aides. A study of the General Orders shows that Burr was not sacked by Washington but traded for Webb.[23] The pertinent General Orders dated June 22, 1776, states, "Aaron Burr Esqr: is appointed Aide-du-Camp to Genl Putnam in the room of Major Webb promoted—He is to be obeyed and regarded as such." Washington politely rid himself of Burr by pawning him off on Putnam and getting Webb in return. Note that Burr is identified in the general orders as esquire. The term was a generalization used at the time to identify an educated and well-mannered person. If Burr refused his transfer, he would probably have been dismissed by Washington and reverted to be a volunteer with the honorary title of captain. No matter what rank an aide-de-camp held, it is important to understand that it was an administrative (staff) position with no authority to command troops (line command). To clarify this important point, aides-de-camp were not authorized to command troops in combat. The idea that Burr wanted to be transferred to Putnam's staff so he could see action is unthinkable.

Cutting through all the theories about Burr's brief service on Washington's staff is that Burr switched from handling the routine office work of one general for another. While Putnam was more congenial and less demanding than Washington, Burr was still saddled with an administrative position. Putman's son, the general's other aide, was unable to draft communications and the burden fell upon Burr who was an excellent penman. Burr had plenty of tedious paperwork to handle in his new position. Putnam was the senior major general in New York in 1776, which made him second in command to Washington of the American forces defending the city.

Putnam was also an anachronism in the Continental Army. He was a fifty-eight year old, barely literate veteran of partisan warfare (called guerilla warfare today) during the French and Indian War. Affectionately called "Old Put," even by Washington, his exploits during the war were embellished in the retelling until they became folklore. Putnam was appointed a major general in the Continental Army as a political maneuver by Congress to satisfy Connecticut's allotment of officers.

Aggressive young officers like Burr were obsessed with their rank in the army. Higher rank came with additional prestige and added status and social position in their community. Typical of this obsession with rank in the Continental Army is John Adams's famous comment, "They Quarrell like Cats and Dogs. They worry one another like Mastiffs. Scrambling for Rank and Pay like Apes for Nutts.[24]" A compelling fact in concluding that Washington dismissed Burr is that Congress authorized that an aide to the commander in chief of the Continental Army (General Washington) came with the rank of lieutenant colonel while all aides to lower ranking American generals were majors.[25] This accounts for the June 22, 1776, General Orders stating "Major Webb promoted." Webb was promoted from a major to a lieutenant colonel when he became Washington's aide. It is implausible that a status conscious individual like Burr would have voluntarily given up the opportunity of being a lieutenant colonel for the lower rank of major.

A compelling incident that illustrates Burr was not idle when it came to rank and promotions concerns his paranoia regarding the date of his promotion to lieutenant colonel later in the war. His anxiety was that if there were several officers with the same rank, the one who was appointed first was regarded as the senior officer and in command. Officers who were unhappy with the dates of their promotions would often refer to the situation as demeaning to their "honor." The word "honor" at the time was synonymous with reputation. Following his appointment, Burr wrote a letter to General Washington expressing his displeasure with the date of his commission. What happened was that Burr received a letter from General Washington dated June 27, 1777, promoting him to the rank of lieutenant colonel in a line (combat) regiment. Upon receiving his coveted promotion, Burr shot back telling Washington that he was "truly sensitive of the Honor done me . . . [but that] . . . the late date of my appointment [June 27, 1777] subjects me to the Command of many [officers] who are younger." Burr concluded by making the usual reference to his honor, "but as a decent Attention to Rank is both proper and necessary, I hope it will be excused in one who regards his Honor next to the welfare of his country."[26] If Burr voluntarily gave up the opportunity to be appointed a lieutenant colonel as an aide to Washington in 1776 why would he be obsessed about the date of a promotion a year later?

Burr's aggressive interest in rank and prestige is evidence that his brief service and sudden departure from headquarters was not mutual but initiated by Washington. What happened to cause the falling out between Washington and Burr was a clash of personalities. Burr was a competent penman but, as he admitted, he tended to "indulge himself in pleasures and amusements," which irritated Washington.[27] Burr apparently also had an air of superiority based on his family lineage, which displeased Washington who demanded deference and obedience.[28]

Burr's short tenure and abrupt departure as Washington's aide is glossed over as a minor incident in Burr's life. Some of Burr's biographers, including Samuel L. Knapp (*The Life of Aaron Burr* published in 1835) don't even mention Burr working at Washington's headquarters. However, the incident actually had a major, and devastating, impact on Burr's military and political career as Washington's prestige and political power increased culminating in his election as the first president of the United States. For example, years later, when Burr was lobbying to be appointed a general in the preparations for a possible war with France, Washington rejected Burr calling him an "intriguer and villain." In addition, serving as an aide to Washington proved to be a path to a coveted promotion to command a regiment in the army and lifelong friendship and help from Washington. Hamilton is a perfect example of an aide who benefited from his service to Washington during wartime. Burr failed at headquarters while Hamilton succeeded, and their experience impacted the rest of their lives.

In retrospect it would have made a big difference in Burr's life if he had shallowed his pride and buckled down and worked hard drafting and copying Washington's correspondence. Or, perhaps Burr could have adopted the artifice that the American artist John Trumbull used in his old age. Trumbull was appointed an aide to Washington at the start of the war. He was a restless nineteen year old at the time and was overwhelmed by the long and demanding workday at headquarters. Trumbull resigned after only nineteen days on the job. He went on to become an eminent artist whose work included the paintings in the rotunda of the Capital Building in Washington, DC. Trumbull lived until 1843, long after many of the people who knew that he only served for nineteen days as Washington's aide-de-camp. Trumbull took advantage of the situation and enhanced his reputation by promoting himself as Washington's Revolutionary War aide-de-camp. He even carried the charade to the grave. The inscription on his tombstone includes "Friend and Aide to Washington." Burr worked for about fourteen days at headquarters, but he was never appointed as one of Washington's aides-de-camp.

6

THE BATTLE FOR NEW YORK

General Putnam was in charge of defending Manhattan Island's thirty-two miles of shoreline when Burr was appointed his aide-de-camp. Putnam faced an enormous undertaking when Burr went to work for him. The problem was that Manhattan's shoreline had numerous coves, inlets, and level ground where the British could land troops. In addition, the City of New York, located at the bottom of the island, could become a battleground.

Some additional background information about Putnam is appropriate as Burr worked as his aide for a year. Of interest is that General Washington overlooked Putnam's homespun roughness in favor of his military experience, aggressiveness, and courage calling him "a most valuable man and a fine executive officer."[1] Washington assigned the difficult assignment of defending Manhattan Island to "Old Put," for despite his rustic manners and being barely literate, Putnam was a no-nonsense, hands-on leader who was uniquely talented in inspiring his men to work and fight. Helping their relationship was that Washington and Putnam had a lot in common. They both had fought as Provincial officers in the French and Indian War. They were also both successful businessmen and farmers despite the fact that neither of them had much formal education. Putnam's business interests included owning a tavern and growing tobacco in Connecticut.[2]

"Old Put's" visible battle scars and gregarious personality made him a folklore hero and the subject of numerous stories. Perhaps the best known is from the start of the American Revolution. The story is that Putnam was plowing his fields when he was told that Massachusetts militia had fought British regulars outside of Boston. Upon hearing the news, Putnam unhitched his team, left his plow in the field, and without changing his clothes, he rode off on one of his farm horses to join the fight.[3] It was said that "Old Put" rode one hundred miles in eight hours to Cambridge where he joined the Patriot army and was appointed a general. As an aide-de-camp to General Putnam, Burr held the brevet rank of major. Burr recalled years later that Putnam had appropriated a building in the center of New York for his headquarters. Burr said that it was a "large brick house [the Warren House at One Broadway] at the corner of Broadway and the Battery."[4] Putnam's wife, Deborah, and their three daughters lived with him there while the city was in no immediate danger of being attacked. Putnam's affable personality and semblance of family living must have been a welcome change for Burr from Washington's stuffy headquarters. Even His Excellency admitted in an April 1776 letter to John Hancock (written a month before Burr's brief tenure at headquarters), "I give into no kind of amusements myself, consequently those about me [his aides-de-camp] can have none, but are confined from morn till Eve . . . and no hours for recreation."[5]

Putnam had a reputation for telling stories and Burr, his new aide, was a perfect audience for the anecdotes from his soldiering during the French and Indian War.[6] His military exploits during the war included serving as a captain in Rogers Rangers. This elite detachment of American colonists was organized by the British Army for dangerous scouting missions and raids deep into hostile Indian Territory. It was said that when it's commander, Robert Rogers, needed an officer for a particularly hazardous mission he would pick Captain Putnam. Putnam also learned Indian tactics during the war, which included killing enemy officers first. Eliminating the officers resulted in confusion and disorder among the common soldiers. It is questionable that Putnam encouraged this ungentlemanly tactic during the American Revolution. But clearly Putnam was no gentleman when it came to fighting and young Burr must have been influenced by his close association with the grizzly old general.

Burr served as one of Putnam's aides for a year, from June 22, 1776, to June 27, 1777. Some of the major events of the American Revolution took place during the twelve months that Burr was on Putnam's staff, including preparing New York City during the spring and summer of 1776 for an anticipated British assault. Washington put Putnam in charge of fortifying the thirteen-mile-long Manhattan Island. Putnam had the arduous task of fortifying New York City, located at the bottom tip of the island, as well as every inlet, cove, and beach along the waterfront where the British might attempt to land troops. As Putnam's aide-de-camp, Burr learned the island's geography by riding from one location to another carrying his commander's orders. Burr's familiarity with the island's country lanes and farm

paths would help save Captain Alexander Hamilton from being captured
or killed later in the war.

Storytellers relate Burr's womanizing in every phase of his life, and his
living and working at Putnam's New York headquarters was no exception.
His romantic interest at the time was Margaret Moncrieffe, the attractive
fourteen-year-old daughter of a British officer. Her father, Major Thomas
Moncrieffe, was a prewar friend of General Putnam. The major asked
Putnam to care for his daughter until he could arrange for her to join him.
Putnam agreed and Margaret lived at the general's New York headquarters
with his family until she could be reunited with her father. The story is
that she became passionately in love with Major Burr. Fueling the story was
her memoirs, which were published in 1794 in which she "bursts forth in
expressions of rapture for a young American officer, with whom she had
become enamoured." Although Burr is not named as her lover, his living
in the same house as her and his "propensity for intrigue" have raconteurs
identifying him as the young American officer who Miss Moncrieffe said
"seduced my virgin heart. With this conqueror of my soul, how happy
should I now have been."[7] The story gets better as Burr is credited with re-
alizing that the watercolor landscapes that the duplicitous Miss Moncrieffe
was painting at the time were actually details of the American fortifications
erected to defend New York City. After Burr exposed her treachery, she
was sent to the countryside, away from the city, and eventually rejoined
her father.

According to some storytellers, Burr's liaison with Miss Moncrieffe
was not his first wartime philandering. In an implausible story, an Indian
princess named Jacataqua fell in love with Burr when the Arnold Expedition reached Maine. She was supposed to have followed him to Canada
where she had the first of his many love children, a girl named Chestnutiana. Leaving the fictional world and returning to reality, the events that
followed are important to describe in order to understand the roles that
Burr and Hamilton played in the American defense of New York.

The Patriots conviction that the British would attack New York City
was justified on June 25, 1776, when British warships were seen approaching New York's harbor. Within days additional warships and transports
arrived and anchored near Staten Island in such large numbers that to some
American observers, their masts looked like a floating forest. The British
began landing troops on Staten Island on July 2 under the command of
General William Howe. Their occupation of Staten Island was unopposed
by Washington who continued his strategy (defined as a plan designed
to achieve an overall goal) of holding New York City by defending the

Brooklyn waterfront, facing the East River, and fortifying key positions on Manhattan Island.[8] Among his tactics (how men and equipment are employed) for defending the city was to place his riflemen in heavily wooded Brooklyn where they could be effectively used as skirmishers and scouts. Washington's strategy and tactics were predicated on the fact that he had no navy.

The same day that General Howe landed his first troops on Staten Island, the delegates to the Continental Congress declared their independence from Britain. The delegates in favor of independence wanted to bring the issue to a vote before a big British army and navy build-up aimed at New York might make the more conservative members of Congress apprehensive to sever all ties with the mother country. The congressmen voted in favor of the so-called Lee Resolution on July 2 that stated, "That these United Colonies are, and of right to be, free and independent States, that they are absolved from all allegiance to the British Crown." Congress adopted a formal Declaration of Independence on July 4. Upon hearing the news, one Englishman wrote "Congress announced the Colonies to be independent states that proclaim the villainy and the madness of these deluded people.[9]

The situation remained unchanged through the summer of 1776 as more ships arrived with additional troops swelling General Howe's army camped on Staten Island to 25,000 men. They included the first German mercenaries, or Hessians as they were called, hired by the British government to crush the rebellion. In comparison, the Patriots had assembled an army of 12,333 present and fit for duty under Washington's immediate command and an additional 3,667 officers and common soldiers stationed in New Jersey commanded by General Hugh Mercer.[10]

On July 12, Admiral Lord Howe arrived in New York Harbor aboard his flagship the new and splendid Third Rate, sixty-four gun, HMS *Eagle*.[11] He was the older brother of General William Howe. After being reunited, the Howe brothers worked well together in coordinating Royal Navy and British Army operations whose immediate objective was to seize the City of New York.

As Lord Howe's ship, the HMS *Eagle*, sailed into the harbor the Royal Navy staged a demonstration in his honor. It began when two nearby Royal Navy frigates suddenly raised their anchors, unfurled their sails, and began heading toward rebel held New York City. Ambrose Serle, Lord Howe's secretary, recorded the event from the deck of the *Eagle* writing, "Nothing could exceed the joy that appeared throughout the Fleet and Army upon our arrival. We were saluted by all the ships of war in the harbor. What added to our Pleasure was, that this very Day, about Noon the Phoenix of 40 Guns & the Rose of 20, with three Tenders forced their Passage up the [Hudson] River in Defiance of all their [rebel] Batteries." The action was initialed as a display of British seamanship and courage to impress Lord Howe.

Captain Hamilton was among the American officers who saw the two warships and their tenders heading toward the city. The rebel artillerymen rushed to man their cannons as the enemy flotilla approached and began steering toward the mouth of the Hudson River. This was the moment that Hamilton had been training for. Every American cannon within range blasted away at the enemy warships as they sailed past the city. But the ships had the tide and a steady wind blowing in their favor and they quickly sailed past the thundering rebel artillery with little damage. The only serious carnage that the Patriot artillery inflicted during the incident was to themselves. What happened is that some of the rebels' old cannons blew up under the pressure of live ammunition killing or wounding their crews. Among the casualties were members of Hamilton's artillery company who were inexperienced in firing their cannons with gunpowder. The commodity was in short supply and could not be wasted in training exercises. A lack of discipline among the rebel artillerymen added to their failure to stop the enemy flotilla. American lieutenant Isaac Banks described the event in his journal, "The cannon of the City did but very little execution, as not more than half the number of men belonging to them were present. The others were at their cups [drinking liquor] and at their usual place of abode, Viz., on the Holy Ground [a section of the city near Trinity Church housing brothels and street-walking prostitutes]." Lieutenant Bangs said that "some of these intoxicated men apparently reported to their stations" killing themselves or their comrades when they drunkenly rammed down gunpowder into their cannons before sponging the barrel to extinguish any sparks left from the previous round.[12] One eyewitness reported seeing five American artillerymen killed and three wounded "with our own cannon by neglect of swabbing."[13] But Captain Hamilton was never knowingly reprimanded for his gun crew's poor performance because the discipline problems he faced were problematic throughout the Continental Army. In fact, Hamilton's men were probably better trained and equipped than the rest of the army. Captain Alexander Graydon, a young Philadelphia merchant turned soldier, summarized the character of the Patriot troops defending New York. The appearance of the army, Graydon said, "was not much calculated to excite sanguine [optimistic] expectations of a sober observer." He described the army as a "motley army of unpromising specimens" whose "irregularity, want of discipline, bad arms and defective equipment gave no favorable impression of its prowess."[14] Compounding the problem was the inexperience of the officers, including Hamilton, who despite his soldier-like appearance had never been in combat.

General Howe methodically enlarged and equipped his army throughout the summer. After assembling twenty-five thousand men, Howe began embarking part of his army from their camps on Staten Island aboard ships on August 18 and landed unopposed on the south shore of Brooklyn on the morning of the 22nd. It was a textbook amphibious landing with more than fifteen thousand men and forty pieces of artillery securing a beachhead and moving inland. Washington responded to diverting more troops from Manhattan Island to Brooklyn.

On August 24 there were approximately nine thousand American troops manning the forts on Brooklyn Heights and in the outlying woods and farmlands. Based on this large number of troops, Putnam exercised his rank as the senior major general by asking Washington to put him in command in Brooklyn. Washington had confidence in Putnam and agreed to his demand.[15] Joseph Reed wrote to his wife from New York City on the date that Putnam was put in charge of Brooklyn, "General Putnam was made happy by obtaining leave to go over—the brave old man was quite miserable at being kept here."[16]

His Excellency gave Putnam detailed orders for defending Brooklyn. In his orders Washington warned Putnam to be alert, "nothing being more probable than that the enemy will allow little enough time to prepare for the attack." Washington concluded by telling Putnam that "the distinction between a well-regulated army, and a mob is the good order and discipline of the first."[17] The Patriots troop and artillery deployment in Brooklyn was established prior to Putnam taking command. He used his aides Putnam Jr. and Burr to assist him in inspecting the American positions and reporting their observations back to him. One chronicler claimed that Burr "rode about the American camp, and visited every post and out-post" and reported his observations to Putnam.[18] What Burr saw was that the American troops were deployed along the crest of a line of rocky ridges called the Guan (a variant of Gowanus) Heights. This high ground formed a natural defense line south of the Patriots East River forts. It prevented the British from attacking the forts from the rear. There were four passes through the Guan Heights. They were all guarded to prevent the British from using them to break through the American's defense line. The eastern most of the four was called the Jamaica Pass. It was remote and seemed least likely to be used by the British. Five American officers on horseback were assigned to observe the distant pass. "Old Put" never got the time to comprehend the details of Brooklyn's defenses, including the vulnerability of Jamaica Pass, as the British attacked on August 27, just days after he took charge.[19] Howe's strategy was to stage several diversionary attacks while his major thrust was made at the isolated Jamaica Pass. His troops captured the five horsemen at the pass before they could give the alarm and came behind (outflanked) the American defenses along the Guan Heights with a force of ten thousand troops and fourteen pieces of field artillery.

The Patriots were overwhelmed and battered by the British flanking movement and retreated to their forts on Brooklyn Heights facing the East River. Based on the function of a general's aide in a general engagement (a battle in which generals command the opposing armies; a big battle) we can be reasonably certain that Putnam Jr. and Burr were delivering General Putnam's orders to his line officers throughout the day as well as observing the enemy's movement and reporting what they saw to their commander. In the midst of the fighting, Putnam's instructions might have been verbal and it was up to Burr to correctly relay his orders. To assure the line officers that a verbal order came from their commanding officer, Continental Army aides-de-camp wore a distinctive sash-like device to identify them as a general's deputy. The General Orders of the Army dated July 14, 1775, specified that all general's aides were "distinguished [identified] by a green ribband . . . wore across his breast, between his coat and waistcoat [vest]."[20] A ribband is not a ribbon or a sash. It was about a four to six inch wide fabric device. An officer wearing a green ribband was readily identified as the personal representative (aide-de-camp) of a general and the aides verbal instructions were to be obeyed without question. Conveying orders in the midst of a battle was dangerous work but Burr managed to escape being killed, wounded, or captured in what became known as the Battle of Long Island. Although there are glamorized stories of Hamilton participating in the battle, he was actually far from the scene. His artillery company continued to man their cannons at the Grand Battery in lower Manhattan in case the fighting on Long island was a diversionary tactic with the enemy's main attack aimed at landing troops along the New York City waterfront.

As the exhausted remnants of the rebel army lay huddled in their East River forts, the Crown forces were celebrating their victory a short distance away. A British officer wrote home following the Battle of Long Island saying "we have given the Rebels a deadly crush. On the 27th we had a very warm action but we flanked and overpowered them with numbers . . . and we shall soon take New York. I expect the affair [the rebellion] will be over this campaign, and we shall all return covered with American laurels."[21]

The Howe brothers had shown Mr. Washington and his amateurs the futility of opposing the best navy in the world and one of the foremost armies. Their verdict that Washington was an inept opponent whose poor planning included an absence of mounted troops.[22]

Washington's regiments seemed hopelessly trapped in Brooklyn with Howe's army facing them on the land side and the Royal Navy about to blockade the East River to prevent their escaping to Manhattan. In a daring move, the entire Patriot Army in Brooklyn, estimated at nine thousand men, were ferried across the East River to Manhattan in a providential fog during the night of August 29–30. Burr claimed that he was actively engaged in the evacuation and helped rescue many men "by his intrepidity [sic] and perseverance." But General Washington never acknowledged his role in the retreat. As a result of the snub, Matthew Davis said, "Burr's prejudices against Gen. Washington became fixed and unchangeable; and to the latest hour of his life he recurred to the retreat from Long Island with acrimonious feelings towards the Commander-in-Chief."[23]

In a terse report to his superiors in London, General Howe concealed his carelessness in allowing the rebels to slip away writing, "on the 29th, at night, the rebels evacuated their entrenchments with the utmost silence, leaving their cannon and a quality of stores in all their works. At daybreak on the 30th, their flight was discovered. The enemy is still in possession of the town [New York City] and the island of New-York [Manhattan Island]."[24]

Washington's army was now concentrated on Manhattan Island. Fortunately, General Howe was a cautious and methodical planner who seemed to be consolidating his forces on Long Island before attacking the rebels on Manhattan and seizing New York City. But General Howe and his older brother Lord Admiral Howe had an alternative reason for delaying their attack, which was to negotiate an end to the war. They were empowered by the king and his ministers to offer generous terms to the Continental Congress to end the war. The Howe brothers invited a delegation from Congress to meet with them on Staten Island to discuss ending the war. However, both parties at the time were unaware that General Washington had a top secret plan to blow up Admiral Lord Howe's flagship, the HMS *Eagle,* with a submarine.

Of all the anecdotes about Aaron Burr, perhaps the most fascinating is the possibility that he saw the submarine known as *American Turtle* and met its inventor, David Bushnell. The plan was for the one man crew of the *American Turtle* to fasten kegs of gunpowder to the hulls of Royal Navy ships anchored in New York harbor. Bushnell's first target was the *Eagle*. Although there is no known record that Major Burr was involved in the secret project, the circumstantial evidence points to his participation. Favoring Burr's involvement was that, as author David Humphreys points out in his 1788 biography of Putnam, "Old Put" was responsible for the defense of Manhattan Island following the Battle of Long Island. His duties included "the direction of the whale-boats, fire-rafts, flat-bottomed boats and armed vessels" available to defend the island. Although an "underwater machine altogether different from anything hitherto devised by the art of man" (to quote Humphreys) was never imagined, the submarine became Putnam's responsibility when it arrived in New York City on the deck of a costal sloop from Connecticut. The sloop reached the city from Long Island Sound, which was not blockaded by the Royal Navy. The machine's potential to sink enemy warships excited Putnam and he "afforded his patronage" to the project.[25]

The existence of Bushnell's submarine was known to only a handful of men including General Washington. Other American officers involved in the project were most likely Putnam's trusted aides Israel Putnam Jr. and Aaron Burr. Evidently, as the story unfolds, Putnam was too preoccupied with strengthening New York's defenses to personally assist Bushnell. He assigned the job to his aides to go the pier at the end of Whitehall Street where the "underwater machine" was docked and help Bushnell prepare for his mission. It is fascinating to speculate that Burr saw the sub and met Bushnell and robust Sergeant Ezra Lee who volunteered to operate it. Equally intriguing is that Burr was among the handful of American officers who joined General Putnam on the night of September 6, 1776, to witness the *American Turtle* being towed out into New York harbor to commence its daring attack. Two longboats with muffled oars were used to tow the contraption as close as possible to the *Eagle*. Then the tow lines were released, and the *American Turtle* dived under the *Eagle's* hull. Unseen by the American officers on the dock, Sargeant Lee was unable to attach the lethal explosive keg to the hull of the *Eagle*. He raced back to New York at dawn to the disappointment of the American officers who had vainly waited through the night. Apparently, the crew of the *Eagle* were unaware how close their ship came to be sunk during the night of September 6–7. Ambrose Serle, who was aboard the *Eagle* only mentioned in his journal entry for September 7, "A slight alarm happened last night from the enemy's boats approaching too near."[26]

The Howe brothers were no more successful in their efforts to end the war through negotiation than David Bushnell was in sinking the *Eagle*. On September 11, 1776, they met with a blue-ribbon delegation from Congress. The Howe's offered the apostate Congress generous terms to end their rebellion. But the meeting failed when the congressional delegation insisted on recognition of the United States as an independent nation as a condition for ending the war.

The lull in the fighting during the so called peace conference gave Washington valuable time to reorganize and decide what to do next. His Excellency used the opportunity move part of his army to the rugged high ground of northern Manhattan, known as Harlem Heights, where his army had constructed Fort Washington earlier in the year. He subsequently decided to abandon New York City following a council with his senior line officers on September 12. But evacuating the city and the lower part of the island to Harlem Heights was a slow process due to a lack of wagons and teams of horses to pull them. The result was that the rebels continued to occupy their earthworks in New York City and along the length of Manhattan Island until they could be evacuated.

Across the East River, General Howe was making plans of his own following the failed diplomatic effort to end the war. He reasoned that another example of Britain's military power would convince the rebels of the futility of their upstart rebellion. This time Lord Howe cooperated using a tactic that the Royal Navy had perfected: an amphibious assault against an entrenched enemy position. The British commanders selected Kips Bay (today the foot of East 34th Street), a small cove facing the East River for their attack. Kips Bay was chosen because it was on level ground and defended by inexperienced militia entrenched behind shallow earthen trenches. General Howe's objective was to quickly march south after coming ashore and seize New York City before the rebels could burn it.

Howe implemented his plan in the early morning hours of September 15. It began with rolling broadsides from five Royal Navy warships anchored in the river, which devastated the rebel's earthen works and traumatized the militia. The powerful naval bombardment continued as the first wave of four thousand British and Hessian troops began crossing the East River from Long Island on specially constructed shallow-draft flatboats. Connecticut militiaman Joseph Plumb Martin witnessed the spectacle from the trenches, which he described in his memoirs, "we saw their boats coming out of a creek on the Long Island side of the water, filled with British soldiers. When they came to the edge of the tide, they formed their boats in line. They continued to augment their forces until they appeared like a large clover field in full bloom."[27]

The British Army troops hit the shoreline with fixed bayonets and quickly established a secure beachhead. The tactic resulted in panic among the militia who dropped their weapons and ran for safety. After securing the beachhead, the Crown forces whose numbers were increased to fifteen thousand, advanced inland across the island. This put the American troops south of Kips Bay in peril of being cut off from retreating to Fort Washington. Among the troops threated were a detachment of several hundred artillery men who were manning an earthen work named Fort Bunker Hill. The fort was situated on commanding high ground called Bayard's Hill.[28] The site (located today at the intersection of Center and Grand Streets in lower Manhattan) was about three miles south of Kips Bay. From the top of Bayard's Hill, the Patriot garrison could see clouds of dust and smoke from Kips Bay. They concluded that they were about to be hopelessly trapped in their earthworks by the advancing British. At this point, Major Burr arrived at the fort on horseback with verbal orders from General Putnam to abandon the fort and retreat north to Fort Washington. Burr convinced the desperate garrison that he knew the terrain and insisted that he could guide them to Harlem Heights along the western edge of the island if they moved quickly.

Burr led the retreat from Bayard's Hill Fort across Manhattan to Monument Lane, today Greenwich Avenue. It was at about this point that the remaining troops from New York City joined Burr's column. Captain Hamilton and his artillery company were among them. He had been awakened at dawn that morning by the sound of cannon fire coming from north of the city. General Putnam arrived on the scene and ordered everyone to evacuate the city and march north to Harlem Heights. All the artillery and other valuable equipment and supplies were abandoned; there was no time to save anything. The city's garrison, including Hamilton's company, headed north almost at a run through the suburb of Greenwich Village where they encountered Burr and the retreating artillerymen from Fort Bunker Hill. Hamilton and the others coming up from the waterfront gratefully joined Burr's column, which headed north along a narrow trail through a wild section of Manhattan known as Bloomingdale (Dutch for valley of flowers). The rough terrain spiked with rock outcroppings forced the fleeing Americans to spread out in a line that was two miles long as Major Burr led them through the woods toward Fort Washington. Several American officers on horseback assisted Burr by reconnoitering inland watching for the approach of enemy troops. It turned out that the main party of British and Hessian infantry were less than a half a mile away at some points along their ten mile wilderness retreat route. There is a creditable account, however, that the column was fired upon by some Royal troops. Burr was reported to have "galloped directly to the spot the firing came from, hallooing to the men to follow him." It proved to be a small enemy detachment that fled as the rebels approached. Concerned that they would give an alarm, Burr and several other officers on horseback pursued and killed them.[29] At dusk Burr delivered the column to Harlem Heights to the surprise and relief of their comrades who had given them up for lost. Burr was among the exhausted survivors of the day's harrowing events. Author David Humphreys describes the scene, "That night our soldiers, excessively fatigued by the sultry march of the day . . . lay upon their arms, covered only by the clouds of an uncomfortable sky." He concluded by saying, "we had every reason to fear the final ruin of our cause."[30]

After carefully researching if Burr actually saved Hamilton from being captured on September 15 historian Michael E. Newton concludes, "there is little doubt that Aaron Burr helped rescue the men . . ., including Hamilton and his artillery company.[31]

There are several creditable sources confirming Burr's heroic deed. They include an eyewitness account by common soldier Nathaniel Judson who wrote that "Burr effected a retreat with the whole brigade" (three or more regiments). Judson said that "we had several brushes with small parties of the enemy. Maj. Burr was foremost and most active where there was danger, and his conduct was afterwards a constant subject of praise, admiration and gratitude."[32]

As the long irregular column of American troops was fleeing north, the disciplined regiments of the Crown forces marched swiftly south and occupied New York City. "And thus," said a jubilant Loyalist, "the city was delivered from these Usurpers who had oppressed it so long."[33]

The heavy artillery that Hamilton's company had manned on the waterfront was among the ordnance left behind. After reaching Harlem Heights, Captain Hamilton's big cannons were replaced with two mobile fieldpieces. Field artillery companies in the American Revolution typically consisted of two cannons. Hamilton was given two 6 pounders supplied by the State of New York that continued to administer and finance his company. The state's government also authorized Hamilton's company to continue as part of Colonel Knox's Continental Artillery Regiment.

While supplying Hamilton with just two field cannons appears to be a modest expenditure, it actually represented a major investment and an ongoing expense in men, horses, food, ammunition, and maintenance. The gun barrels were made of iron or brass (actually bronze, which consists primarily of copper with a small amount of tin). Brass cannons were considered superior as they could handle a bigger charge and fire a longer distance than their iron equivalents. Brass cannons were also lighter than iron cannons of the same caliber. A brass 6 pound cannon barrel weighted about

550 pounds and, depending on the projective being fired, had a maximum range of about 1,200 yards. It is unknown if Hamilton's company was supplied with brass or iron cannon barrels.[34]

The Americans tended to follow the organization and techniques of the British Army especially during the first years of the American Revolution. The British used four horses to pull a 6 pound field gun. In the British system, the horses were harnessed in tandem, one behind the other, to a two-wheeled carriage (called a limber), which was attached to the field gun. The Americans employed these same arrangements for their field artillery. Also, copying from the British, the Americans kept a small amount of ammunition in boxes attached to each side of the field piece. Additional ammunition and equipment were carried in a horse-drawn, four wheeled ammunition wagon or in a two-wheeled cart, called a tumbrel, pulled by one horse. The British Army painted their gun carriages lead gray throughout the American Revolution and the Americans followed the British dictum, at least during the first years of the war. It can therefore be assumed that the carriages of Hamilton's field guns, delivered to him in 1776, were painted lead gray. A fine point of history is that the Americans began painting some of their gun carriages a dark red color called Spanish Red later in the war. A full gun crew for a 6 pound field gun consisted of fourteen men. Each of them had a specific task involved in loading and firing the cannon. They drilled constantly to be able to perform their function safely and quickly. The result was a well-trained gun crew should be able to load and fire their cannon four times in a minute.[35] When the gun was fired, the recoil propelled it backward requiring it to be brought back to firing position for the next shot. This was done with two specially designed ropes called bricoles (French for rope) by artillerymen. Bricoles were ropes with attached links of iron chain near the wheels of the cannon that prevented the ropes from being torn if the cannon was turned. Six members of a complete 6 pounder gun crew were called matross (probably derived from the French word matelot for sailor). Their job was to use the bricoles to move the gun back into position after it fired a jarring round of ammunition. British artillery officers benefited from formal instruction at a school in Woolwich, England, while their American counterparts, including Hamilton, learned their trade from military manuals and on-the-job training.

Replacing Hamilton's big, immobile cannons with smaller caliber mobile field guns gave the young captain the ability to provide advantageous close-in artillery support to the Main Army's line regiments. In combat, small caliber field artillery was most effective by aiming high speed solid cannon balls (called round shot or solid shot) low to the ground. This technique caused the cannon balls to bounce along the ground, ploughing through the enemy ranks causing gruesome injuries and spreading mayhem. Even more lethal was to fire canister shot (bags filled with small lead balls) at close range. The British used cloth bags for canister shot during the Revolutionary War, but the Americans were also firing canister shot in crude tin cans. Canister shot in cans was more lethal than using bags. The difference was that the flimsy bags would explode in midair scattering the balls, while the cans would remain intact until they hit the ground, detonating the balls in a concentrated blast. Grapeshot is similar to canister shot. The term grapeshot at the time of the Revolution meant small balls in a mash bag. It took a skillful and courageous artillery officer to use these techniques effectively. From all accounts, Hamilton was an expert at all of them. Commanding field artillery would give Hamilton an opportunity to impress the army's senior line officers. His first opportunity to prove his valor in combat took place when a series of events brought the Patriot Army to the village of White Plains, in rural Westchester County, New York.

The move to White Plains started when General Howe decided that a frontal attack against the rebel's strong position in the chiseled hills of Harlem Heights was too hazardous. Instead, Howe gave Washington another lesson in generalship when he outflanked Harlem Heights by landing troops in what is today the Bronx section of New York City. The maneuver was the opening move to capture Fort Washington, the rebel's main position on Harlem Heights. Their plan was to surround the fortress and then destroy it in a siege or starve its garrison into surrendering.

Howe's flanking maneuver forced Washington to abandon northern Manhattan Island on October 21 and retreat to the open country around the village of White Plains. However, assured that Fort Washington could be defended, Washington agreed to leave 1,500 troops there and retreat with the rest. Captain Hamilton's artillery company, consisting of two horse-drawn field cannons, accompanied the withdrawal. The British followed Washington's army to White Plains where the opposing armies clashed on September 28. Washington's Main Army consisted of about fourteen thousand men entrenched along a three mile line of hills overlooking the village and the nearby Bronx River. Opposing the Continentals was a splendidly well equipped army of thirteen thousand troops commanded by General Howe. If necessary, Howe could be reinforced by thousands of additional troops from British-held New York City.

After studying the terrain and the rebel positions, Howe directed his main attack against what he correctly perceived to be the rebel's weakest position. It was one of the hills surrounding White Plains. Called Chatterton Hill, it was lightly defended by two inexperienced militia regiments. Howe decided that a frightening bayonet charge by his British and Hessian infantry would chase the militiamen off the hill. Washington quickly realized Howe's intentions and ordered veteran Continentals and artillery to defend the hill while the Crown forces prepared their assault.

Many accounts of the ensuing Battle of While Plains, fought mostly on Chatterton Hill, state that Hamilton's artillery was there. They claim that at one point in the fighting Hamilton maneuvered his two field pieces on his own initiative to a position where he blasted away at the advancing enemy column. Author Washington Irving (whose works included *The Legend of Sleepy Hollow*) described the action in his *Life of George Washington*. Describing how British troops were constructing a temporary bridge across the narrow Bronx River to reach Chatterton Hill, Irving wrote, "In doing so, they were severely galled by two field-pieces planted on a ledge of rock on Chatterton's Hill and in charge of Alexander Hamilton, the youthful captain of artillery." The British managed to finish their bridge, "formed, and charged up the hill to seize Hamilton's two lethal field-pieces. Three times his two field-pieces were discharged, ploughing the ascending columns from hill-top to river, while Smallwood's "blue and buff" Marylanders kept up their volleys of musketry." He continued,

> Gen. McDougall ordered Hamilton to open his artillery upon them as the enemy advanced. Hamilton forthwith descended the hill, planting his two field-pieces upon a ledge of rock bearing upon the bridge. . . . Thence he poured his fire upon the bridge. Then British regiments resumed the attack. . . . They crossed the little river by a ford [a point on a river or stream that had a stable river bottom and an unobstructed firm gradual slope on both shorelines] and, resolved to capture Hamilton's guns, rushed up the hill with bayonets fixed. Again and again Hamilton's pieces flashed, driving the ascending columns down to the river's edge.[36]

Hamilton's skillful handling of his two field guns was commended by his prewar friend Alexander McDougall who was a Continental Army brigadier general at the time. Besides McDougall, other American officers became aware of Hamilton's courage and initiative.

Despite fierce American resistance, the Battle of White Plains was another British victory. The British and Hessian troops captured the village and forced Washington to retreat further into Westchester County. After retreating, Washington dug in on the north side of the Croton River. The

Return for Washington's Main Army on November 3 reported a total of 16,969 officers and common soldiers present and fit for duty. However, this number included about 2,500 men left behind to garrison Fort Washington.[37] General Howe unexpectedly cutoff pursuit of Washington's army and began to march his troops west toward Dobbs Ferry, New York, and the Hudson River. According to one eyewitness account, their route was "marked by the licentiousness of the troops, who committed every species of rapine and plunder."[38] With the exception of Fort Washington, which a young and brilliant Continental Army brigadier general named Nathanael Greene insisted on holding, the British occupied the rest of Manhattan Island, including New York City.

Stories abound that both Hamilton and Burr were opposed to defending New York City at the outset of the campaign and expressed their opinions to the army's senior officers. For example, in his 1836 biography of Burr, author Matthew Davis states that Burr advised General Putnam on strategy: "Major Burr, previous to the action, [the Battle of Long Island] had expressed to General Putnam the opinion that a battle ought not to be risked; and that much was to be gained by placing the troops in where the navy of the enemy would not be so serviceable to them." According to Davis, Burr offered advice to other senior officers after the Battle of Long Island: "Burr continued to urge upon General Putnam and Mifflin [Brigadier General Thomas Mifflin] the necessity of a retreat."[39] Today's scholars continue to believe that generals sought the opinion of their aides-de-camp on matters of strategy. An example is Nancy Isenberg's biography of Burr published in 2007,"he [Gen. Putnam] relied heavily on Burr's advice in coordinating military operations."[40]

Hamilton's advice to abandon New York also appears in a book published in 1860 titled *Recollections and Private Memoirs of Washington*, written by General Washington's self-proclaimed adopted son George Washington Parke Custis. In his book, Custis claims that Hamilton wrote General Washington a letter strongly recommending abandoning New York City early in the1776 campaign. Custis claims that Hamilton's letter "detailed many and forcible arguments against risking an action, and warmly recommending a retreat to the strong grounds of the mainland." Washington's failure to heed Captain Hamilton's advice resulted in the "disastrous Battle of Long Island."[41]

The idea of a junior officer offering advice to a general is preposterous. Hamilton was a mere captain of artillery in1776 with little combat experience who never commanded more than one hundred men. Burr had some combat experience leading small detachments during the failed

Canadian campaign. He was also a captain with the brevet rank of major in his capacity as an aide-de-camp to General Putnam. Generals did not seek the advice of junior officers nor did junior officers, who never commanded more than a detachment of soldiers, presume to give their opinions to senior commanders. The men responsible for strategy and tactics were senior officers who were mature, experienced in commanding large numbers of troops, and judicious. To get their opinions, Washington typically organized councils of war to consult with his high-ranking officers. For example, in deciding whether to abandon his strong position in northern Manhattan, Washington organized a council of war on October 16 to discuss the situation with his senior officers. Five Continental Army major generals and ten brigadier generals and Colonel Knox, the army's senior artillery officer, attended the meeting.[42] Washington sought the opinions of his generals throughout the war and his reliance of them increased as they gained combat experience. Washington typically had one of his aides attend his war councils. But they were present for the sole purpose of taking notes and preparing reports and correspondence pertaining to the meeting. They did not participate in the discussions or dare to interrupt the council to offer their opinion or advice. However, some historians infer that Washington consulted Hamilton regarding strategy. One such example is, "And none of Washington's aides had more military knowledge and skill than Hamilton. In this area, Hamilton even rivaled and exceeded many of the army's top generals."[43] Washington's aides were also expected to maintain strict confidentiality and never to discuss what they heard at headquarters.

In retrospect, Washington made some serious strategic mistakes attempting to defend New York City in 1776. Fundamental to his errors was that he yielded to the wishes of the members of Congress who wanted the city to be defended. Instead, he should have followed the advice of General Charles Lee, his most experienced officer, who warned him "that to fortify the city against shipping [enemy warships] is impartible."[44] The rebels had no warships to defend the waterways surrounding New York while the British had the best navy in the world at the time. Adding to his problems was that Washington had little experience implementing broad strategy at the outset of the New York campaign. He acknowledged this when he told Congress of his "want of experience to move upon a large scale" at the beginning of the war.[45] Perhaps his most questionable operational decision during the campaign, besides attempting to defend New York at all, was dividing his inexperienced and outnumbered army between Brooklyn and Manhattan. What saved Washington was that the Howe brothers were slow in following up on their victories. Their methodical preparations and

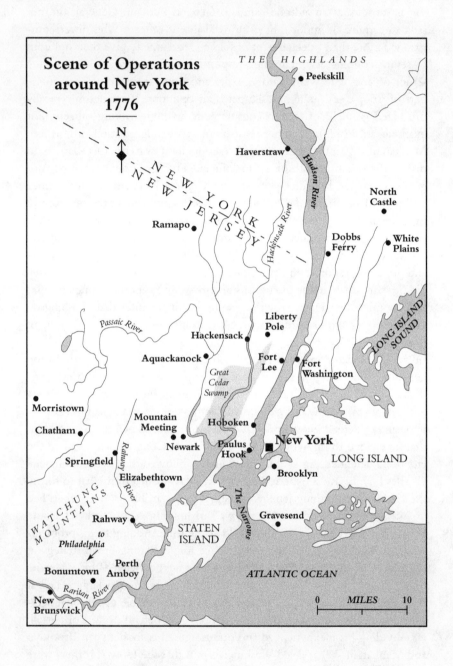

Scene of Operations around New York 1776

N

THE HIGHLANDS

Peekskill

Haverstraw

Hudson River

Hackensack River

NEW YORK / NEW JERSEY

Ramapo

North Castle

Dobbs Ferry

White Plains

LONG ISLAND SOUND

Passaic River

Liberty Pole

Hackensack

Aquackanock

Great Cedar Swamp

Fort Lee

Fort Washington

Morristown

Mountain Meeting

Hoboken

Chatham

Newark

Paulus Hook

New York

LONG ISLAND

Springfield

Rahway River

Elizabethtown

Brooklyn

WATCHUNG MOUNTAINS

Rahway

to Philadelphia

STATEN ISLAND

The Narrows

Gravesend

Bonumtown

Perth Amboy

New Brunswick

Raritan River

ATLANTIC OCEAN

0   MILES   10

attempts at peacemaking contributed to Washington's survival throughout the summer and fall of 1776. Also helping Washington was that he gained valuable experience and learned important lessons from the campaign. Among them was that he would never again get near any body of water where the Royal Navy could be deployed against him. He also shifted his strategy to what he called "a war of posts." In a letter dated September 8, 1776, Washington explained his new defensive policy to Congress, "that we should on all occasions avoid a general action [battle] or put anything to the risqué unless compelled by a necessity."[46] Washington's new policy was also referred to as a Fabian strategy, named after the Roman general Fabius Cunctator whose ideals included a war of attrition; wearing down the enemy through small scale actions, ambushes, and cutting supply lines and communications. These highly mobile hit-and-run tactics were called partisan warfare, petite guerre (small war), or Fabian tactics. The modern term is guerilla warfare.

Washington's new strategy required a change in the way his army used artillery. Colonel Knox took the lead in replacing cumbersome big cannons that had to be dragged into fixed positions with mobile, lighter weight field artillery that could be shifted quickly and fired rapidly. The emphasis on field artillery by the Continental Army effected Captain Hamilton's artillery company. No longer would they be firing big cannons in fixed positions. Instead, they would be using horse-drawn mobile field artillery operating in close support of infantry. Colonel Knox implemented another innovation, which was to mass his field artillery to support an attack. Hamilton's company was assimilated into Knox's tactic of consolidating his guns that would be successfully employed as the war continued.

Washington also learned which of his senior officers he could rely on during the New York campaign. Henry Knox, the bookish artillery virtuoso, emerged from the campaign as one of his best officers. Another was Nathanael Greene, a thirty-six-year-old, brilliant organizer who had risen through the ranks to become a brigadier general. Washington learned that he could count on some of his other generals as being less talented than Knox and Greene but reliable and loyal. They included William Heath, John Sullivan, and Benjamin Lincoln. General Charles Lee, still considered the army's most experienced officer, rejoined the Main Army after leading a successful defense of Charleston, South Carolina. But while Putnam was still active and respected, his reputation had suffered during the New York campaign. Specifically, Putnam had failed to adequately defend the Jamaica Pass during the Battle of Long Island despite Washington's orders that he was to "prevent the Enemy's passing the Wood and approaching your

Works."[47] It was whispered throughout the army that Putnam's best days were behind him. Besides being past his prime, "Old Put's" rough hand-to-hand frontier fighting style from the French & Indian War was out of date. Instead, during the American Revolution the dominant military thinking was to maneuver large numbers of troops and artillery to force an enemy to retreat or surrender. Even Silas Deane, a member of Congress from Connecticut and an admirer of his state's popular folk hero, admitted that Putnam "was totally unfit for everything, except fighting."[48] As a result, Washington diplomatically reassigned the illiterate "Old Put" to rudimentary administrative assignments as the war continued. The change resulted in Burr being removed from the Main Army and the chance for recognition and advancement. Burr became as isolated as Putnam. As for General William Howe, the commander of the Crown Forces during the Battle of Long Island, he was rewarded for his part in the victorious campaign with the prestigious Order of the Bath by King George III. The award gave him the honor of being addressed as General Sir William Howe, the name with which he is commonly called by historians.

7

THE 1776 BRITISH INVASION
OF NEW JERSEY

Both Burr and Hamilton were participants in the events of late 1776. Their involvement began when General Sir William Howe suddenly broke off pursuing the rebels in Westchester County. Washington had a good idea where Sir William was headed with his army. The reason was that behind his conservative facade, Washington was a dynamic warrior who was particularly aggressive in gathering and analyzing intelligence. Washington's interest in obtaining information about the enemy's movements can be traced to the army's first General Order, dated July 4, 1775, in which he stated, "All prisoners taken, deserters coming in, Persons coming out of Boston, who can give any Intelligence; any Captures of any kind from the Enemy, are to be immediately reported and brought up to Headquarters in Cambridge."[1]

The supervision of intelligence-gathering by the Continental Army, which included the interrogation of deserters and prisoners, the reading of captured documents, and the analysis of reports from spies was done at headquarters by Washington's aides. Their intelligence-gathering in late 1776 pointed to the enemy crossing the Hudson River to seize the rich farmland along northern New Jersey's Hackensack River Valley. Called the "Garden of America" at the time, the British wanted the crops and livestock from these bountiful farms to feed their soldiers, sailors, and horses. Based on his intelligence-gathering, Washington decided to transfer part of his army to protect northern New Jersey. However, to allow for any contingencies, Washington decided to leave part of his army in Westchester County to block any move by Sir William aimed at New England. Splitting his weak army against a superior force was a dangerous strategy, but Washington's plan was to quickly consolidate his troops once the enemy's intensions became clear. To this end, he put General Charles Lee in charge of the 7,500 troops remaining in Westchester with instructions to cross the Hudson River with his army to reinforce Washington if the British moved in force into New Jersey. Washington's instructions to Lee were clear and important to keep in mind as events unfolded. Dated "Head Quarters near the White Plains this 10th day of Novr 1776," it reads, "If the Enemy should remove the whole, or the greatest part of their Force to the West side of Hudsons River, I have no doubt of your following with all possible dispatch, leaving the Militia and Invalids to cover the Frontiers of Connecticut."[2]

Washington decided that he would take only 5,000 men from Westchester, believing that he would be reinforced upon arriving in New Jersey by the 2,000 troops at Fort Lee, 1,500 at nearby Fort Washington, and thousands more from the New Jersey militia. Having made his decision, the first Patriot troops began crossing the Hudson River on November 8, 1776. General Putnam crossed the river the next day with additional troops and his two aides: Israel Putnam Jr. and Aaron Burr. Washington followed on the morning of November 10 and reached General Greene's headquarters near Fort Lee, New Jersey, on the 13th. Greene commanded both Fort Lee and Fort Washington, which was located directly across the Hudson from Fort Lee. Washington expressed concern for the safety of Fort Washington and its garrison of 1,500 men. Greene assured him that the isolated northern Manhattan Island hilltop post could withstand a siege or frontal attack. Washington decided to let Greene decide when and if to evacuate the fortress. Having made his decision, Washington rode six miles west to the farming village of Hackensack, New Jersey, where he established his headquarters. Meanwhile, Greene decided on his own to reinforce Fort Washington with more than one thousand men. On November 15, just two days after Washington met with Greene, General Howe's army surrounded Fort Washington and demanded that it surrender. Alerted to Howe's ultimatum, Washington hurried back to Fort Lee where he conferred with Generals Greene, Mercer, and Putnam, all of whom had just returned from inspecting Fort Washington. They informed him "that the Troops were in high Spirits and would make a good defense." Putnam, for one, expressed "supreme confidence" that the garrison could hold out based on his experience at Bunker Hill the previous year.[3] The fortress, reportedly flying a flag consisting of thirteen red and white stripes, refused to surrender and the next morning the British and Hessians stormed the place from four directions. Washington and Putnam were among the American officers who looked on helplessly through their glasses (i.e., telescopes) from Fort Lee as the British attacked. The sound of distant cannons and muskets being fired, and the sight of gun smoke showed the Americans at Fort Lee that the fighting across the river was intense. But after just four hours the gun-fire fell silent and the sky cleared. From across the river, Washington and his generals watched in disbelief as the rebel stripes were lowered from the flagpole atop Fort Washington and the Union Flag (also called the Union Jack) raised in its place. The stunned Americans at Fort Lee learned that 2,800 men had surrendered. It is interesting to speculate that Putnam's aide, Major Aaron Burr, witnessed the surrender of Fort Washington. The answer may have been included in Burr's trunk full of his personal papers, which were lost at sea in 1813. Perhaps that same trunk of papers would have also established that Burr saw the *American Turtle* submarine and met its inventor David Bushnell.

Four days after capturing Fort Washington, General Howe invaded New Jersey on the morning of November 20. The assault was led by Major General Charles, Earl Cornwallis, described as the most aristocratic of the British commanders in America.[4] He was also one of the most aggressive. He occupied Fort Lee later in the day. The fort was actually several gun batteries facing the Hudson River. It was abandoned as the British approached and its garrison retreated in haste to Hackensack. According to one British officer, the rebels "fled like rabbits" leaving behind "some poor pork" and "a few greasy proclamations which we can read at our leisure, now that we have got one of the impregnable redoubts of Mr. Washington's to quarter in."[5] From his temporary headquarters in Hackensack, Washington sent an urgent message to General Lee to quickly reinforce him with his 7,500 men. Then, with no other option, Washington ordered his Continentals to retreat deeper into New Jersey to start what became known as "The Long Retreat."

Washington retreated from Hackensack across the Passaic River and marched his army southwest to Newark where he felt confident that he would be reinforced by Lee's corps and the New Jersey militia. Washington waited five days in Newark for reinforcements to arrive, but the New Jersey militia failed to turn out in large numbers and General Lee continued to hold his position claiming that the British might still launch an attack aimed at New England. Additional urgent messages to General Lee only brought more excuses and delays. Washington had to make a decision at Newark. He could either march west to the relative safety of the village of Morristown, which was sheltered by the Watchung Mountains or continue southwest toward New Brunswick. Following the latter route would position his army between the British and the rebel capital of Philadelphia. Heading to Morristown was tempting, especially since he could see the

Watchung Mountain range from Newark. But he decided to head to New Brunswick, which was located on the main road that connected New York City with Philadelphia. Washington's retreating army had followed local roads and farm lanes in northern New Jersey to reach Newark. At Newark, the army picked up the main road, called the High Road (or the Kings Highway), which ran southwest across New Jersey from Newark through the towns of Elizabeth, Rahway, New Brunswick, Princeton, and Trenton.

It is probable that Hamilton's company, with its two horse-drawn field cannons, was the only artillery that accompanied Washington's troops during the start of its epic retreat across New Jersey. However, when the retreating column reached Elizabeth, a few miles south of Newark, it was joined by Captain Daniel Neil's Eastern Company of New Jersey Artillery. Neil's company added two additional horse-drawn field guns to Washington's arsenal. Neil, a resident of Acquackanonk (today's Passaic, New Jersey) commanded one of the two artillery companies raised by the New Jersey Provincial Congress in February 1776. Neil took command of the Eastern Company in April 1776. His detachment was deployed along the New Jersey coast throughout the New York City campaign. As a result, Neil's company had no combat experience when it joined Washington's army at Elizabeth.[6] Washington only lingered briefly at Elizabeth before resuming his march along the High Road to the Raritan River and the town of New Brunswick.

New Brunswick was located in central New Jersey on the far side of the Raritan River. The American troops began crossing the Raritan at noon on November 29, 1776, and occupied the river town. Washington was hoping to find reinforcements waiting for him when he arrived at New Brunswick but there were only a few stragglers from the army and a handful of New Jersey militiamen. Even more critical was that the enlistment of thousands of his troops would expire in a few days (December 1) and they were determined to leave. They felt that they had served the Patriot cause and it was time for other men to take their place. With the van (advance detachment) of Cornwallis's column reported to be five miles away, Washington wrote Congress from New Brunswick on November 30, "the situation of our affairs being truly alarming."[7] Washington established his temporary headquarters at Cochrane's Tavern where he spent the night. He awoke the following morning, December 1, 1776, to a truly desperate situation. Scouts reported that ten thousand enemy troops were approaching while 2,060 of his own troops had walked off at dawn without an apology or backward glance. A hasty return showed a total of a little more than 3,500 officers and common soldiers remained.[8] Some regiments had been reduced after months of fighting, illness, and desertions to just a handful of men. Most shocking of all was the Virginia and Maryland Rifle Regiment commanded by Lieutenant Colonel Moses Rawling. The regiment counted 250 men as late as November 1776. It was reduced to 44 officers and common soldiers at New Brunswick on December 1.[9] By 1:30 in the afternoon the Crown forces were arrayed across the shallow Raritan from New Brunswick and only the rebel's artillery was discouraging them from crossing the river. Archibald Robertson, a British Army officer was on the scene on December 1 and wrote in his diary that the rebels had "five pieces of Cannon with which they gave us a Cannonade."[10] The artillery Robertson saw were the field guns of Hamilton's and Neil's companies. At two guns for each company, it accounts for four of the cannons Robertson claimed were in the American arsenal. Assuming that Robertson is correct, the fifth rebel gun might have been a small cannon or mortar owned by a militia company. The position of Neil's company is another mystery. As for the location of Hamilton's unit, tradition places his two guns on a hilltop in New Brunswick where they swept the river below with artillery fire. There is a historic marker on the site, which is today on the campus of Rutgers University in New Brunswick.

The American artillery and marksmen armed with rifles managed to keep Cornwallis's troops from crossing the Raritan on December 1. At dusk, with no news from General Lee, Washington began withdrawing part his little army from New Brunswick south toward Princeton. General Greene was with them and he later wrote Governor Cooke of Rhode Island, "when we left New Brunswick, we had not 3000 men, a very pitiful army to trust the Liberties of America upon."[11] His Excellency stayed in New Brunswick until 7:30 in the evening before riding off to join his main force, which was already halfway to Princeton.[12] To trick Cornwallis, Washington resorted to leaving a few hundred men behind. They marched around enormous campfires and made noise as if they were digging earthworks to defend New Brunswick. Then they marched off in the middle of the night to join Washington's shadow of an army as it moved toward Princeton. Washington wrote a hasty message to Congress that night explaining that he had no option but to continue to retreat through Princeton and Trenton and across the Delaware River into Pennsylvania, "It being impossible to oppose them with our present force with the least prospect of success, we shall retreat to the West side of Delaware [Pennsylvania] . . . where it is hoped we shall meet a reinforcement sufficient to check their Progress."[13]

What is significant about Washington's brief defense of New Brunswick is that, in retrospect, December 1, 1776, was the closest that the

British came to a military victory in the American Revolution. If the Crown forces had managed to cross the Raritan River that day, they would have been opposed by a rebel army of only 3,500 men. The defeat of Washington's Main Army, added to the series of American defeats earlier that year, might have forced Congress to seek a negotiated peace to end the war. It is staggering to realize that only Hamilton's and Neil's field artillery saved the American cause from potential disaster.

On the morning of December 2, Cornwallis realized that all the rebels were gone, and his army occupied New Brunswick. They did not pursue the rebels further as his orders from General Howe were to advance no further than New Brunswick where he was to await further instructions.

As the ragged Patriot army passed through Princeton on the Long Retreat, a resident of the college town is reported to have noticed Captain Hamilton among the retreating Americans. "Well do I recollect the day" the villager recalled, "when Hamilton's company marched into Princeton. It was a model of discipline, at its head was a boy, and I wondered at his youth.[14] Perhaps Hamilton turned to look at Nassau Hall, the home of the college in Princeton, as he scurried through the village with his two precious field cannons. How different his situation was when he applied to the school just three years earlier. There was another purported sighting of Hamilton on the retreat toward the Delaware River. The source is identified as a "veteran officer" who saw Hamilton trekking alongside one of his field pieces. The officer said that he "noticed a youth, a mere stripling, small, slender, almost delicate in frame, marching with a cocked hat pulled down over his eyes, apparently lost in thought, with his hand resting on a cannon, and every now and then patting it, as if it were a favorite horse or a pet plaything."[15]

There is no known record that Burr was with the Main Army as it retreated across New Jersey. However, his boss, General Putnam, was definitely at Fort Lee on November 16 where he witnessed the fatal attack on Fort Washington and in Pennsylvania on December 9 with the Main Army. If Putnam was with the army as it withdrew across New Jersey, then his two aides were probably with him. This puts Burr on the Long Retreat, one of the most dramatic events of the American Revolution.

Washington's army arrived in Trenton on December 7 where it began to cross the Delaware River into Pennsylvania. Cornwallis reached Trenton too late to prevent their crossing the river. Washington had taken the precaution of removing all boats for miles up and down the river from Trenton, which discouraged Cornwallis from pursuing the rebels further. But the possibility remained that Cornwallis would eventually cross the

Delaware and march on to Philadelphia. To deal with this possibility, Washington decided to send one of his senior officers to help organize that city's defenses.

His Excellency had become anxious regarding the competency of some of his generals.[16] Helping to organize Philadelphia's defenses was an administrative rear echelon job. It was a good opportunity for Washington to tactfully purge his army of one of his least competent senior officers. Probably the most inept of the lot was the aged and nearly illiterate Israel Putnam. The old, white haired, grizzly general was courageous and an excellent motivator, but his crude fighting style was out of date at a time when American officers were studying military science. They were reading the latest European military treatises and interested in how to best employ artillery and maneuvering their armies to force an enemy to retreat or surrender rather than bring on a general engagement.[17] Washington was creating a disciplined, professional army and Putnam's rough-edged, belligerent temperament was out of date. Captain Alexander Graydon perhaps best summed up Putnam's declining standing in the army when he said "he was not what the time required."[18]

Probably the first indication that Washington was dissatisfied with the inveterate Putnam was when he relieved "Old Put" of his command of Manhattan Island with General Greene on November 8, 1776. Washington specifically instructed Greene to "give such orders as to evacuating Mount Washington [Fort Washington] as you judge best."[19] Washington took action to completely eliminate Putnam from a field command in the Main Army on December 9 when he gave the aged general the Philadelphia assignment.[20] His instructions to "Old Put" were to "put that town into a posture of defense."[21] As Putnam's aide, Burr joined his "good old general" in exile in the rebel capital.[22] As Putnam's aide, Major Burr was obligated to join his commander in backwater Philadelphia where his chances for recognition and a commission as a line officer were slim. At the same time, Captain Hamilton remained at the center of the action with the Main Army on the banks of the Delaware River.

The amiable Putnam turned out to be the right man for the job of cooperating with the local authorities to organize Philadelphia's defenses. Working with his small military family, Putnam was able to rally the local militia and send supplies to Washington's beleaguered army camped along the Delaware River. He helped muster Philadelphia's male population to dig trenches and fortifications to defend the city. To help maintain order, his headquarters issued a number of proclamations including one declaring martial law on December 12 and imposing a curfew. A few days later Congress voted to leave Philadelphia and move to Baltimore. Before departing, Congress ordered Putnam to defend Philadelphia "to the last extremity." The news that Congress was evacuating the city resulted in residents packing up their most precious belongings and leaving in droves. Those that remained were panicky as rumors of the enemy's approach spread through Philadelphia. Responding to hearsay that the Continental Army was going to set fire to the city, Putnam's headquarters issued a notice on December 13,

> The General has been informed that some weak or wicked men have maliciously reported that it is the design and wish of the officers and men in the Continental Army to burn and destroy the city of Philadelphia. To counteract such a false and scandalous report, he thinks it necessary to inform the inhabitants who propose to remain in the city that he has received positive orders from the honourable Continental Congress, and from his Excellency General Washington, to secure and protect the city of Philadelphia against all invaders and enemies.[23]

Who wrote this notice that originated from General Putnam's headquarters? Most likely it was Burr who was Putnam's aide and an able penman. In fact, Burr was probably writing everything that was emanating from "Old Put's" headquarters, including this brief excerpt from a nicely composed letter Putnam wrote to Washington on December 12, 1776, "My Dear General : Your favor of yesterday I have received. All things in this city remain in confusion for want of men to put them in order. The citizens are generally with you."[24]

Besides preparing correspondence, it was customary for a general to be accompanied by one or both of his aides on official business. One story tells how Putnam visited the upholstery shop of Betsy Ross while he was in Philadelphia supervising the city's defenses. The purpose of the alleged meeting was to discuss a design for the American flag. It was not uncommon for upholsters to sew flags, and there are receipts proving that Ms. Ross made flags during the war. Burr may have been present at this historic meeting between General Putnam and Betsy Ross. In one version of the story, Putnam suggested a flag with six pointed stars to Ms. Ross during their meeting. In response, Betsy cut a piece of paper with a pair of scissors to demonstrate that it was easier to make a five pointed star. This story allegedly accounts for the eventual adoption of the five-pointed star in the American flag.[25]

Another famous Revolutionary War character who was in Philadelphia when Putnam and Burr were there was Thomas Paine. On December

19, Paine published a pamphlet in Philadelphia entitled *The American Crisis—Number One.* The pamphlet began, "These are the times that try men's souls. The summer soldier and the sunshine patriot will, in this crisis, shrink from the service of his country; but he that stands it now, deserves the love and thanks of man and woman."

Paine's pamphlet mentioned the likelihood that General Sir William Howe's army would cross the Delaware River and march to Philadelphia, "Howe, it is probable, will make an attempt on this city; should he fall on this side the Delaware River [Pennsylvania], he is ruined; if he succeeds, our cause is ruined.[26]

Unknown to Paine, or anyone else among the Americans, General Howe had no intention of pursing the rebels beyond Trenton. He reasoned that his army had conquered far more of New Jersey than originally planned. Thus, on December 13, 1776, Howe decided to end campaigning for the winter believing that his army would finish off Mr. Washington and his shabby army, capture Philadelphia, and end the war in the following spring.[27] Howe also decided to garrison part of his army throughout the subjugated parts of New Jersey to maintain control and forage locally for food and firewood while he returned to New York City for the winter. Author Washington Irving graphically described the foreboding situation in New Jersey as large numbers of its disheartened citizens appeared at the newly established garrison towns to sign affidavits affirming their fidelity to Royal authority,

> Many of them . . . thought it a ruined enterprise; the armies engaged in it had been defeated and broken up. They beheld the commander-in-chief retreating through their country with a handful of men, weary, way worn, dispirited; without tents, without clothing, many of them barefooted, exposed to wintry weather, and driven from post to post by a well-clad, well-fed, triumphant force, tricked out in all the glittering bravery of war. Could it be wondered at, that peaceful husbandmen, seeing their quiet fields thus suddenly overrun by adverse hosts . . . should instead of flying to arms, seek for the safety of their wives and little ones. A proclamation, dated 30th of November, commanded all persons in arms against his majesty's government, to disband and return home offering a pardon to all should comply.[28]

The Patriot cause suffered another blow when General Charles Lee, now second in command of the army was captured in New Jersey on Friday, December 13, 1776. Lee was captured after leaving the safety of his army at Bernardsville, New Jersey, on the afternoon of December 12, 1776.

Accompanied by a few guards, Lee spent the night at the isolated Widow White's Tavern. Loyalists alerted the British to his position and a detachment of intrepid light dragoons (mounted troops that were lightly equipped and particularly useful for reconnaissance and raids) surrounded the tavern on the following morning. After the dragoons chased off his bodyguards, Lee surrendered and was brought to British-held New Brunswick. Author Thomas Fleming calls the date of Lee's capture the luckiest Friday the 13th in American history. To explain, Lee was a capable commander, but he was arrogant and ambitious. He purposely marched his column as slow as possible to reinforce Washington in New Jersey to maintain an independent command. At the same time, he was criticizing Washington's leadership with his credulous friends in Congress. His capture put an end to his plotting and allowed General John Sullivan, his second in command, to quickly join Washington's beleaguered army in Pennsylvania.

Encouraged by the arrival of Sullivan's troops, artillery, and other reinforcements, Washington was planning a counterattack. His target was Trenton on the Delaware River. It was at the western end of the line of towns occupied by the British and their Hessian hirelings. Trenton was garrisoned by three Hessian regiments and a detachment of British light dragoons. Commanding at Trenton was fifty-year-old Colonel Johann Gottlieb Rall. A tough combat officer, Rall had no respect for Mr. Washington and his ragtag army. As a result, Patriot spies informed Washington that Rall had erected no earthworks to defend Trenton. When, Major Von Dechow, a veteran Hessian officer stationed at Trenton, proposed that some gun batteries should be constructed where cannons could be placed against a rebel assault, Colonel Rall was reported to have replied, "Works!—pooh-pooh, an assault by the rebels! Let them come! We'll at them with the bayonet."[29] Rall should have realized early on how dangerous his isolated position was. One reason for Rall to have been alarmed was that detachments of rebel militia were cutting off his communications with the nearest Crown forces winter garrison at Princeton. On December 20, just days before Washington's Main Army attacked, Colonel Rall sent two dragoons with dispatches to Princeton. An hour later one of them returned to report that his companion was killed in a rebel ambush. Fearing for his life, the dragoon turned back to Trenton. Rall had to send a captain and a hundred men with a field gun to deliver his letters.[30]

Washington decided that Trenton was a tempting target for a badly needed victory. Following careful planning, he launched his attack on Trenton on the night of December 25. His daring plan was to approach Trenton at night with 2,400 men and 16 cannons.[31]

The Patriot army crossed the Delaware River nine miles above Trenton at McConkey's Ferry.[32] Hamilton's company was camped a few miles from the ferry in Upper Makefield, Pennsylvania. His unit, which boasted one hundred men earlier that year, was down to three officers, including Hamilton, and thirty-two enlisted men. It was still an adequate force to handle the company's two 6 pounders. They made their way to McConkey's Ferry during the afternoon of December 25. The company's second in command, Lieutenant James Moore, was too ill to join them. He was left behind in the home of Robert Thompson (today's Thompson-Neely House Museum) where he died on the morning of December 26.

Washington planned to convey his entire army across the Delaware by midnight and reach Trenton by 5:00 a.m., but ice floes in the river struck the boats, at times pushing them off course. Adding to the delay was that Colonel Knox insisted on bringing a large number of cannons and the numerous horses to pull them. The artillery and horses were brought across the river on flatboats, and precious time was lost maneuvering the heavy guns and coaxing the skittish horses on and off the boats.[33] Then, the weather suddenly worsened, slowing down the operation still further. Conditions deteriorated further around midnight with increasing winds, freezing rain, followed by snow. As the night wore on the snow turned to blinding sleet, soaking the men and covering the ground with ice. It was well after one o'clock in the morning before Hamilton's company crossed the river. Washington's timetable became impossible to maintain in the storm, and it took until 3:00 a.m. just to get his 2,400 sodden and freezing men and sixteen canons across the ice-choked river. Another hour was lost assembling the troops and hitching up the artillery horses. Everything was done in the dark as the light from a single lantern might alert an enemy patrol or some local Loyalist to the rebel's presence. The men and artillery were finally assembled and ready to move by 4:00 a.m.[34] The delay meant that the army would not arrive outside of Trenton until around 8:00 a.m. But Washington was determined to push on. He gathered his senior officers and instructed them set their watches to his. The revised plan was for the Continentals to strike Trenton at exactly 8:00 a.m. Part of the army, under General John Sullivan, would attack along a road close to the river, but the major thrust was led by General Greene whose objective was to occupy the high ground facing the town. Hamilton's company was assigned to Greene's division. Besides Hamilton's company, Greene's command included the artillery companies of Captains Thomas Forrest and Sabastian Bauman.[35] Forrest was the senior artillery officer of the division. He commanded the Second Company, Pennsylvania State Artillery, which consisted of two brass 6 pounders and two howitzers (a small cannon that fired a shell at a high trajectory). The three artillery companies were distributed throughout Greene's division on the march to Trenton. Hamilton's guns were in the middle of the column. Everyone had to keep moving to avoid freezing to death.

When the rebels reached the outskirts of Trenton, they encountered Hessian guard posts. The soldiers manning these guardhouses were quickly scattered and although they were able to warn the town's garrison of the rebel's presence it was too late. The artillery in Greene's division was quickly deployed on the high ground above the town and went into action. Their cannons had a clear field to fire down King and Queen Streets (the two major streets in Trenton) as the Hessians struggled to form in the open and fight back. Hamilton's company was credited with disabling the two Hessian cannons that managed to be brought into action.[36] Following the initial artillery barrage, rebel infantry stormed into the center of town from different directions. The Hessians broke rank under the intense rebel firepower. Colonel Rall was mortally wounded while bravely leading his troops. Some of his men were more fortunate and managed to escape but over eight hundred surrendered.

Washington and his victorious army remained in Trenton only briefly. They gathered up their captured weapons, equipment, and prisoners and returned to Pennsylvania. The captured Hessians were marched to Philadelphia where they were imprisoned under Putnam's authority. Their arrival gives us another rare example of Putnam's poor writing ability when he penned a hasty order to an American officer to have his men vacate a barracks for the captured Hessian. The order reads, "You are immedatly to remove your men out of the Barrok to make room for the hashon [Hessian] prisoners."[37] His aide Major Burr was probably present when "Old Put" invited the captured Hessian officers to his headquarters for some refreshments. One of them left an account of the meeting, "He shook hands with each of us, and we all had to drink a glass of Madeira with him. This old gray-beard may be a good, honest man, but nobody but the rebels would have made him a general."[38] Entertaining the Hessian officers captured at Trenton was the closest Burr came to participating in one of the greatest events of the American Revolution.

Washington was encouraged by his stunning victory at Trenton and the rallying of the New Jersey militia in response to the devastation of the state by the occupation troops. General Greene described the situation in a letter to Governor Nicholas Cooke of Rhode Island, "The enemy's ravages in the Jerseys exceeds all description. . . . The country are in high spirits and breathe nothing but revenge.[39] Encouraged by the surge of Patriot resistance in New Jersey, Washington crossed back over the Delaware River on December 29 and occupied Trenton. It was a bold move as he was aware that General Cornwallis was marching from British-held New York City with nine thousand troops to retake Trenton. Cornwallis left two regiments at Princeton while he advanced with the bulk of his army to American-held Trenton. The two armies clashed on the afternoon of January 2 at Assunpink Creek just south of the town. After intense fighting, Cornwallis withdrew at dusk believing that he would renew his attack in the morning and overwhelm the rebels. One again, Washington reverted to his trick of leaving a few hundred men to man his defenses at Assunpink Creek while he took off with most of his army. They marched through the night to surprise the British at Princeton. There were reports that the Patriot's nighttime march was slowed down by their field artillery. The story is probably true as the rebels brought thirty-five cannons with them on the night march including Captain Hamilton's two 6 pounders.

Early the next morning, January 3, 1777, General Cornwallis awoke to find that the rebels were gone and the sound of cannon fire coming from the direction of Princeton. He immediately formed his army and started back down the road toward Princeton. Washington had tricked Cornwallis. After learning what happened, British General Sir Henry Clinton said that the Americans had escaped through Cornwallis's negligence, "the most consummate ignorance I ever heard of [in] any officer above a corporal."[40]

The two British regiments at Princeton were under the command of Lieutenant Colonel Charles Mawhood. They were marching to Trenton when they were attacked outside of Princeton. Mawhood was an experienced officer who reacted calmly to the situation. He deployed his infantry and two 6 pound field guns in the Clarke farm fields where he successfully fought off rebel troops commanded by General Hugh Mercer. Washington personally led a successful counterattack.

Following the American victory at the Clarke farm, the action shifted to the center of Princeton where about two hundred British Redcoats barricaded themselves in Nassau Hall. From this stronghold the British intended to hold off the Americans until reinforcements arrived. However, their hopes were short-lived when the Americans encircled the building with their field artillery and commenced firing. A legendary story from the Battle of Princeton is that an American cannonball is alleged to have decapitated the portrait of King George II hanging inside Nassau Hall. Captain Hamilton is cited as firing the shot that decapitated King George's head. The British barricaded in the building viewed the lucky shot as an admonition and they surrendered.

Historian John C. Miller quipped in his Hamilton biography, "Although Hamilton had been denied admission to Princeton, he left his mark upon that institution: he put a cannon ball through Nassau Hall where some British troops were holed up."[41]

Reflecting on the successful New Jersey campaign, General Greene wrote, "The two late actions at Trenton and Princeton have put a very different face upon affairs. Within a fortnight past we have taken and killed of Howe's army between two and three thousand men—Our loss is trifling."[42]

Washington marched his army into winter quarters in Morristown, New Jersey, following the Battle of Princeton. At the same time, the British abandoned wintering troops throughout New Jersey. They withdrew from the western section of the state and consolidated their forces for the winter in New Brunswick and Perth Amboy, both located in eastern New Jersey. Washington wanted a detachment of troops to occupy Princeton to protect the region and warn him of any enemy movement from New Brunswick aimed at outflanking his position in Morristown. Not surprisingly, His Excellency selected "Old Put" for this latest perfunctory and forsaken assignment. Putnam was available as the threat to Philadelphia temporarily ended when the British withdrew to the eastern part of New Jersey. Following Washington's order, Putnam crossed the Delaware River at Bristol, Pennsylvania, to New Jersey on January 4. He brought six hundred Pennsylvania militiamen with him and temporarily occupied the village of Crosswicks, New Jersey. From Crosswicks he dispatched spies and mounted patrols to watch for any British strike aimed at Trenton or Princeton. Washington warned Putnam of this possibility, "As we have made two successful Attacks upon the Enemy—by way of surprise [Trenton and Princeton]—they will be pointed [sic] with resentment and if there is any possibility of retaliating will Attempt it."[43]

With no reports of enemy movement, Putnam felt safe to move his headquarters to Princeton, which was just sixteen miles southwest of New Brunswick. He arrived there on January 19, 1777, and occupied the battle-scared village for the next four months. Putnam's situation was perilous. The enlistment of many of his militiamen expired and they went home. With no replacements or reinforcements forthcoming, Putnam's command was reduced to a few hundred men with only a days' march separating them from thousands of Royal troops camped in New Brunswick. From Princeton, Putnam implemented His Excellency's instructions to be vigilant, as "a number of horsemen in the dress of the Country [wearing civilian clothing] must be Constantly Kept going backwards & forwards" to watch for any enemy movement.[44] Putnam made Nassau Hall his head-quarters. Burr had studied in the building as a college student but now he was occupied there with Putnam's office work including scribbling letters, orders, and keeping records. "Old Put" and his son seemed incompetent as administrators and must have appreciated Burr's ability to handle their paperwork. In fact, a study of Putnam's generalship during the American Revolution shows that he always had one aide who was a ready penman such as Webb or Burr.

If Burr was not miserable enough in isolated Princeton, a letter he received in early March 1777 from his boyhood friend Matthias Ogden probably made him more depressed. Ogden wrote that he was recently promoted to colonel and commanding officer of the 1st New Jersey Regi-ment. After congratulating him, Burr expressed his hopeless clerical situa-tion. "As to expectations of promotion, I have not the least," Burr wrote Ogden, "either in the line or the staff. I should have been fond of a berth in a regiment." Burr lamented to his friend "that my former equals, and even inferior in rank, have left me [been promoted]." But trying to put a positive outlook on his situation, Burr said, "I am at present happy in the esteem and entire confidence of my good old general."[45]

There was one incident during Burr's boring winter in Princeton that livened things up. It began when Putnam arrived in Princeton and discovered that a seriously wounded British army captain named James McPherson was residing in a house in the village. Captain McPherson was left for dead during the Battle of Princeton. Described as a "worthy Scots-man and a captain in the 17th British regiment," McPherson believed that his wounds were fatal and asked Putnam if he would allow a fellow British officer wintering in New Brunswick to come to Princeton to help him make out his will. Putnam agreed and a message was sent under a flag of truce to McPherson's officer friend, but Putnam did not want the visitor to see how few troops he had in Princeton. What Putnam did was to insist that the British officer arrive in Princeton after dark. Putnam had candles lit in every room in Nassau Hall to make it look like it was a barracks full of off-duty troops. Next, he ordered his small garrison to march around the house where Captain McPherson lay all night, sometimes all together and sometimes in small detachments. The trick worked. It was heard that the British officer returned to New Brunswick where he reported that General Putnam's army "could not consist of less than four or five thousand men."[46] To finish the story, Captain McPherson recovered from his wounds. He was exchanged and retired from the British Army in 1780.

In the spring of 1777, Washington sent Putnam to yet another distant outpost, this time to Peekskill, New York, on the lower Hudson River. His orders were to guard that section of the river. Burr joined him there. A few months later, on July 14, Putnam sent Burr from Peekskill on a mission to the Connecticut coast to observe and report on any Royal Navy ships operating on Long Island Sound. Burr was to ask the "committees and selectmen" of the towns along the coast for information. Burr's orders were to transmit to Putnam "the intelligence you shall from time to time receive of the movements of the enemy." After gathering information, Burr was instructed to "return with all convenient speed to this place." His mission was actually implemented by General Washington who was gathering intelligence about the enemy's positions and strength.

Burr returned from his mission on July 20 to find a letter waiting for him from General Washington. Much to his surprise and joy, His Excellency's letter announced Burr's promotion to lieutenant colonel and second in command of a Continental Army regiment. Burr bid farewell to his "good old general" and headed to his new regimental assignment. As for Putnam, he was fortunate to replace Burr with David Humphreys, one of the most accomplished penmen of the American Revolution. Putnam continued to be assigned isolated commands until he suffered a paralytic stroke in December 1779 that put an end to his military career. Following Putnam's forced retirement, General Washington invited Humphreys to join his military family as an aide-de-camp. Humphreys accepted and his appointment as one of Washington's aides, with the rank of lieutenant colonel, appeared in the General Orders for June 23, 1780. Humphreys is a good example of one of Washington's sources for talented men to serve as aides at headquarters, which was to take them from his generals. Washington had written and verbal communication with his general's aides, and he commandeered the best ones for his headquarter's staff. As previously mentioned, Washington got rid of Burr by swapping him (perhaps pawning Burr off is more appropriate) for Putnam's aide Samuel B. Webb. Another example is William Palfrey who Washington took from General Charles Lee early in the war. But Humphreys was special as he was arguably Washington's favorite wartime aide. This is a good point to introduce Humphreys and understand his warm association with Washington; a personal relationship that Hamilton would never enjoy with Washington. Humphreys will appear again later in this narrative when I discuss who was the most important member of Washington's wartime staff.

David Humphreys was born in the village of Derby, Connecticut, on July 10, 1752. He was the youngest son of the Reverend Daniel

Humphreys, a Congregational clergyman. David's higher education was at Yale College where he graduated in the class of 1771. His graduating class consisted of nine men. It was the custom in Connecticut that recent Yale graduates devote a few years to teaching in the local schools as a public service before pursuing other interests. Because of this tradition, Connecticut towns sought out Yale graduates as they were educated young men who could be employed at low wages. Humphreys was no exception. Following graduation, he worked as a schoolmaster in Wethersfield, Connecticut. In 1773, he took a new position as a private tutor at the Philipse Manor on the Hudson River. The wealthy Colonel Frederick Philipse had eleven children for Humphreys to educate. Living at Philipse's opulent mansion gave Humphreys an introduction to aristocratic tastes and luxury. It led to his life-long love of pomp and affluence. Humphreys also found the time to earn a master of arts degree from Yale in 1774. Following the start of the Revolutionary War, Humphreys volunteered as adjutant in the 2nd Connecticut Militia Regiment. He proved to be a talented and courageous officer and he quickly rose through the ranks and attracted the attention of Connecticut's celebrated General Putnam. Humphreys replaced Burr as one of Putnam's aides. Humphreys remained loyal to Putnam even as the old general's reputation and responsibilities diminished ending in Putnam's stroke and retirement from the army.

No introduction to Humphreys would be complete without the story of his employment years later as a senior member of Washington's presidential staff. It will be recalled that Humphreys served as Thomas Jefferson's secretary in France for a short time following the end of the Revolution. Because of his experience abroad and his love of stately formality, Humphreys was put in charge of ceremonies and official protocol when George Washington became president. President Washington and the new nation had little experience in such things. Humphreys orchestrated them to be an imitation of the King of France's receptions that he attended in Paris with Jefferson. At President Washington's first levee, Humphreys aped the French court by throwing open the doors to a reception with great pomp and in a loud voice announced, "the President of the United States." Washington was shocked by this silly display of European pomp and told Humphreys not to do it again. "Well," said Washington, "you have taken me in once, but by God you shall never take me in a second time."[47]

Despite this incident, George and Martha Washington adored Colonel Humphreys. The colonel was named the American minister to Spain during the administration of John Adams. When Jefferson became president, he replaced Humphreys with his own appointee. Before leaving Spain,

Humphreys secretly purchased a flock of Merino sheep. This breed of sheep was originally brought to Spain from North Africa in the twelfth century and valued for its fine wool. The Spanish government maintained strict regulations over Merino sheep and prohibited their exportation under penalty of death. But political unrest in Europe at the time made it possible for Humphreys to clandestinely purchase one hundred Merino sheep and herd them across the Spanish border to the seaport of Lisbon, Portugal. From Lisbon, he transported his sheep to Connecticut aboard a sloop appropriately named *Perseverance*. A demand for Humphrey's Merinos quickly developed and he made a fortune selling some of his flock and kept others to use to start his own woolen mill. President Jefferson ordered sufficient fabric from Humphreys to make a Merino wool coat, which it is believed Jefferson wore for the first time on New Year's Day 1809.[48]

David Humphreys followed Burr's example by diligently working for the antiquated General Putnam. Humphreys' dedication and competency were noted by General Washington who eventually invited Humphreys to join his military family. As for Burr, he was finally promoted in 1777 to a line command in a Continental Army regiment. That same year also witnessed a dramatic change in Alexander Hamilton's life that began with an invitation to join General Washington's military family.

8

HAMILTON JOINS
WASHINGTON'S STAFF

The story of how and where Captain Hamilton first met General Washington has become part of the folklore of the American Revolution. One story is that Washington first learned about Hamilton from Hamilton's friend Elias Boudinot. Another possible source was Lord Sterling (General William Alexander) who it is purported to have invited Hamilton to serve as his aide-de-camp early in the war. The story goes that Hamilton declined Lord Sterling's offer preferring instead to take command of the New York artillery company.[1] Another possibility is that General McDougall mentioned Hamilton to General Washington. McDougall knew Hamilton before the war and tried unsuccessfully to recruit him as his aide.[2] From these plausible explanations the literature of the Revolution takes a turn to legends about how Washington first met Hamilton. There are two stories worth even seriously considering. One first appeared in William Johnson's 1822 book *Sketches of the Life and Correspondence of Nathanael Greene*. According to Johnson, General Greene was walking in New York City in the spring of 1776. While rambling along he observed a young officer "disciplining a juvenile corps of artillerists." Greene did not know who the young artillery officer was "but his attention was riveted by the vivacity of his motion, the ardor of his countenance, and by the proficiency and precision of movement of his little corps." Greene sent one of his aides to learn more about this officer and found out that his name was Alexander Hamilton. Greene later invited Hamilton to dine with him one evening. Greene befriended Hamilton and "soon made an opportunity of introducing his young acquaintance to the commander in chief."[3]

The other famous legendary source for how Hamilton first met Washington comes from George Washington Parke Custis. In his book *Recollections and Private Memoirs of Washington*, published in 1860, Custis said that

General Washington first took notice of Hamilton at New Brunswick on December 1, 1776. It will be recalled that Hamilton's field guns were instrumental in thwarting the Crown Forces from crossing the Raritan River. According to Custis' story, General Washington "was charmed by the brilliant courage and admirable skill displayed by a young officer of artillery." His Excellency ordered one of his aides to find out who this young officer was and invited him to headquarters "at the first halt of the army." From that interview, wrote Custis, "Washington marked him for his own."[4]

The earliest known creditable reference to Hamilton's joining Washington's headquarters is believed to be a letter from General Washington, dated Morristown [New Jersey], January 20, 1777, addressed to his stanch military secretary Robert Hanson Harrison. Lieutenant Colonel Harrison was in Philadelphia at the time undergoing immunization against smallpox. Hamilton was also in the city recovering from an illness reputed to be the result of the arduous campaigning in New Jersey during the final months of 1776. In his letter Washington asked Harrison about his health, and concern that his adversary, General Howe, was planning to "either rout this Army [wintering at Morristown] or to move towards Philadelphia." Washington concluded his letter by asking Harrison "To be so good as to forward the enclosed to Captn Hamilton." The message to Hamilton is believed to be an invitation for the young artillery officer to work at headquarters.[5] Lieutenant Colonel Harrison did not know where Hamilton was staying in Philadelphia at the time and placed the following advertisement in the January 25 issue of the *Pennsylvania Evening Post* newspaper, "Captain Alexander Hamilton of the New York Company of Artillery, by applying to the printer of this paper, may hear of something to his advantage."[6] Harrison found Hamilton and give him Washington's invitation to work at headquarters.

Hamilton accepted the coveted offer and was appointed to Washington's staff in the General Orders dated "Head-Quarters, Morristown March 1, 1777: Alexander Hamilton Esquire is appointed Aide-De-Camp to the Commander in Chief; and is to be respected and obeyed as such."[7]

Historians seem to have ignored the fact that Hamilton was invited to work at headquarters in late January 1777 but was appointed as aide in early March. Where was Hamilton during the month of February? Maybe he was slow in arriving at Washington's headquarters in Morristown. Or perhaps he was working at headquarters for several weeks in February on a trial basis similar to Burr.

Hamilton's appointment came at a time when Washington's reputation had recovered from the debacle of the previous year's failed defense of New York. His Excellency had scored a stunning victory against the Crown forces in the Battles of Trenton and Princeton. An appointment as one of his aides following his victories had become a particularly desirable position. Its attraction was not only due to the prestige of working closely with the commander in chief but the opportunity for advancement in the army. Washington had already been instrumental in rewarding four of his aides with promotions as senior line officers. They were George Baylor, Stephen Moylan, Samuel Blatchley Webb, and William Grayson. Their departure from headquarters in early January 1777 left Washington with an official headquarters staff consisting of Robert Hanson Harrison, George Johnston Jr. (Harrison's brother-in-law), and John Fitzgerald (one of Washington's prewar business associates). Serving in an unofficial capacity was volunteer aide Tench Tilghman. Prior to the war Tilghman was a successful Philadelphia merchant. Washington also pressed Caleb Gibbs and George Lewis into service, drafting and copying letters for him at headquarters. Gibbs and Lewis were the officers who commanded the Life Guards (also called the Commander in Chief's Guard). The Life Guards was an elite detachment assigned to protect headquarters' baggage (tents, copies of letters, and orders and personal articles such as clothing and dinnerware from being stolen) as well as any attempt to kill or capture Washington. Gibbs was from Massachusetts and served as a regimental adjutant prior to his appointment as commanding officer of the Life Guards. Lewis was the detachment's junior officer. He was known as Washington's favorite nephew. His mother was Washington's sister Elizabeth (Betty) who married Colonel Fielding Lewis. Colonel Lewis was a member of the House of Burgesses who devoted much of his time and money during the war to manufacturing weapons for the Continental Army.

Hamilton was a welcomed addition to Washington's military family. There are numerous descriptions of Hamilton during his years in the army. The most interesting and reliable was written by his sister-in-law Catharine Schuyler (1781–1857) whose nickname was Caty. She was the youngest daughter of General Phillip Schuyler and the sister of Hamilton's wife Elizabeth. Caty described Hamilton as a "small, lithe figure, erect and steady in gait; . . . his general address was graceful and nervous, indicating the beauty, energy and activity of his mind. A bright, ruddy complexion; light colored hair; a mouth infinite in expression; and the whole countenance decidedly Scottish in form and expression."[8]

Continental Army captain Alexander Graydon knew Hamilton during the war and gave some insightful additional details about his appearance. Graydon described him as "remarkable erect and dignified in his department." He said that despite being "under middle size and thin," when Hamilton entered a room "it was apparent that he was a distinguished person."[9] Graydon wrote that he dined one afternoon with Washington and his staff. There were also ladies present and Graydon said that Hamilton "acquitted himself with an ease, propriety and vivacity, which gave me the most favorable impression of his talents and accomplishments."[10]

Hamilton's first recorded letter following his appointment as Washington's aide was addressed to Lieutenant Colonel Archibald Campbell. Colonel Campbell was a captured British officer who was being held in close confinement by Massachusetts officials. Campbell wrote Washington asking his help in getting better treatment. The reply was in Hamilton's handwriting and signed by Washington. The letter reads in part,

> Morris Town March the 1st 1777
>
> I last night received the favor of your letter of the 4th instant [February 4], and am much obliged by the opinion you are pleased to entertain of me.
>
> I am not invested with the powers you suppose; & it is as incompatible with my authority as my inclination to contravene any determination Congress may make. But as it does not appear to me that your present treatment is required to any resolution of theirs, but is the result of misconception.

The letter goes on to state that Washington wrote "my opinion on the matter to Col. Bowdoin [James Bowdoin, president of the Massachusetts Provincial Congress]." It concludes, "I shall always be happy to manifest my disinclination to any undue severities towards those whom the fortune of War may chance to throw into my hands."[11]

In comparison to Hamilton's letter, three days later, on March 3, Washington wrote to British general Sir William Howe. This letter is in the handwriting of aide Robert Hanson Harrison and signed by Washington. It reads,

> On the 1ˢᵗ Instt I received the favor of your Letter of the 27ᵗʰ Ulto. I had heard the day before of Lt Col. Campbell's confinement and wrote him and the president of the Council of the Massachusetts State respecting it, and I trust his situation will be made more agreeable, it being my wish that every reasonable indulgence and act of Humanity should be done to those whom the fortune of War has or may put into our hands.[12]

Note that both letters include similar closing sentences. Both letters are respectful, clear, and to the point and include actions that Washington took regarding Campbell's imprisonment. The letters read as if they were written by the same person although they were not. They are examples of the strict control that Washington exercised in his communications. He gave Hamilton, as well as all his other aides, verbal instructions about the contents of a letter, wrote an outline, or edited a draft, but all the letters read the same. It is erroneous to believe that Hamilton, or any of Washington's aides-de-camp, wrote his letters for him. They drafted his letters following a strict format and under close supervision. The finished letters are in the aide's handwriting and signed by Washington because of his heavy workload. Washington could not have possibly penned each of the estimated twelve thousand letters and orders he produced during the American Revolution.

It is believed that Hamilton became indispensable to Washington during the war. One of the most famous stories regarding this was told by George Washington Parke Custis in his book *Recollections and Private Memoirs of Washington*. It describes how His Excellency, "the man of mighty labors," was asleep late one night when a courier arrived on horseback with important communications for him. Washington was awakened and handed the dispatches. What happened next, according to Custis, is so theatrical that it is worth quoting in its entirety, "The dispatches being opened and read, there would be heard in the calm deep tones of that voice, so well-remembered by the good and the brave in the old days of our country's trial, the command of the chief to his now watchful attendant, 'Call Colonel Hamilton!'"[13]

One problem with this story is that Hamilton served as Washington's aide for only part of the war. To clarify this point, Washington was commander in chief of the Continental Army for eight years, from June 1775 until the end of the war in December 1783. Hamilton served as Washington's aide for just four of the eight years, from March 1777 to March 1781. Are we to assume that Washington was befuddled for half of the American Revolution?

What is accurate and significant about Hamilton is that he was the most intelligent and dynamic person in Washington's military family. His appointment in 1777 was the addition that gave Washington an outstanding headquarters team during a critical period of the American Revolution. It also consisted of Robert Hanson Harrison and Tench Tilghman. They were the key members of Washington's headquarters staff from 1777–1780. Harrison's specialty was administration. He could be counted on to keep the routine functions of the army operating smoothly if Washington was away. Harrison was also the best of all the aides at communicating Washington's ideas. The general frequently entrusted Harrison to write Congress on his behalf. Tilghman was arguably Washington's best all-around aide. Congressman James Duane said "he had a penetrating intellect that flies like an arrow from a bow."[14] Washington respected Tilghman, and they had an excellent working rapport and a close friendship. Washington also seemed to be on friendly terms with Harrison. However, Washington had a different kind of relationship with Hamilton. They worked closely together for four years but they never had the same warm and congenial relationship that Washington had with Tilghman and Harrison. Washington respected Hamilton's intelligence and abilities and entrusted him with tasks that he would give few others. Hamilton did his share of the routine work at headquarters, but Washington tended to use him for important military and political missions. Young Hamilton also exuded ambition. Unlike Washington's other wartime aides, Hamilton had no wide circle of family members to help his career. Harrison and Tilghman, for example, were from distinguished wealthy families when they joined Washington's staff. As a result, Hamilton was more of a go-getter than any of Washington's other aides.

Soon after joining Washington's staff an excellent opportunity arose for Hamilton that would enhance his reputation. The story begins when the Provincial Convention of New York (forerunner of the New York State Legislature) appointed a Committee of Correspondence whose activities included getting regular news reports from Washington's headquarters.[15] The committee needed someone from headquarters who was well informed and willing to cooperate with them. One of Washington's aides-de-camp was the logical choice for the job and with His Excellency's approval, the New Yorkers approached Tench Tilghman. The Marylander agreed to help, however he was only able to write them reports sporadically. When the New York Committee of Correspondence learned of Hamilton's appointment, they approached him to replace Tilghman as their correspondent at headquarters. The committee considered Hamilton to be a New Yorker because of his tenure at King's College and his service as an officer in the state's Independent Artillery Company. Hamilton was busy but accepted their offer. He was happy with the arrangement as it gave him access to New York State's political leaders. Hamilton accepted their offer in a letter dated Morristown, New Jersey, March 20, 1777. His acceptance letter reads in part, "With cheerfulness, I embrace the proposal of corresponding with your convention." Hamilton continued his letter with his first of many reports to the committee that included,

> There are daily little skirmishes, arising from attempts of the enemy to forage [from their winter encampments at New Brunswick and Perth Amboy]. . . . They are indeed of great service in the general scale, as they serve to harass and distress the enemy, and by keeping them from forage will put them under difficulties, as to the transportation of their baggage and cannon whenever they shalt think of making any capital movement [an offensive campaign].[16]

These periodic reports that he wrote the committee while still a member of Washington's staff helped establish his reputation with influential New York State government officials.

Hamilton's fluency in French may have also influenced Washington to invite the young artillery officer to join his staff. Prior to Hamilton's appointment, the only member of Washington's staff who spoke some French was Tench Tilghman. Due to the influx of French officers, Washington needed someone at headquarters who was fluent in the language. The need was serious, and the story is worth describing in detail as it is an overlooked aspect of the American Revolution and of Hamilton's exceptional service to Washington. Here is what happened.

The French defeat in the Seven Years War resulted in a major reorganization and rearmament program of the French Army. Superfluous and mediocre officers were purged from the ranks and thrown out of work. Europe was at peace at the time and these jobless officers were hard-pressed to find employment as mercenaries on the Continent. Other French career officers who survived the purge were frustrated by their inability to be promoted or gain valuable combat experience. In order to find employment and gain experience, the war in America was ideal for these unemployed and often destitute French and other European officers. They began to arrive in America soon after the Revolution began and offered their services to the Patriot cause. They arrived on their own with no encouragement or support from the French government. For example, in 1777 a French merchant ship was intercepted and boarded by a Royal Navy cruiser. The British found three French officers and two sergeants onboard bound for America. The British arrested the lot. When confronted with the incident, the Comte de Vergennes (the French foreign minister) replied, "having left France without permission to serve the Americans, the representatives of the [French] King cannot involve himself in their situation."[17]

Just how many Frenchmen volunteered to join the Continental Army in the first years of the American Revolution is difficult to determine because some of them failed in their efforts to be appointed as officers in the Continental Army. Having failed, they returned to France or to the French West Indies. Another problem was that Americans at the time were unfamiliar with foreign languages. As a result, they were spelling the names and titles of the same French volunteer's different ways. Washington, for example, spelled Kosciuszko's name eleven different ways.[18] However, there are clues to their numbers, including a letter Washington wrote to Congress from Morristown on February 20, 1777. In his missive, Washington said that the aspirants were, "coming in swarms from old France and the [West Indies] Islands."[19] In another letter written during the same period, Washington described them as "*t*he shoals of French Men that are coming on to this Camp."[20] Citing another example, written in August 1777, Washington referred to them as "the numberless applications for Employment by Foreigners.[21]

The first French volunteers arrived randomly during 1775 and 1776. Many of them came from the French West Indies. To improve their chance for a commission in the fledging Continental Army, they arrived with glowing letters of recommendation, inflated resumes, and wearing elegant uniforms. They had to make a favorable impression as they paid for their voyage and expenses. They headed for Philadelphia where they lobbied the members of the Continental Congress, which gave them commissions as officers and sent them on to Washington's headquarters. Washington described his experience when they arrived,

> Men who in the first instance tell you that they wish for nothing more than the honor of serving in so glorious a cause as Volunteers—the next day solicit rank without pay—the day following want money advanced them—and in the course of a week want further promotion, and are not satisfied with anything you can do for them.[22]

The trickle of French officers who arrived in 1775 and 1776 increased to a torrent in early 1777 in part through the activities of Silas Deane. He arrived in Paris in July 1776. Posing as a merchant, Deane was actually dispatched by the five-man Committee of Secret Correspondence of the Continental Congress to purchase war materials and make contact with the French government. Deane was also given printed Continental Army commissions to take with him to France. They were blank commissions and Deane was authorized by the Secret Committee to use them to appoint officers for the Patriot army. The rationale behind this action can be traced back to a July 10, 1775, letter Washington wrote to Congress in which he mentions "a want of engineers to construct proper works." Deane was supposed to recruit French Army engineers to help the rebels. When Deane's real identity become known, he was inundated by a procession of French officers who called upon him. Deane was mesmerized by their tailored uniforms, claims of military prowess, and connections to the French government and the royal family. Deane believed that he was aiding the rebel cause by issuing commissions to many of the French officers he met in Paris. His disciples arrived in Philadelphia where they presented Congress their bona fide commissions signed by Deane appointing them as majors, colonels, and even generals in the Continental Army. The delegates were befuddled and solved the problem by sending the Frenchmen to Washington's headquarters. Washington quickly discovered that many of them knew little or no English. Washington first mentioned this problem early in the war. Writing to Congress from headquarters in October 1776, "I must take the liberty, to observe that I am under no small difficulties on account of the French Gentlemen that are here. . . . Their want of our language is an objection to their being joined to any of the Regiments.[23] Writing again in greater detail on the subject from Morristown in February 1777 and just prior to French-speaking Hamilton joining his staff, Washington vented his frustration to Congress, "You cannot conceive what a weight these kind of people are upon the service and upon me in particular; few of them have any knowledge of the branches which they profess to understand and those that have, are entirely useless as officers from their ignorance of the English language."[24] Understanding the situation, Burr's fluency in French should have made him a valuable addition to Washington's staff months before Hamilton arrived on the scene.

Washington must have been grateful to have Hamilton at headquarters to converse with the army's French-speaking officers. But Hamilton, along with the rest of Washington's personal staff, were much more occupied in the spring of 1777 with "obtaining the earliest and best intelligence of the designs of the enemy."[25]

Alarming reports from American spies operating in New York City during the first months of 1777 were arriving at Washington's headquarters in Morristown. Written in code or invisible ink, they reported seeing reinforcements, provisions, and equipment arriving in ships from England. Washington's covert techniques included having his aides compare the reports from different sources to see if their information matched. The aides gleaned additional intelligence by interrogating prisoners and deserters, reading intercepted mail, and scrutinizing Loyalist newspapers for clues to the enemy's plans. Hamilton, for example, submitted the following report (the original document, in Hamilton's handwriting, is in the Library of Congress) to General Washington after questioning two British deserters. The deserters were (former) members of the Royal Highland Emigrants Regiment. They had recently been stationed at the important Royal Navy base at Halifax, Nova Scotia, which they described in detail to Hamilton. They told Hamilton that Halifax's garrison consisted of about three hundred infantry and seven hundred to one thousand British Marines. The report when on to say,

> On Sideral Hill, which commands the Harbour, on the West side—a block house with 6 six pounders and 6 or 8 four pounders. A mile from ye Hill were two forts, Neidham and Good, half a mile distant from each other—3 heavy cannons in the former two in the latter, with a block house in each.[26]

The intelligence analyzed at headquarters in early 1777 pointed to General Sir William Howe preparing for a big offensive against the rebels to begin that spring. The problem was that Washington could not uncover Howe's plans. Howe had several options. The most prevalent was that Howe was going to march his army across New Jersey and seize Philadelphia. Another was that he was planning to board his army on the numerous ships reported to be docked in New York. Once onboard, he would sail north on the Hudson River to cooperate with another British Army under the command of General John Burgoyne. Burgoyne's army was advancing south from Montreal to capture strategic Albany, New York, on the upper Hudson River. There was also the possibility that Sir William would launch an attack into New England from British held Newport, Rhode Island.

Unsure of General Howe's intensions, on May 28, 1777, Washington began moving his army south from Morristown to an excellent defensive position in the Watchung Mountains of central New Jersey. This move placed his army in a position to move safely behind the mountains toward Philadelphia or the Hudson River once Sir William's plans became clear.

Howe finally revealed his intensions on June 14 when he marched from his base at New Brunswick toward Washington's position in the Watchung Mountains. Howe wanted Washington to come down from his mountain stronghold and fight him. Defeating Washington's Main Army would clear the way for Howe to advance unhindered across New Jersey to Philadelphia. An early historian of the Revolution, Mercy Otis Warren, describes what happened next, "Confident of his success from his superior numbers in the field, General Howe exercised all the artifices of an experienced commander to bring General Washington to a decisive engagement . . . but the American chieftain defeated every measure to bring him to a general action [battle]."[27]

Howe could not risk crossing New Jersey with Washington's army nearby. He knew that his adversary would send raiding parties and stage ambushes to cut his communications and supply lines. After a futile effort, and wasting valuable campaigning weather, Howe embarked his army of more than eighteen thousand abroad 267 warships and transports anchored in New York Harbor over several days—July 7–10, 1777. Only a handful of senior British and Hessian officers knew their destination. Although the British fleet was ready to set sail on July 10, it mysteriously remained at anchor for nine days. The explanation for the delay can be found in a journal kept by Hessian captain Friedrich von Muenchhausen. He spoke English fluently and was one of Howe's aides-de-camp. In his journal he explains that Howe was waiting for definite word that Burgoyne had captured Fort Ticonderoga from the rebels. The fort was the major American obstacle blocking Burgoyne's route to Albany. On July 14, Muenchhausen wrote in his journal, "We have no longer any reason to doubt the news of the capture of Ticonderoga, for my General [Howe] personally received letters today from Burgoyne."[28] Howe believed that the news meant that Burgoyne was safely on his way to Albany. The informal cooperation between Burgoyne and Howe is an example of the lack of cohesive planning by the king and his ministers who were in London, three thousand miles and months away from the fast moving war in America. After sharing the news of Burgoyne's capture of Fort Ticonderoga with his older brother, Admiral Lord Howe, the Royal fleet finally set sail for the Atlantic Ocean with the first favorable wind. Washington and his staff could only guess where Howe's 267 ships were headed.

The British fleet was sighted sailing south off the coast of New Jersey, which convinced Washington that their objective was to seize Philadelphia. His assessment was correct. The flotilla arrived at the mouth of the Delaware River. However, it was discouraged by Royal Navy warships blockading the river from approaching the city as it was heavily defended by the rebels. The fleet then continued further south to Chesapeake Bay. Bad weather hampered its progress and it took thirty-two days to sail from the Delaware River to the Chesapeake Bay. The Howe brothers selected Maryland's Elk River, which emptied into Chesapeake Bay, as their landing place. General Howe had wasted most of the good campaigning weather maneuvering in New Jersey and transporting his army to Chesapeake Bay. In doing so, he had eliminated any chance of reinforcing Burgoyne if necessary.

Howe finally offloaded his sickly army, who had been crowded together in the hot ship's holds for weeks. Most of his army's horses were dead or weak from the long voyage and lack of food and water. The troops staggered ashore on August 23, 1777, at Head of Elk, which was the furthest point, or *head* in nautical terms, on the Elk River that a ship could navigate. After establishing a beachhead, Howe's army moved cautiously inland toward Philadelphia; a distance of fifty-five miles. Howe had finally forced Washington to fight a general engagement by threatening the rebel capital. Hamilton explained this in a report he wrote to the New York State Committee of Correspondence on September 1, 1777, "The enemy will have Philadelphia, if they dare make a bold push for it, unless we fight them a pretty general action [battle]. I opine [opt] we ought to do it, that we shall beat them soundly if we do."

In the same letter, Hamilton explained that "This country [the region south of Philadelphia] does not abound in good posts [defensive positions]. It is intersected by such an infinity of roads, and is so little mountainous that it is impossible to find a spot not liable to capital defects."[29]

Forced to fight, Washington wanted a strong defensive position to meet Howe's thrust toward Philadelphia. Washington was experienced enough from the previous year's New York campaign to select an inland location that was distant from any navigable waterway where the powerful Royal Navy could be used against him. His Excellency marched his army through Philadelphia on August 24. From there, the Continentals moved through southern Pennsylvania and into Delaware. After maneuvering in the Newport, Delaware, area, Washington withdrew into Pennsylvania where he chose to defend Philadelphia from high ground facing Chad's Ford on Brandywine Creek. The ford was where the strategic Great Post Road (today's US Route 1) leading to Philadelphia crossed the Brandywine. The creek was a tributary of the Christina River. The Brandywine was a shallow waterway twenty-five miles southwest of Philadelphia. But it was like a moat; sufficiently deep to force a large number of troops, field artillery, and heavily-laden wagons to use fords to cross it. The problem was that there were a number of fords up and down the length of the stream. The surrounding area was farmland dominated by a knoll called Birmingham Hill. It was a bare mount with some scattered clumps of trees. Across Brandywine Creek was another key feature. It was a road that paralleled the creek called the Great Valley Road. Washington established his headquarters one mile east of Chad's Ford in a house owned by a Quaker named Benjamin Ring. The house was typical of the neat stone farmhouses in this prosperous farming region.

From the outset, Washington was vigilant to guard against General Howe's moving behind the American's right flank by crossing the Brandywine at one of the upstream fords. Outflanking the rebels and coming at them from behind was Howe's favorite tactic. He had used it successfully at the Battle of Long Island in 1776 and Washington was determined not to let him do it again.

The British arrived at Chad's Ford in force early on the morning of September 11, 1777, and immediately began exchanging artillery fire with the Continentals entrenched across the creek. The opposing armies were equally matched; about fifteen thousand men faced each other across Brandywine Creek.

American major Samuel Shaw was among the defenders and gave a good account of the ensuing day-long battle. Shaw wrote in his journal,

> On the 11th . . . a considerable body of their army appeared opposite us. Immediately a heavy cannonade commenced and lasted with spirit for about four hours, and more or less the whole day . . . a large column, consisting of the British and Hessian grenadiers [elite troops; the tallest and most vigorous soldiers] light infantry [also elite troops whose equipment and weapons were lighter than regular troops allowing them to be more mobile] and some brigades [three or more regiments operating together], took a circuitous route of six miles to our right and crossed the creek at the forks of Brandywine.

Racing to prevent the flanking column to get behind his army, Shaw said that Washington ordered "three divisions" (a division consisted of three or more brigades) to face the new threat. "These divisions," wrote Shaw,

> having advanced about three miles fell in with the enemy, who were also advancing. Both sides pushing for a hill situated in the middle [Birmingham Hill]; the contest became exceedingly severe, and lasted without interruption for an hour and a half, when our troops began to give way. Night coming on, his Excellency, the General, gave orders for a retreat, which was regularly effected, without the least attempt by the enemy to pursue. Our troops that night retired to Chester and will now take post in such manner as best to cover Philadelphia.[30]

To elaborate on Shaw's eyewitness account, Washington was suspicious from the outset that the enemy troops, mostly Hessians, facing Chad's Ford were a diversion. He believed the real thrust would be a substantial part of Howe's army trying to sneak across the Brandywine behind his right flank (upriver) and attacking his positions at Chad's Ford. To guard against this possibility, Washington posted troops at all the fords along a six mile front. The most northern ford being guarded was Buffington's Ford. It was located six miles from Chad's Ford. Mounted couriers were stationed at each ford to quickly report any enemy activity to headquarters. Two divisions were positioned near Buffington's Ford to quickly respond to an attempt to outflank the main American defenses at Chad's Ford. Washington was assured by local militiamen that the creek north of Buffington's Ford was difficult to cross. However, Washington ordered Colonel Theodorick Bland, one his most reliable officers, to patrol both sides of the Brandywine above Buffington's Ford with his light dragoons. Bland was instructed to report any enemy activity immediately and directly to headquarters.

It seems that Washington took every precaution to prevent General Howe from outflanking Chad's Ford. But Washington failed to carefully reconnoiter the creek north of Buffington's Ford. If done, he would have discovered that the Great Valley Road led to Jefferis's (modern spelling is Jefferies) Ford, which was two miles north of Buffington's Ford. A local Loyalist named Curtis Lewis knew the route and led an 8,200 man flanking column, commanded by General Cornwallis, to the unguarded ford.[31] General Howe accompanied Cornwallis's troops during the seventeen-mile, nine hour march.

Washington, attended by several of his aides, was out inspecting his positions facing Chad's Ford during the morning of the battle. According to historian James Thomas Flexner, Hamilton was at the Ring House to "correlate dispatches and give any instructions immediately required."[32] Flexner's statement that Hamilton was at headquarters is in keeping with Washington's command style. He always kept at least one of his aides-de-camp at headquarters to receive and evaluate all messages and verbal reports. Fellow aide Robert Hanson Harrison was with Hamilton based on a report that Harrison wrote that morning to Congress.[33] A detachment of light dragoons were stationed at headquarters to forward any critical information from Harrison and Hamilton to Washington.[34] However, nothing of consequence occurred during the morning.

Washington returned to headquarters around 11:00 a.m. just as conflicting reports began arriving. One was from Lieutenant Colonel James Ross dated "Eleven oclock A.M.," which begins, "A large body of the enemy—from every account 5000 with 16 or 18 field pieces, marched along this Road [Great Valley Road] just now."[35] At about the same time another report arrived from Major Joseph Spear, a local militia officer who reported that "he was from the upper country [returned from the area north of Buffington's Ford] that he had come in the Road [the Great

Valley Road], where the enemy must have passed to attack our right [the American right flank] and that there was not the least appearance of them in that Quarter."[36] Baffled by these and other conflicting reports, Washington was annoyed that he had not heard anything from Colonel Bland. He sent a hasty note to Bland at 11:20 a.m., which read in part, "I wish you to gain satisfactory information of a body [enemy troops] confidently reported to have gone up to a Ford Seven or Eight miles about this [Chad's Ford]. . . . You will send up an intelligent—sensible Officer immediately with a party to find out the truth. The note is in the handwriting of aide Robert Hanson Harrison. "[37]

Colonel Bland finally sent Washington a message at 1:15 p.m. confirming that Crown troops were across the stream. Washington had been outflanked again but he took quick action to prevent a rout. At 2:00 p.m. he ordered his two reserve divisions near Buffington Ford to fall back and take up positions on Birmingham Hill. At 2:30 p.m. he ordered a third division to join them. This accounts for Shaw's mentioning that three divisions "had engaged the enemy." Washington rode to Birmingham Hill in the afternoon accompanied by Hamilton as Cornwallis's troops were advancing to seize the hill.

The late afternoon fighting for strategic Birmingham Hill was fierce. The rebels were driven from the hill five times and retook it four times.[38] Although Hamilton had no authority to command troops, according to the historian Flexner, Hamilton was on the battlefield and "assisted in reorganizing companies that had become ragged and placing them on partially wooded hillsides from which they could slow the enemy."[39]

Eventually the Americans gave way and, at dusk, began retreating toward Chester, Pennsylvania, in good order. Howe's army was exhausted, and he did not pursue the retreating rebels. Brandywine was an American defeat, but Howe failed to trap them as he did at the Battle of Long Island.

There were two people who had recently joined the Continental Army and fought in the Battle of Brandywine. They both became Hamilton's close friends. They were John Laurens and the Marquis de Lafayette. We will discuss Laurens first as he was the more important of the two in terms of his influence on Hamilton.

John Laurens joined Washington's military family as a volunteer aide-de-camp on September 6, 1777. Young Laurens proved to be as passionate and aggressive as Hamilton and they quickly became intimate friends despite their different backgrounds. Hamilton, it will be recalled, was the illegitimate son of an itinerant Scotsman while Laurens was the son of one of the wealthiest and most influential men in colonial America. John

Laurens father was Henry Laurens, a shrewd Charleston businessman whose holdings included large plantations in South Carolina farmed by hundreds of black slaves laboring in brutal captivity. Henry Laurens was also in the lucrative business of importing and selling slaves.

His son, John, was born on October 28, 1754. John's earliest education was by private tutors. His father next accompanied his teenage son to Europe where he arranged for his advanced education. John studied with tutors in London before settling in Geneva, Switzerland, where he attended school for two years. Geneva was the center of liberal education in the Western world at the time. It is ironic that Henry Laurens, whose fortune was built on slave labor, chose to have his son study in altruistic Geneva where he became an opponent to slavery. Young Laurens next returned to London where he studied law.

John was studying in London when the American Revolution began. He passionately wanted to return home and join the Continental Army. His father finally agreed and John sailed for America from France arriving in Charleston on April 15, 1777. His father believed that an appointment as an aide-de-camp to General Washington was a safe and honorable position for his son. Henry was a delegate to the Continental Congress at the time but arranged for John Rutledge, president of the South Carolina General Assembly to recommend twenty-two year old John to General Washington. Young Laurens promptly received an invitation to join Washington's staff as a volunteer aide. His appointment was unofficial, but his father mentioned his starting date in a letter to John Lewis Gervais (a fellow South Carolina Patriot and plantation owner) dated August 5, 1777, "This morning John joined Gen Washington at headquarters as one of his family."[40] Once at headquarters, John met Hamilton. They had similar personalities and quickly became close friends. Hamilton admired Laurens for his wealth, education, polished manners, and European travels. Both were romantics who viewed the Revolution as a mission to defend the liberties of mankind and as a way of attaining personal glory.

At times, Hamilton and Laurens became separated. They kept in contact through letters one of which Hamilton wrote to Laurens, which reveals their heartfelt attachment to one another. The letter is undated but believed to have been written by Hamilton in April 1779. Hamilton was at Washington's headquarters at the Wallace House in Middlebrook, New Jersey (today's Somerville), at the time. Laurens was in South Carolina. The noteworthy text reads, "Cold in my professions, warm in my friendships, I wish, my Dear Laurens, it might be in my power, by action rather than words, to convince you that I love you."[41]

Henry Laurens was sadly mistaken if he thought that a staff position at Washington's headquarters would keep his son out of danger. Although Lauren's location during the Battle of Brandywine is not known, an eyewitness to the fighting wrote his father, "It was not his fault that he was not killed or wounded. He did everything that was necessary to procure one or the other."[42] It is not unusual that aides-de-camp Laurens and Hamilton were exposed to enemy gunfire at Brandywine. Typically, Washington would ride into battle accompanied by several of his aides. He would dispatch them, as needed, with verbal orders to various senior officers as the enemy deployed and the fighting continued. The aides were exposed to enemy fire as they delivered the commander in chief's orders. Hamilton and Laurens were selected to convey orders at Brandywine as they were among the youngest, most energetic, and intrepid of Washington's aides. At Brandywine both young men remained on the battlefield into the late afternoon to offer assistance to regimental (line) officers during the fighting.

Another person who first saw combat at Brandywine, and befriended Hamilton, was Marie-Joseph-Paul-Yves-Roch-Gilbert du Motier, Marquis de La Fayette. He was born in France on September 6, 1757, and was twenty-one years old when he fought in the Battle of Brandywine. Lafayette's father was killed in the Battle of Minden in 1759 and his mother died in 1770. Following their death's young Lafayette inherited a large fortune. He wanted to be a solider like his father and his military career began at the age of fourteen when he was appointed a junior officer in the King's Musketeers. Lafayette was stationed with his regiment at Metz, France, where he attended a dinner in 1775 during which the Duke of Gloucester spoke about the revolt of the American colonists. Lafayette became an enthusiastic supporter of the rebellion and he signed an agreement with Silas Deane in Paris on December 7, 1775, appointing him a major general in the Continental Army. Lafayette next bought a ship named *La Victoire* and sailed for America on April 20, 1777, bringing fifteen other European officers with him. He arrived in Philadelphia on July 31, 1777, and promptly presented his credentials to Congress. By that time Congress had grown suspicious and weary of newly arrived French officers who were claiming that they came to America to join the rebellion out of their love of liberty. But Lafayette was different; he was wealthy, spoke some English, and seemed sincere. Congress confirmed Silas's appointment and commissioned Lafayette as a major general in the Continental Army. However, he was given no troops to command and served as a volunteer at Washington's headquarters until a division of Virginia troops was assigned to him in December 1777.

It was while serving at headquarters that Lafayette befriended Laurens and Hamilton, both of whom spoke French, and helped Lafayette improve his English. Lafayette fought at the Battle of Brandywine where he was wounded in the leg. At one point in the battle, Lafayette fought alongside the Americans who were tenaciously holding their ground on Birmingham Hill. Another French officer on the scene said Lafayette "did his utmost to make the men charge with fixed bayonets. Lafayette personally attached their bayonets for them and pushed them in the back to make them charge. But the Americans are not suited for this type of combat and never wanted to take it up."[43]

The circumstances that led to Lafayette being wounded at Brandywine reveal his personality and why he formed a particular friendship with Hamilton and Laurens; they were all young and high-spirited officers. Hamilton and Lafayette enjoyed a particularly close relationship that continued even after Hamilton resigned from the Continental Army. Their letters include a memorable line in a November 3, 1782, letter Hamilton wrote to Lafayette. Hamilton was a newly appointed lawyer at the time living in Albany with his wife and their first child, "I have been employed for the last ten months in rocking the cradle," Hamilton wrote Lafayette, "and studying the art of fleecing my neighbors."[44]

Besides Lafayette, there were two other former French Army officers who participated in the Philadelphia campaign with the rank of general in the Continental Army. Their involvement in the campaign highlights the problems that Washington faced during the war dealing with Frenchmen who were commissioned by Congress and told to report to headquarters for assignments. One of them was Philippe-Hubert, Chevalier do Preudhomme de Borre. Silas Deane commissioned him as a brigadier general in Paris and Congress approved the appointment. De Borre was an egotistical, sixty-year-old former lieutenant colonel in the French Army who could barely speak English. He was despised by the Maryland troops he commanded at Brandywine who refused to obey his orders. De Borre later claimed he commanded "bad troops" but Congress felt differently. They sacked him. Maryland delegate to Congress Samuel Chase summarized the situation, "Maryland forces gained no Honor. They were Commanded by Gen. Debore who was ignorant of his Duty."[45] The other American general from France was a former portentous French Army major named Philppe Tronson du Coudray. Du Coudray was on his way to join Washington's Main Army a few days after the Battle of Brandywine, but he died while crossing the swollen Schuylkill River on a flatboat. He insisted on remaining on his horse during the dangerous crossing and drowned when

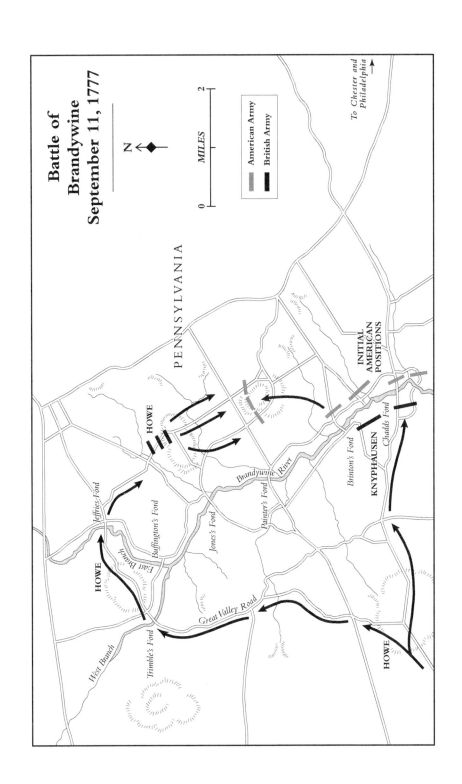

Battle of
Brandywine
September 11, 1777

N

MILES
0   2

American Army
British Army

PENNSYLVANIA

To Chester and
Philadelphia

HOWE

INITIAL
AMERICAN
POSITIONS

Chadds Ford

Brinton's Ford

KNYPHAUSEN

Brandywine River

Jeffries's Ford

Buffington's Ford

Jones's Ford

Painter's Ford

East Branch

HOWE

Great Valley Road

West Branch

Trimble's Ford

HOWE

his skittish mount plunged into the river with the insolent Frenchman still in the saddle.

The Battle of Brandywine was an American defeat. However, Washington's Main Army recovered from the loss and continued to defend Philadelphia. Washington maneuvered his army about ten miles west of the capital a week after the Battle of Brandywine and began skirmishing with Howe's army on the morning of September 16. A general engagement was evolving when the clouds erupted in a torrential rainstorm that flooded roads, reduced visibility, and rendered rain-soaked weapons and ammunition useless. Washington withdrew to Reading Furnace, Pennsylvania. From his headquarters there Washington ordered Hamilton to assist in removing valuable stores, including flour and horseshoes, from a supply depot located along the banks of the Schuylkill River above Philadelphia at Valley Forge. This assignment almost ruined Hamilton's military career.

The problems started when Hamilton and his detachment were attacked at Valley Forge by a large party of British horsemen and light infantry. Hamilton escaped but believed that the British troops that attacked him were part of a larger force about to occupy Philadelphia. He immediately scribbled a hastily written note to John Hancock, the president of the Continental Congress. The note read, "If Congress have not yet left Philadelphia, they ought to do it immediately without fail, for the enemy have the means of throwing a party this night into the city. I just now crossed the valley-ford [Valley Forge] in doing which a party of the enemy came down & fired upon us."[46]

Hancock received Hamilton's message around midnight and panicked. He and the other members of Congress ignominiously fled the city at dawn the following day.[47]

Delegate John Adams described the scene,

> At 3 this Morning was waked by Mr. Lovell and told that the Members of Congress were gone, some of them a little after Midnight. That there was a Letter from Mr. Hamilton Aid de Camp to the General, informing that the Enemy were in Possession of the Ford and the Boats, and had it in their Power in be in Philadelphia before Morning. . . . Mr. Merchant and myself rose, sent for our Horses, and, after collecting our Things, rode off after the others.[48]

Hamilton's warning quickly spread causing pandemonium among the civilian population of the city. But his assessment of British intentions was wrong, and his impulsively scribbled note started a stampede from Philadelphia and the greatest consternation, fright, and terror that can be

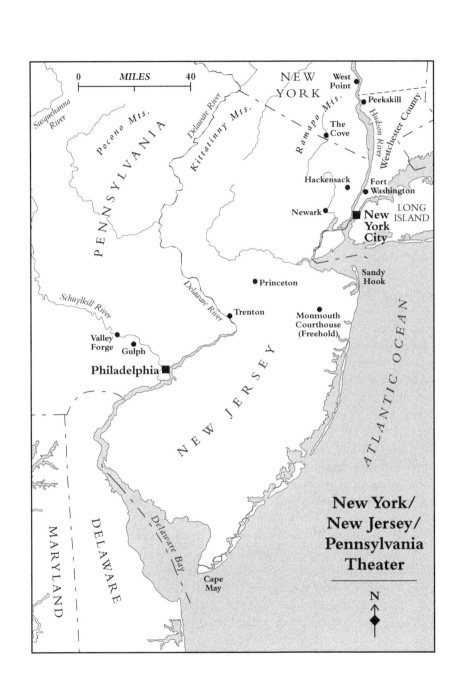

New York/
New Jersey/
Pennsylvania
Theater

The events leading to the establishment of Malcolm's Regiment began in late December 1776 when the Continental Congress authorized Washington to raise sixteen additional regiments for the Continental Army. The wording of their instructions to Washington is important, as Congress allowed him to personally appoint the officers for the sixteen new regiments. The pertinent text of Congress' instructions reads, "That General Washington shall be, and he is hereby, vested with full, ample, and complete powers to raise . . . from any or all of these United States, 16 battalions of infantry and to appoint officers for the said battalions."[54] According to the 1779 *An Universal Military Dictionary*, a battalion is a body of infantry generally from five hundred to eight hundred men. The Americans used the word battalion loosely early in the Revolution to mean the same thing as a regiment.

Washington gave command to one of the sixteen new regiments to William Malcolm, a wealthy New York merchant and militia colonel. Malcolm's appointment was due in part to his providing the money to outfit the regiment and offering bounties for men to join it. The regiment was organized on April 30, 1777, and named in Malcolm's honor. It appears in the records of the Revolution as Malcolm's Additional Regiment. Washington realized that Colonel Malcolm had little military experience and needed an experienced officer as his second in command. Washington picked Burr who, as the regiment's lieutenant colonel, actually commanded the regiment in the field and led it in combat. Burr was twenty-one years old at the time of his appointment. He has the distinction of being the youngest person to be appointed to the rank of lieutenant colonel in the Continental Army during the Revolutionary War. Burr was probably appointed by Washington based on a recommendation he received from William Livingston, the governor of New Jersey. Livingston was one of Washington's most important supporters, and his suggestions were taken seriously. Writing to Washington on February 15, 1777, Governor Livingston said, "May I once more take the liberty to mention to your Excellency Major Burr aid de Camp to General Putnam? I think him a most promising youth & like to do Honour to his Country."[55] Besides Livingston's recommendation, while Washington may not have approved of Burr's personal traits, he knew him to be a competent and courageous officer.

Washington replied to Governor Livingston's letter on February 22, 1777, saying, "I will most assuredly keep Mr. Burr in remembrance, and take the first proper Opportunity of giving him a more permanent Office than the one he now holds." The reference to "a more permanent Office" is an acknowledgment by Washington that Burr's present rank of major was a brevet position that he held only while he was an aide-de-camp to imaged. Hamilton had merely run into an enemy patrol on September 18. The British had no immediate intension of making a move to seize the rebel capital.

The embarrassed members of Congress, who had vaulted from Philadelphia when they received Hamilton's message, soon realized that the city was in no immediate danger. Their anger was evident in the letters they wrote the days that followed their degrading midnight departure from the city. For example, Delegate James Duane wrote his wife on September 21, "Our Removal from Philad. Was owning to information that General Howe was crossing Schuylkill. . . . However tho' this intelligence was from one of the General's family, it was not well found & we wish we had not left Philad."[49] There is no record of Washington's reaction to his aide's rash behavior and the havoc it caused. But Hamilton survived the humiliating incident perhaps because of his acumen and hard work at headquarters.

The opposing armies continued to maneuver near Philadelphia until September 25 when the Crown forces occupied Germantown, just five miles from Philadelphia. They entered the city the following day. A British officer recorded the event in his journal, "[September] 26th. This morning at eight oclock, the british and hessian grenadiers under the command of Lord Cornwallis, proceeded by six twelve pounders . . . marched in a kind of procession with bands of music playing before them, and took possession of the city of Philadelphia."[50]

Having failed to prevent the British from capturing the rebel capital, Washington attempted to defeat the estimated eight thousand Crown troops stationed in the vicinity of Germantown on October 4, 1777. However, Washington's strategy was complicated under the best of conditions. His eleven thousand-man, four-pronged plan of attack began to unravel when a dense fog obscured everything for miles. Some of the attacking columns lost their way in the haze giving the enemy time to rally. Adding to the rebel's problems were the multitude of stone walls, fences, and hedges that slowed down their efforts to move cross-country. At the height of the American attack, part of the British 40th Regiment occupied Cliveden, a two-and-half story substantial stone mansion located on the main road leading to the center of Germantown. The British who barricaded themselves inside Cliveden were exchanging shots with the rebels when Washington and several of his aides rode up. Colonel Timothy Pickering, a learned and experienced officer, was with the general's retinue. According to Captain Henry Lee (an American officer on the scene) he could clearly hear that Colonel Pickering accompanied by Lieutenant Colonel Hamilton "urged with zeal the propriety of passing the house."[51] Pickering recommended leaving a regiment to surround the mansion to keep the British penned up inside. But Captain Lee said that General Knox soon arrived on the scene "insisting that it would be unmilitary to leave a castle in our rear."[52] Washington followed the advice of his artillery chief, and artillery and infantry were diverted to capture the house. But the Redcoats held out even against Knox's field artillery, which was ineffective against the building's thick stone walls. The complicated American assault lost momentum as ammunition ran low and the troops were unnerved by gunfire coming from their rear (Cliveden). The Americans retreated in disarray after briefly overrunning the British troops defending Germantown. As a result of his complicated attack plan and wasting valuable time at Cliveden, Washington lost another battle and any hope of retaking Philadelphia.

There is a bizarre sequel to the story of the Battle of Germantown. What happened was that a handsome dog strayed into the advancing American column during the fighting. The dog had a plate on its collar stating that its owner was General Sir William Howe. Washington returned the dog to Howe with a note in Hamilton's handwriting. The note read, "General Washington's complements to General Howe. He does himself the pleasure to return him a dog, which accidentally fell into his hands, and by the inscription on the Collar appears to belong to General Howe."[53]

Following the Battle of Germantown, Washington continued to maneuver his army north of Philadelphia before going into winter quarters on December 19 at Valley Forge, Pennsylvania.

Aaron Burr was far from the fighting in Pennsylvania following his appointment as a lieutenant colonel in the Continental Army on June 27, 1777. It will be recalled that Washington's Main Army was located in New Jersey's Watchung Mountains in June 1777. He was unwilling to bring his army down from their mountain stronghold to confront General Howe's army in the unbroken farmland of central New Jersey. Washington did not know at the time if Howe's plan was to march across New Jersey and seize Philadelphia or suddenly turn his army to the Hudson River to support General Burgoyne's campaign from Montreal toward Albany. Unsure of Howe's intentions, Washington stationed troops in the lower Hudson River Valley if Howe moved north to cooperate with Burgoyne. Defending the lower Hudson was also necessary to challenge enemy raids and forging parties from operating in the region. These forays were coming from British-held Manhattan Island. Among the American troops defending the lower Hudson was a newly organized Continental Army unit called Malcolm's Additional Regiment. General Washington appointed Aaron Burr as a lieutenant colonel and second in command of the new regiment.

Self portrait of Alexander Hamilton dated 1773. Hamilton was living and working as a clerk in St. Croix at the time. *Library of Congress.*

Alexander Hamilton depicted as a captain commanding a New York colony (after July, 4, 1776, New York State artillery company. *Portrait by George C. Woodbridge. M. Dawson Collection.*

American Revolution field artillery. A six-pound cannon is in the foreground. The smaller piece is a three-pound gun. Hamilton's New York artillery company consisted of a pair of six pounders.

Miniature of Hamilton painted during the Valley Forge encampment by Charles Willson Peale. Hamilton is wearing a ribband across his chest. It would have been green to identify him as an aide-de-camp. His short hair is attributed to a wartime recommendation by Dr. Benjamin Rush advocating keeping hair short for health reasons. Museum of the City of New York.

Portrait of Alexander Hamilton as a young aide-de-camp to General Washington. Portrait by George C. Woodbridge. *Author's collection.*

The home and law school of Tapping Reeve in Litchfield, Connecticut. Reeve married Arron Burr's sister Sally. Arron was studying law with Reeve at the start of the American Revolution. *Author's photo.*

Aaron Burr as a teenage volunteer on the 1775 Arnold Expedition. Burr's clothing and weapons are based on a letter he wrote to his sister at the outset of the campaign. Portrait by George C. Woodbridge. *Author's collection.*

Reproduction of one of the gun batteries at Fort Lee, on the New Jersey side of the lower Hudson River. It is probable that Aaron Burr was at Fort Lee on November 16, 1776, where he witnessed the surrender of Fort Washington located on the opposite side of the river. *Author's photo.*

The Jabez Campfield House, Morristown, New Jersey. The house was occupied by Dr. John Cochran during the winter of 1779-1780. His wife was the sister of Gen. Philip Schuyler. Washington and his staff were living in the nearby Ford Mansion. General Schuyler's daughter, Elizabeth (better known as Betsy) spent the winter with the Cochran's where she met Col. Hamilton. The Colonel courted Betsy that winter and is believed to have asked her to marry him in the house. *Author's photo.*

The Beekman Arms Inn, Rhinebeck, New York. Both Burr and Hamilton lodged at the inn as young lawyers representing clients in the local courts. *Author's photo.*

Portrait of Aaron Burr by James Sharples dated 1797. Sharples was a British artist who came to the United States to paint the portraits of the young nation's leading citizens. *Bristol Museum and Art Gallery, UK/Bridgeman Images.*

Aaron Burr as a successful lawyer and politician. Burr was a fastidious dresser and he is accurately depicted wearing impeccably tailored, fashionable clothing. *Courtesy of George Stuart Historical Figures, Collection of the Museum of Ventura County, California.*

Portrait of Alexander Hamilton by John Trumbull. *Yale University Art Gallery.*

The grave of Hercules Mulligan in the burial ground of New York City's Trinity Church. The elaborate tomb of his friend Alexander Hamilton is in the background. *Author's photo.*

Fictional illustration depicting the Hamilton-Burr duel. *Author's collection.*

A section of the wooden water pipe that Aron Burr's Metropolitan Company (incorporated in 1799) built to bring fresh water to New York City. This small section of the pipe is on exhibit at the New York Historical Society. *Author's photo.*

A row of townhouses built on the site of Aaron Burr's Richmond Hill estate. Located at the edge of modern Greenwich Village in Manhattan, Burr was forced to sell Richmond Hill in 1807 to pay his creditors. John Jacob Astor bought the property and made a fortune building townhouses on the land. *Author's photo.*

Putnam. Should he lose that post he would be a civilian since his rank of captain as General Richard Montgomery's aide was also a brevet posting. Burr was aware of his tenuous situation and that after conspicuous military service for almost two years he had no permanent rank or seniority.

Burr's commission is dated "Head Quarters Middle Brook 27th June 1777." It reads in part, "You are hereby appointed Lieut. Colo. To a Regiment in the Continental Service to be commanded by Colo. Malcolm. . . . I desire you will join him and give every necessary Assistance towards forming the Corps."[56]

Burr did not receive Washington's letter until July 20, almost a month later, appointing him a lieutenant colonel in Malcolm's regiment. Burr acknowledged Washington's letter the following day (July 21, 1777). In his reply Burr flaunted the arrogance that probably originally irritated Washington by complaining about the date of his commission (June 27, 1777). Burr told Washington that he felt that he was entitled to have the date of his commission during "the last campaign" (1776). After venting his displeasure with the date of his promotion, Burr concluded by saying that he would "immediately repair to their [Malcolm's Regiment] Rendezvous, and receive Col. Malcolm's Directions."[57] Washington never replied to Burr's letter.

After saying farewell to General Putnam, Burr reported to Colonel Malcolm whose regimental headquarters was located at Sidman's Cove (today's Suffern), in Rockland County, New York. Malcolm was a middle-aged, wealthy, and influential businessman who preferred to remain at his country home away from the vicissitudes of war. When Malcolm first met Burr, he was disappointed by his youthful appearance, fearing that he be "wanting in judgment and discretion."[58] But Malcolm warmed to Burr and turned over the field command of the regiment to him. Satisfied with his arrangement, Malcolm retired to his pastoral home with his family and sat out the war. Burr lived up to Malcolm's judgment. The regiment had 260 men when Burr joined it. He brought the strength to 500. He also made the regiment one of the best disciplined in the army.

Robert Hunter was an officer in Malcolm's Regiment. Recalling his service years later, Hunter said that "Malcom was never a month with the regiment after Burr joined it." Hunter attributed the regiment's discipline and order to Burr. The regiment, Hunter said, "was a model for the whole army."[59]

Malcolm's Regiment, under Burr's command, remained at Sidman's Cove, which was also called Smith's Cove, the Point of the Mountains, or simply the Cove. Sidman's Cove was the northern section of a pass that ran through a valley in the Ramapo Mountain range from the lower Hudson

River Valley of New York State to northern New Jersey. Its possession was critical to allow Revolutionary War period armies with wagons and artillery to move rapidly through this mountainous section of the lower Hudson Valley. Burr's regiment guarded the strategic pass through the summer and autumn of 1777. His regiment also helped to defend northern New Jersey. Lieutenant Colonel Burr established his headquarters at Suffern's Tavern at the northern end of the pass. While Washington's Main Army was fighting Howe's army in Pennsylvania, Burr was guarding the Cove and fending off nearby enemy raids and foraging parties.

Burr got the opportunity to lead his regiment into combat when two thousand British and Loyalist troops organized a foraging expedition from New York City in mid-September 1777. The foragers crossed the Hudson River into northern New Jersey to gather farm produce and livestock as well as plundering and destroying Patriot property. Burr received news of the enemy's presence soon after it reached New Jersey and pillaged the town of Hackensack. He mustered his regiment and hastened to confront them. Burr's regiment marched south through the Cove, covering sixteen miles in one day, reaching the countryside near Paramus, New Jersey, where the local militia had gathered. However, the militiamen could give Burr "no intelligence of the enemy but from rumor."[60] On September 13, Burr took twenty-two of his best men on a scouting mission to locate the enemy. Burr's detachment cautiously moved south into the night. At about 10:00 p.m. they saw the forager's campfires in the distance. They were camped near Hackensack. Burr went alone to reconnoiter their camp. He returned at dawn (September 14) to where his men were concealed. After sending a message for the rest of his regiment and militia to reinforce him, Burr led his small detachment toward the enemy camp. He warned his men not to speak a word or fire their muskets upon pain of death. Burr had discovered an enemy picket guard during his nighttime reconnaissance. They were stationed at a place called New Bridge. Burr and his detachment managed to sneak up on the guard post, which consisted of about fifty men, without being detected. A lieutenant in Malcolm's regiment named Alexander Dow was there and he recorded that Colonel Burr divided his men into platoons. Dow described what happened next,

> Col. Burr pitched [ordered] mine [Dow's detachment] to enter [the enemy camp] first without any alarm and challenge the whole to surrender which I did. That moment finding them both brave and obstinate, as they flew to their arms, I dropped three of them with my bayonet on

the muzzle of my fusee [an officer's musket]. By this time Col. Burr and the rest of our party had done their part [joined the surprise attack].[61]

Burr's detachment withdrew at dawn on September 14, having killed two and captured thirty British regulars and Loyalists stationed at the guard post.[62] Burr's surprise attack caused havoc in the main British camp. By 10:00 a.m. that morning Lieutenant Dow reported that "the whole of the enemy were gone in great fright." They left behind most of the cattle and plunder they had taken in their haste to withdraw. Burr was unable to pursue them as he received orders that same day to bring his regiment, without delay, to Pennsylvania. One of Burr's early biographers claimed that "for fifty years the events of these exciting days and nights in the Hudson Valley were narrated in the country; where to the last, Colonel Burr had devoted friends."[63]

The order for Malcolm's Regiment to join the Main Army came after the American defeat at the Battle of Brandywine. Washington needed reinforcements to bolster his depleted ranks. Malcolm's Regiment was among the troops instructed to join Washington's Main Army in Pennsylvania. Burr's order was dated September 27, 1777. His regiment joined the Main Army in November 1777 at Whitemarsh, Pennsylvania.

9

VALLEY FORGE

When the twelve thousand soldiers of Washington's Main Army reached Valley Forge, they looked upon an inhospitable countryside. One American officer wrote that the place "must have been selected at the instance of a speculator, or on the advice of a traitor, or by a council of ignoramuses."[1] But, despite its bleak appearance, Valley Forge offered numerous advantages to the Americans including terrain that favored defense. In addition, the area was dry, near an abundant fresh water supply (the Schuylkill River), and nearby forests that could provide fuel and building materials. But perhaps most important is that Valley Forge lay between British-held Philadelphia and the important Continental Army depots and hospitals at Lancaster, Reading, and York, Pennsylvania.

Washington's troops arrived at Valley Forge on December 19, 1777. It was late in the year to be going into winter quarters. The delay was because Washington had campaigned into early winter looking for a favorable opportunity to redeem his reputation following his defeats at Brandywine and Germantown. His failures were in sharp contrast to the spectacular victory won by his subordinate, Major General Horatio Gates. Operating independently of Washington's Grand Army, Gates commanded the Northern Department troops that trapped Burgoyne's army a few day's march from Albany in what became known as the Battle of Saratoga. Contributing to his defeat, Burgoyne had stretched his supply lines from Canada and made the fatal mistake of underestimating Patriot strength and overestimating that of the Loyalists. But perhaps more significant is that Gates had taken the advice of his Polish-born, French trained assistant engineer Thaddeus Kosciuszko who recommended that Gates' Northern Department establish a strong defense position on Bemis Heights, forty-two miles north of Albany.[2] This high ground blocked Burgoyne's route to Albany. After fortifying Bemis Heights, Gates remained embedded in his fortifications. His defensive plan was passionately opposed by Benedict Arnold, one of his chief subordinates, who repeatedly pressed Gates to take the fight to the enemy. Burgoyne tried twice to break through Bemis Heights only to fail. With his retreat route back to Canada blocked and running out of food, Burgoyne surrendered his army of 5,200 men, 5,000 muskets, and 37 cannons to Gates on October 17, 1777. As a result of his victory Gates became the darling of the Continental Congress and some dissent army officers. There were whispers within the Patriot ranks of replacing Washington with Gates, which increased during the Valley Forge winter encampment. As events unfolded, Hamilton and his fellow aide John Laurens were at headquarters and collaborating with Washington to oppose the shadowy movement to replace him while Aaron Burr was exiled to a distant assignment.

After arriving at Valley Forge, Washington and his military family made their headquarters in the Isaac Potts House and adjacent temporary wooden buildings. Burr's regiment was among the troops that wintered at Valley Forge. His Excellency gave Lieutenant Colonel Burr what appeared to be a difficult assignment that winter. Burr was ordered to take command of a large detachment of local militia guarding a strategic narrow section of a road leading to Valley Forge. The defile was called the Gulph Road or the Gulph (an archaic spelling of Gulf). It was located eight miles from Valley Forge on a route that the British might use to stealthily approach to the rebel winter encampment. Burr's assignment can be interpreted as either His Excellency having confidence in the young colonel's abilities or an opportunity to banish an insolent officer to a distant command. Washington was a skilled politician who may have tactfully banished outdated Putnam to Philadelphia in 1776 and impertinent Burr to the Gulph in 1777 to avoid upsetting their influential patrons and friends.

The orderly book kept by Burr for Malcolm's Additional Regiment indicates the dates that Burr was stationed at the Gulph. The orderly book shows that he made no entries from November 27, 1777, to March 2, 1778. This break in his record keeping was probably due to his being absent from Valley Forge and in command of guarding the Gulph.

After arriving at the Gulph, Burr the consummate soldier, carried out his responsibilities with great vigor. According to Burr, the inexperienced militiamen he commanded "fancied they heard the tramp of British columns in every nocturnal noise, and were continually sending false alarms to headquarters."[3] Burr put an end to this problem by instituting strict discipline and personal late night inspections of the various guard posts.

Burr claimed that some of the militiamen he commanded became weary of his strict discipline and plotted to kill him. Informed that the conspirators planned to murder him one night during a formation, Burr said that he armed himself with a well sharpened sword. He watched for any sudden movement as he walked along the line of men. Suddenly, one of the dissidents raised and leveled his musket at Burr. The young colonel claimed he responded quickly. He raised his sword hitting the extended arm of the mutineer above the elbow, breaking the bone, and leaving the limb hanging by little more than the skin. There were no more attempts on Burr's life after that, and it was said that the army slept in their huts at Valley Forge undisturbed by the jittery militiamen defending the Gulph.[4]

Colonel Burr was also involved with preventing local farmers from smuggling their produce to the British in Philadelphia. The British were paying for food and animal fodder with hard currency while the Patriot Army could only pay with depreciated paper money. General Washington had mounted patrols out, known as "market stoppers," to intercept farmers trying to sell their produce to the British.

From his outpost at the Gulph, Burr was involved in preventing the illicit trade with the enemy. There is an order from Washington's head-quarters, dated February 3, 1778, instructing Burr to guard a road "much frequented by the rascally inhabitants." The same order instructed Burr to secretly change the location of his guards and dispatch constant patrols to "prevent such a criminal intercourse with the enemy."[5]

While Burr was dutifully manning his dull outpost far from General Washington's view, Hamilton's star was rising. Washington's growing confidence in his young aide's abilities is evident when His Excellency selected him for an important assignment following General Gates victory at Saratoga. Gates's popularity was enormous at the time, particularly in New England. Gates, a former British Army major, was making the most of his military prowess by bypassing Washington, his commander, and corresponding directly with Congress. Washington gave twenty-two-year-old Hamilton the tactful job of getting the emboldened Gates to send the bulk of his troops to Pennsylvania to reinforce Washington's army. Gates, puffed up with arrogant pride, had given Washington excuses for continuing to retain a large army.

On October 30, 1777, Washington gave Hamilton a long letter of instructions, which started with his traveling to Gates' headquarters in Albany. The crux of his orders was to "point out, in the clearest and fullest manner . . . the absolute necessary that there is for his detaching a very considerable part of the Army at present under his [Gates'] command to the reinforcement of this."[6]

Hamilton left that same day for Gates's headquarters accompanied only by Captain Gibbs. The pair rode fast and arrived in Albany on November 5. Hamilton met with General Gates that same day. His command consisted of three brigades. The shrewd general pretended cheerful compliance with Hamilton's mission but tried to take advantage of his perceived youth and inexperience by offering him Brigadier General John Patterson's brigade, the smallest and weakest of the three brigades he commanded. But Hamilton was not fooled and wrote a letter to Gates later that day after reviewing his proposal, "By inquiry, I have learned that General Patterson's brigade, which is the one you propose to send is, by far, the weakest of the three now here." Hamilton used strong language telling Gates "I did not imagine you would pitch upon a brigade little more than half as large at the others." He concluded his letter by stating that "Gen. [John] Glover's brigade should be the one."[7] Hamilton later wrote to General Washington that he gave Gates "a little time to recollect himself" after which "I renewed my remonstrances on the necessity and propriety of sending you more than one Brigade."[8] Gates reluctantly yielded to Hamilton's demands and ordered both Glover's and Patterson's brigades to reinforce Washington's Main Army in Pennsylvania. Hamilton had proven himself to be a skillful negotiator adding to his good reputation with General Washington.

Illness delayed Hamilton's return to Valley Forge until late January 1777. Eighteenth-century armies typically stopped fighting during the frigid winter months and went into a stoical period of military hibernation. But the winter at Valley Forge was an exception as the bleak Pennsylvania encampment was teeming with activity. For starters, Hamilton arrived back at headquarters to learn that there were whispers of a plot to appoint Gates commander of the army. The mysterious plot became known as the Conway Cabal. It was allegedly composed of a group (a cabal) of dissident politicians and army officers who wanted to replace Washington with Gates as commander in chief. Hamilton was zealously loyal to Washington throughout the episode and used his acerbic pen to help squash the shadowy plot. The existence of an organized plot to replace Washington with Gates remains a conundrum, but Washington and his supporters were convinced of its existence and moved quickly to crush it. The alleged conspiracy was named for Continental Army major General Thomas Conway. He was an Irishman who had served as a colonel in the French Army. Conway came to America to add to his military experience and enhance his reputation.

Congress appointed him a general and shipped him off to Washington's headquarters. Conway proved to be a capable officer and a gossipy critic of Washington's generalship. He found a ready audience among some members of Congress following Gates's victory at Saratoga. Fueling Washington's anxiety was the news that Colonel James Wilkinson, who was one of Gates's aides-de-camp, was overheard boasting in a tavern that Conway had written Gates calling Washington a "weak general." Conway denied the allegation while the crafty Gates tried to switch the subject by claiming that someone had rifled through his personal letters. Gates accused Hamilton of reading his confidential correspondence when left alone in Gates's office during his mission to Albany.[9] Gates alluded to Hamilton when he wrote Washington on December 8, 1777, asking His Excellency's help in "detecting a wretch, who may betray me."[10]

General Conway was believed to be at the center of the plot to depose Washington, and Hamilton's efforts to discredit Conway included a fiery assault on his character in a personal letter to New York State governor George Clinton. The letter is dated Valley Forge, February 13, 1778. In his missive, Hamilton first attacked the feckless Continental Congress for being "resolute enough to withstand the impudent importunity and vain boasting of foreign pretenders." Further, Hamilton accused the delegates "of being bullied by every petty rascal, who comes armed with ostentatious pretensions of military merit and experience." Hamilton then refers specifically to Conway, "Have you heard anything of Conway's history? He is one of the vermin bred in the entrails of the chimera dire, and there does not exist a more villainous calumniator and incendiary."[11] According to Matthew Davis *Memoirs of Aaron Burr*, Colonel Burr claimed that the "difficulties between General Washington and General Gates was well-known among the officers wintering at Valley Forge." Davis said that Burr admitted to being "a friend of Gates" primarily because of Burr's belief that Washington "was exceedingly hostile towards him." It is not known if Washington or any of his allies were aware of Burr's favoring Gates. It they did, it would have further soured Burr's relationship with the commander in chief. But, by March 1778, the so-called Conway Cabal had fizzled out. After studying what is known about the plot, historian Lee Boyle concludes, "Whatever the facts were, they were lost in the tempest which ensued as Washington loyalists rallied around him."[12]

Another movement that had the Valley Forge encampment active was a crusade to raise and arm a regiment composed of black slaves. Hamilton's friend and fellow aide John Laurens led the movement of allowing blacks to earn their freedom by serving in the army. Individual blacks were already serving in the manpower-starved Continental Army. The British were also using them but primarily for menial jobs such as laborers and teamsters and not as combat troops. Lauren's proposal met with little support. But the state of Rhode Island, desperate to provide troops for its 1st Rhode Island Regiment, recruited a large number of black slaves during the winter. The regiment arrived at Valley Forge on May 29, 1778.[13]

Laurens would periodically resume his "black scheme" with Hamilton's support and encouragement. But Hamilton was realistic in understanding the stiff opposition the idea of arming slaves and teaching them soldiering. He lectured Laurens, telling him "Even the animated and persuasive eloquence of my young Demosthenes will not be able to rouse his countrymen from the lethargy of voluptuous indolence, or dissolve the fascinating character of self-interest."[14]

Adding to the activity at Valley Forge were the intense efforts by Washington and his aides-de-camp to relieve the sufferings of the army. The winter was relatively mild but the roads leading to the encampment were muddy making it difficult to bring food and equipment into the encampment. In addition, there was a shortage of wagons and teamsters to haul the provisions to Valley Forge plus lax and inept management of the supply system. The aides drafted impassioned letters for Washington to members of Congress and state officials describing the terrible conditions in the camp. Hamilton's personal efforts that winter included a letter to his friend and confidant, Governor George Clinton of New York. Hamilton's letter is dated February 13, 1778, during what was probably the most horrific period of the Valley Forge encampment. His letter reads in part,

> By injudicious changes and arrangements in the Commissary's department, in the middle of a campaign they [Congress] have exposed the army frequently to temporary want, and to the danger of dissolution, from absolute famine. At this very day there are complaints from the whole line, of having been three or four days without provisions; desertions have been immense, and strong features of munity begin to show themselves.
>
> If effectual measures are not speedily adopted, I know not how we are shall keep the army together or make another campaign.[15]

The hardships suffered by the army at Valley Forge were not due primarily to the weather but to a breakdown of the supply system. Sickness added to the misery of the encampment. The situation at Valley Forge slowly improved through the efforts of Washington and his aides and the appointment of the capable General Nathanael Greene as quartermaster general. Greene quickly reorganized the department and supplies finally began to reach the encampment in quantity in the spring of 1778.

The coming of warmer weather finally allowed Washington to turn his attention to another pressing problem, which was negotiating a prisoner exchange with the British. His Excellency appointed the capable Colonel Hamilton to a committee to parley with the enemy. The effort to free American prisoners in March 1778 can be traced to July 1776 when General Washington communicated with his adversary, General Howe, regarding an exchange of prisoners. It was a complicated issue and both commanders finally agreed that representatives from their armies would meet at Germantown at the end of March 1778 to "fix the exchange and accommodation of Prisoners of War, upon a more certain, liberal, and ample foundation."[16] Hamilton was appointed as one of the American commissioners (representatives) along with another member of Washington's inner circle, his competent military secretary and prewar lawyer Robert Hanson Harrison. Colonel William Grayson was also a member of the American delegation. Grayson was also a prewar lawyer and a former aide to Washington. General Howe appointed Colonel Charles O'Hara as his chief negotiator.

Prisoner exchanges during the American Revolution were a thorny issue because King George III and his government viewed the colonists as rebels. They did not recognize American independence or the sovereignty of the United States. Because of this, prisoner exchanges were individually negotiated as one-time gentleman agreements between two opposing military commanders who pledged their personal honor that all parts of the agreement would be faithfully executed.

The negotiators met for the first time on March 31, 1778. As agreed, they met in British held Germantown. The British removed their garrison from the town and no troops, except for a military escort of fourteen men from each side, were present while the negotiations were in progress. Nothing of consequence was accomplished during their initial meeting and both sides agreed to meet again on the following day. Again, nothing was concluded, and the commissioners met again on April 6 in Newton, Pennsylvania. This time Hamilton took the lead. He drew up a lengthy draft calling for a cartel for the exchange of prisoners. A cartel was a general treaty that, in this situation, would establish the terms and conditions for all future prisoner exchanges. The Newton negotiations continued for several days but became deadlocked as the Americans continued to insist upon a prisoner exchange endorsed by the British government.

On April 11, following days of discussions, both sides realized that they were hopelessly deadlocked, and they broke off negotiations. However, during the time they spent together the British and American officers met socially and they became friendly with one another. When the two sides had their final meeting, Colonel Charles O'Hara declared that if any of the American delegates were captured, the British commissioners would make sure they were well treated. On the other hand, if any of them were ever taken prisoner by the Americans, they would call upon Colonels Harrison, Grayson, and Hamilton to help them. The two sides agreed, and they parted company.

At the surrender of the British Army at Yorktown three years later, General Cornwallis the British commander, claimed illness and Colonel O'Hara, his second in command, delivered up his sword on the parade ground to the Americans. O'Hara immediately called out for Colonel Hamilton, whom he recognized among the American officers. Hamilton came forward, "now sir," said O'Hara, "perform your promise." Hamilton kept his word and made sure that O'Hara was well treated as a prisoner of war.[17]

Hamilton was also busy assisting a former German officer who arrived at the Valley Forge encampment on February 23, 1778. The foreigner called himself Baron Friedrich Wilhelm August Heinrich Ferdinand von Steuben. Promenading as a former general in the service of the King of Prussia, with great knowledge of military organization, he was warmly received by the Americans who gave him the name that he would be known throughout history, Baron von Steuben. The truth was that he was a retired captain in the Prussian Army, acknowledged as the best army in Europe at the time. But what made von Steuben unique was that he was also a graduate of an elite Prussian Army school where he was taught strategic planning and leadership. The baron only spoke German and French, and Washington's fluent French-speaking aides Hamilton and Laurens became his translators. The Baron was shocked by the deplorable condition of the rebel army and particularly its lack of a standard system for maneuvering. Von Steuben discussed with Hamilton and Laurens the idea of creating an uncomplicated drill manual for the army. They not only encouraged the idea but worked with von Steuben to create the manual making "alterations they deemed advisable."[18] General Washington enthusiastically supported von Steuben's manual, which was written in French. Hamilton and Laurens translated it into English and made handwritten copies. The baron began teaching his new system of drills to a small detachment of troops. The manual was a huge success and eventually taught to the entire army at Valley Forge.

Turning to Burr, he rejoined Malcolm's regiment in March 1778 from his assignment at the Gulph and spent the balance of the winter at the Valley Forge encampment.

The coming of warmer weather in 1778 also brought the long hoped-for news of a treaty of alliance between the United States and France. Washington first learned of the treaty at Valley Forge on May 4, 1778. The terms of the treaty, signed in Paris on February 6, 1778, provided for a defensive alliance between the United States and France. The treaty also recognized the United States as an independent nation. On March 17, the British government declared war on France after learning that the French had officially acknowledged the United States as a sovereign nation. The British declaration of war meant that the French Army and Navy would fight alongside the Americans. France was a formidable adversary in this new war with Britain. She had lost valuable colonies to Britain in the Seven Years War. France had also lost prestige and influence in Europe as a result of her defeat by England. Desperate to regain her past glory, France had been modernizing and rearming its army and navy for years. The American Revolution was a great opportunity for France to cripple the overstretched British Army and Navy as a prelude to invading and conquering Great Britain.

The French alliance was a reason for a celebration at Valley Forge. The festivity was not unique to the camp as there was some semblance of social life among the officers at Valley Forge during the miserable winter. Foremost were dinners and dances organized by the officer's wives, including Martha Washington, in the encampment. As both Hamilton and Burr were lieutenant colonels, it is probable that they were invited to these social gatherings. Even more compelling is that they both undoubtedly attended a feu de joie (a salute fired by muskets in succession along a line of troops) on May 6, 1777, at Valley Forge to formally celebrate the alliance between the United States and France. One eyewitness described the joyous event saying that there was "a general invitation of the officers of the army to dine with His Excellency in the center of the camp, where several remarkable toasts were drunk. The day was spent in mirth and rejoicing."[19] Burr biographer Nancy Isenberg states that Burr was there "and marched off, arm-in-arm, with his fellow officers to a sumptuous buffet, joined by a group of fawning females."[20]

The entry of France into the war as America's allies brought foreboding possibilities for the British. Among them was that the new warships of the French Navy would blockade the Delaware River and isolate

British-occupied Philadelphia. Even worse, the French would launch a combined attack with the Americans against New York or Philadelphia. New York, serving as the principal naval base for the Royal Navy in America, was the more important of the two cities. As a result, General Sir Henry Clinton, now in command of the Crown Forces in America, was ordered by the king's ministers to abandon Philadelphia and bring his troops to reinforce New York.

10

THE BATTLE OF MONMOUTH

The first indication that the Crown Forces were going to abandon Philadelphia came from American spies who reported that British officers in the city told the women washing their clothes to quickly finish their work. By mid-June (1778) it was evident that the British were preparing to leave. General Clinton decided to take the best regiments at Philadelphia and march overland across New Jersey toward New York. The rest would be transported by ships. Clinton's thinking was that perhaps he could bring on a general engagement with Washington's army in New Jersey. Clinton's army of more than seventeen thousand troops purposely moved slowly across the state to lure Washington to leave Valley Forge and attack his column. Washington decided to cautiously follow Clinton and ordered New Jersey militia to harass the enemy. The militia went into action, skirmishing with the British along with destroying bridges and felling trees across their route. Meanwhile, Washington advanced with the Main Army from Valley Forge on June 19. The Continentals crossed the Delaware River into New Jersey at Coryell's Ferry (today's Lambertville, New Jersey) on June 21 and 22 maintaining a respectable distance from Clinton's column.

While shadowing Clinton's army, Washington summoned a council of war at which Hamilton was present as well as eleven of Washington's generals. The council took place on June 24, 1778, at the home of John Hunt in Hopewell, New Jersey. Washington was using the Hunt House at the time as his temporary headquarters. The purpose of the meeting was to decide if the Americans should fight a pitched battle with Clinton's army. It was one of the most important councils of war that took place during the American Revolution. The major generals at the meeting were Lee, Greene, Sterling, Lafayette, and Von Steuben. The brigadier generals who were present included Henry Knox and Anthony Wayne. The majority of the generals were opposed to bringing on a general engagement with Clinton's army. Hamilton was disgusted with their timidity. He later wrote his famous comment about the meeting saying it "would have done honor to the most honorable society of midwives, and to them only."[1]

From this description of the council of war at the Hunt House, it is assumed that Hamilton took an active part in the meeting. However, this is incorrect. Hamilton was only there to take notes and write a report of the proceedings. Hamilton and Washington's fellow aides-de-camp were not consulted regarding planning and executing strategy during the American Revolution. This is despite comments by some historians who claim, for example, that "Hamilton became one of Washington's principal military advisors."[2]

Despite the majority of his generals opposing a general engagement with Clinton's army, Washington was characteristically aggressive. He decided to move closer to Clinton's column, which was stretched out for more than ten miles with a baggage train of 1,500 wagons. Washington also dispatched Continental troops to join the New Jersey militia who were skirmishing with Clinton's men and cutting down trees to block his route. The weather was unseasonably hot, and the militiamen were also filling wells with tree trunks and dead livestock to deny water to the enemy's thirsty men and horses. Washington reinforced the militia harassing the enemy with General Maxwell's New Jersey brigade and Daniel Morgan's riflemen. He soon added an additional 1,500 Continentals commanded by General Charles Scott to scuffle with Clinton's army. At the same time, Washington marched the Main Army even closer to the slowly moving enemy. Washington and his Continentals arrived at the village of Kingston, New Jersey, on June 25. Malcolm's regiment, commanded by Burr, was with them. Until now, Washington was unsure of Clinton's route across the eastern portion of New Jersey, but a courier arrived at Kingston on June 25 with the news that Clinton was following a route that would take his army to Sandy Hook, on the New Jersey coast. It was evident that Clinton was going to rendezvous with Royal Navy warships and transports at Sandy Hook that would convey his army on the final leg of its journey to New York. Based on Clinton's route the last good opportunity to engage the British was in the rolling farmland surrounding the village of Monmouth Courthouse, New Jersey. Once the enemy was past Monmouth they would be in hilly country and better able to defend themselves.

Washington had almost 4,000 troops nipping at Clinton's long column when he arrived at Kingston on June 25; 800 New Jersey militia; 1,000 Continentals under the command of General Maxwell; 1,500 Continental led by General Charles Scott; and 600 riflemen commanded by

Daniel Morgan. From Kingston, on June 25, Washington dispatched an additional 1,000 men to skirmish with the British under the command of General Anthony Wayne. Washington took an additional aggressive move when he ordered Major General Lafayette to take command of all the American troops in the field with orders to attack the rear of Clinton's column instead of skirmishing and harassing them. Lafayette's force was designated the advance corps.

Washington instructed Hamilton to accompany Lafayette to obtain accurate information on the enemy's strength and movements and send frequent reports back to headquarters. Hamilton was selected for this important mission because he could converse with Lafayette in French. In addition, Hamilton was young and had the stamina that the assignment required. But perhaps the most compelling reason for picking Hamilton for the job was that Washington could rely on him to provide precise and detailed reports. From his close observations of how Clinton had cunningly organized his army, Hamilton sent a courier to Washington in the evening of June 26 describing what Lafayette and he had observed. Hamilton's message read in part,

> Their march to day has been very judiciously conducted:— their baggage in front and their flying army [a strong body of mounted troops and infantry that can maneuver quickly] in the rear, with a rear guard of one thousand men about four hundred paces from the main body.[3]

Hamilton conveyed to Washington the advice of Lafayette and other senior American officers in the field,

> To attack them in this situation [the presence of a flying army that could swiftly counterattack] without being supported by the whole army, would be folly in the extreme.[4]

Events now moved fast. Based on Hamilton's report and other information reaching headquarters, Washington marched the Grand Army closer to Clinton in support of Lafayette's advance corps. Washington arrived at Cranbury, New Jersey, on June 26. Clinton's army was camped twelve miles away at Monmouth Courthouse. At Cranbury, Major General Lee, who rejoined the Main Army at Valley Forge, suddenly decided that he was entitled to command the advance corps. Washington respected Lee's rank as the senior major general of the army and acceded to his request. Lee took charge of the advance corps from Lafayette on the following day, June 27, in the village of Englishtown, New Jersey. Englishtown was only three miles west of Clinton's army at Monmouth, which was resting that day in the intense heat. Washington reinforced Lee on the twenty-seventh with an additional three hundred men, artillery, and mounted troops, giving his advance corps a total of five thousand men. It was apparent that Clinton would resume his march the following morning, and Lee's instructions were to attack the rear of Clinton's column as it departed Monmouth.

Hamilton rejoined Washington on the night of the twenty-seventh. On the following morning, His Excellency instructed three of his aides, including Hamilton, to observe Lee's attack and report back as events unfolded. Hamilton returned later in the morning to report that Lee was about to engage Clinton's rear guard. He had also scouted the terrain and told Washington of a hill that dominated the surrounding countryside.[5] General Knox, who had also been reconnoitering, confirmed Hamilton's news and a recommendation to position artillery on the hill. Washington followed their advice. Positioning the artillery on the knoll, known locally as Combs Hill, proved to be an excellent decision.

Lee attacked Clinton's rear guard at 10:00 a.m., but fell into a trap when Clinton's ten-thousand-man flying army counterattacked. Lee's troops retreated in confusion. Washington was too far away to reinforce

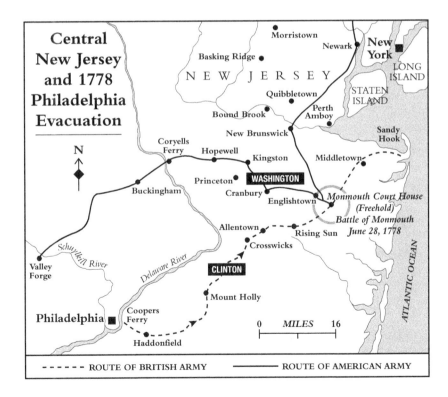

Lee with the eight thousand troops under his immediate command, but marched toward the sound of musket and artillery fire. As noon approached Washington was still two miles away from Monmouth when the sounds of gunfire suddenly ceased.

Washington continued to advance and encountered troops from Lee's corps retreating in confusion. None of the officers he met seemed to know what was happening. Washington met Colonel Ogden, Burr's boyhood friend, whose regiment was fleeing with the others. When Washington asked Ogden why Lee's corps was retreating, the exasperated colonel gave his famous reply, "By God! They are flying from a shadow."[6] Lee would later be accused of failing to reconnoiter the enemy's position and understand the local terrain (streams, swamps, roads, etc.) before attacking.

In the early afternoon Washington found Lee and ordered him to rally his troops behind a hedgerow (a line of closely placed shrubs) near the Rhea Family Farm west of Monmouth. At this point, according to George Washington Parke Custis, Hamilton rode up in great heat and told Lee, "I will stay here with you, my dear General, and die with you; let us all die here rather than retreat."

Washington was much more composed than his aide. Colonel David Rhea's family farm was close by and Rhea knew the area. He advised Washington to occupy a hill on the nearby Perrine Farm (Perrine Hill). Washington agreed and at 1:30 in the afternoon he formed a defense line on Perrine Hill supported by the artillery. Burr's regiment was with them. Meanwhile, the British seized the hedgerow from the Americans after a brief but intense firefight. From the hedgerow, the elite British 2nd Grenadier Regiment launched a flanking movement to get behind the American defense line on Perrine Hill. The Grenadiers reached a prominence (known today as Grenadier Hill), which was about a half mile from American-held Perrine Hill. General Lord Sterling spied the Grenadiers from Perrine Hill and ordered Colonel Burr to lead three regiments to drive the enemy troops off the knoll. Burr, who was on horseback, led his men forward at 1:45 in the afternoon, passing over a rush bridge (large bundles of rushes bound together over which planks are laid) to pass over a morass (boggy ground) and engaged the Grenadiers at close range. Volleys of musket fire followed with the proud Grenadiers fighting tenaciously to hold the hilltop. In the midst of the fighting Major William Barber, aide to General Lord Sterling, arrived on the scene with orders for Burr to retreat. The reason was that the Americans on Perrine Hill had moved field artillery into position to bombard the Grenadiers. Burr reluctantly ordered a retreat exposing his men to British artillery from the hedgerow, which was concentrating on

Burr's brigade as it withdrew. Burr's *Memoirs* describe how his detachment "suffered severely" as it retreated back to Perrine Hill. Burr's horse was "shot under him" during the retreat.

It will be recalled that Burr's *Memoirs* was based on his dictating much of the text to his friend Matthew Davis. *Memoirs* describes the events following the firefight with the Grenadiers,

> The movements and firing of the armies continued until dark. The Americans remained on the battle-ground . . . but vigilant of renewed fighting. Burr was up all night, visiting his own pickets and taking the necessary precautions for avoiding a surprise. The weather was intensely hot [the temperature reached 98 degrees on the day of the battle with men dying from heat exhaustion and dehydration]. Exhausted with fatigue, and worn out for the want of repose, on the 29th, Colonel Burr lay down under the shade of some trees and fell asleep. When he awoke, he was exposed, and had been for some time, to the rays of the sun. He found himself unable to walk without great difficulty; and so severely was he afflicted, that he did not recover from the effects for some years afterwards.[7]

The Americans technically won the Battle of Monmouth because they seized and held the battlefield, but it was a contentious victory at a time when Washington wanted a major victory to silence his critics. When General Lee sent His Excellency a disrespectful letter demanding a court-martial to clear his name from the failed morning attack, Washington was ready to accommodate his request. Lee, who was then the Continental Army's senior major general, had become a pretentious nuisance. His court-martial was an opportunity to both relegate Lee and make him responsible for the Continental Army's shortcomings during the battle including making "an unnecessary, disorderly, and shameful retreat."[8]

Washington's clique, and Hamilton in particular, gave damaging testimony against Lee at his court-martial. When called to testify Hamilton told the court that when he found Lee's corps retreating, "they seemed to be marching without system or design, as chance should direct: in short, I saw nothing like a general plan." Hamilton then described Lee as "under a hurry of mind [confused]." Lee handled his own defense and tried to discredit Hamilton's testimony by describing how the young aide was "flourishing his sword on the battlefield" and swearing that "we will all die here on this spot."[9] Colonel Burr followed the proceedings and reported that "Lee was found guilty and sentenced to be suspended from any command in the armies of the United States for the term of twelve months." Burr felt that Lee had been railroaded and wrote him a sympathetic letter. Burr's letter has never been found but Lee's reply is known and includes a caustic reference to General Washington who was a tobacco planter prior to being appointed the Commander-in-Chief of the Continental Army; "It is my intent," Lee wrote Burr, "to resign my commission, retire to Virginia, and learn to hoe tobacco, which I find is the best school to form [make] a consummate general."[10]

Another of Lee's supporters was Major John Eustace. When the trial ended, Eustace charged loudly, in the presence of many officers, that he believed Colonel Hamilton had lied in his testimony. Eustace later wrote Lee a letter about a conversation he had with Hamilton. The letter included the following compelling text,

> I met Hambeton [a purposeful misspelling] the other day in company with the favorite Green [General Nathanael Greene], the Drunkard Stirling [another purposeful misspelling of General Lord Sterling] and their several classes of attendants . . . . I cou'd not treat him much more rudely—I've repeated my suspicions of his veracity on the tryall [Lee's court-martial] so often that I expect the son of a bitch will challenge me [to a duel] when he comes.[11]

The June 28, 1778, Battle of Monmouth proved to be the last major battle of the American Revolution in the North. The war moved to the southern states following Monmouth as Britain altered its strategy in the face of the entry of France into the war as America's ally and the belief that there was a strong allegiance to King George in the South.

11

AARON BURR'S
FINEST COMMAND

The Continental Army turned-out on the morning of June 29, 1778, on Monmouth battlefield to find that Clinton's army had vanished during the night. Reports arrived at headquarters late that afternoon that the British were on the road toward Sandy Hook where "a great quantity of small brigs and cutters" could be seen "from towards New York."[1] Washington decided that his army was too exhausted from the previous day's fighting to pursue Clinton's column. Influencing his decision not to follow the enemy was the continued heat wave and a shortage of drinking water. The army was ordered to fall back to Englishtown to start a move to New Brunswick. Washington knew that his army could rest and recover along the tree-lined shores of the Raritan River. The army marched from Englishtown to New Brunswick in one day, a distance of twenty miles. Washington described the march "as inconceivably distressing to the troops and horses . . . through a deep sand without a drop of water, except at South River [a meandering tributary of the Raritan River] which is half way."[2]

General Washington knew that Sir Henry Clinton was an aggressive and resourceful opponent who would undertake some new operations against the Americans. Washington already had an expert spy network operating in British-held New York, but ordered Colonel Burr to go immediately to Elizabeth, New Jersey, and "endeavor to get all the intelligence you possibly can from the city."[3] Burr arrived in Elizabeth on July 2, 1778. Two days later he received specific orders from General Washington to ascertain "the preparations of shipping for embarkation of foot [infantry] and horse [mounted troops]; what expeditions on hand . . . whether up the North River [Hudson], Connecticut, or West Indies?" His Excellency also instructed Burr to send spies into New York to gather information.[4]

Elizabeth was a good location for Burr to operate his spy ring because it was close to New York City. Elizabeth was also the home of Elias Boudinot, who Burr knew from his childhood days. Boudinot's official title during much of the war was the American Commissioner of Prisoners.[5] However, Boudinot was also covertly running an American spy ring for General Washington that was operating in New York City and Long Island.

According to Burr biographer Nathan Schachner, the young colonel (Burr) was noted as "a master of intelligence,"[6] but there is nothing in his past that would qualify him to supervise a spy network. General Washington sending Burr off on what appears to be a redundant mission, far from the Main Army, can be interpreted as His Excellency's abhorrence of Burr dating back to Burr's brief tenure at headquarters in 1776. There is a pattern in Washington's wartime assignments of Burr: appointed to Malcolm's regiment stationed in a remote section of New Jersey; commanding a militia detachment at the Gulph distant from Valley Forge; and now his being sent off to Elizabeth while the Main Army was in New Brunswick. These were seemingly important assignments, but each kept Burr far from Washington's presence.

There is another plausible explanation for Washington's behavior toward Burr. Washington knew that Burr had a low opinion of his generalship. In *Memoirs*, Burr states that, following the 1776 Battle of Long Island, in which the Americans were outflanked and badly defeated, "his prejudices against General Washington became fixed and unchangeable." Burr also admitted that he was "the friend of [General Charles] Lee and [General Horatio] Gates in opposition to General Washington."[7] While Washington was not malicious, he valued loyalty and ostracized anyone who was disrespectful toward him.

Burr's remote assignment in Elizabeth ended on July 18 when he resumed the field command of Malcolm's regiment. However, just one day later, his regiment received orders from General Washington to garrison West Point, New York, the American fortifications guarding the lower Hudson River. The fort was under construction at the time under the direction of Colonel Thaddeus Kosciuszko. Burr's regiment left the Main Army on the morning of July 20 and marched off to their new assignment. A *Return* [roster] *of the Continental Army Under the Immediate Command of His Excellency George Washington* dated August 1, 1778, shows Malcolm's regiment stationed at West Point. The unit's total strength is listed as 177 officers and common soldiers.[8] Was Burr's regiment being assigned to distant West Point another coincidence or the latest move by Washington to isolate the young colonel?

Colonel Burr's presence in New York State soon involved him in a mission initiated by the New York State legislature. The undertaking began when the legislature became alarmed following the safe arrival of General Sir Henry Clinton's army from Philadelphia to New York City. It resulted in "much excitement and apprehension" among the New York State authorities who were alarmed by the presence of a large British Army in the city.[9] One response to the danger was to require every male citizen in New York State to take an oath of allegiance. The oaths were administered by the state's Commissioners for Detecting and Defeating Conspiracies. Anyone refusing to take the pledge would be deemed a Loyalist. The consequence for loyalty to the king by New York State authorities was severe: Loyalists would be forced to forfeit their property and escorted under armed guard to British-held New York City. The state's governor, George Clinton, requested General Washington to provide an officer to take charge of the transfer of the "disaffected" to the enemy. His Excellency gave the assignment to Colonel Burr. The colonel was ordered on August 1, 1778, to cooperate with the local authorities and escort those New Yorker's who refused to sign the oath of allegiance to enemy lines.[10] Colonel Burr's *Memoirs* give a good summary of the situation,

> Early in July 1778, in consequence of Sir Henry Clinton having arrived in New-York with his army [from Philadelphia], much excitement and some apprehension existed in the upper part of the state respecting the Tories [Loyalists]. The legislature had previously adopted rigid measures [oath of allegiance] on the subject and it became necessary [here Burr is flattering himself] that an intelligent and confidential military officer should be designated to take charge of them. General Washington selected Colonel Burr for this purpose.[11]

The assignment was another example of a seemingly important, but in reality, lackluster job that Washington thrust on Burr. The first group that Burr transported consisted of three men who boarded the sloop *Liberty* at Fishkill, New York, on the Hudson River. One of them was William Smith, a wealthy lawyer who served as the chief justice of the Province of New York prior to the Revolution. On three occasions Smith had refused to take the required oath of allegiance to New York.[12]

Burr conveyed them, under a flag of truce to New York City. What is particularly interesting about this first mission is that Theodosia Bartow Prevost, the wife of a British Army lieutenant colonel, was among Burr's passengers. She was traveling to New York City with a safe conduct pass signed by Governor George Clinton. The purpose of her visit to New

York is unknown. It was imaged by some starry-eyed authors that Theodosia was an American spy who was going to New York City on a secret mission.[13] Burr noted her presence on the trip, "Mrs. Prevost and Miss De Visme [Theodosia's half-sister Catherine De Visme] with one man servant . . . to pass to N. York and return are admitted on board this Flagg."[14] The significance of this event is that Colonel Burr would marry Mrs. Prevost before the war ended.

Some historians, including Burr biographer Nancy Isenberg, speculate that Burr first met Mrs. Prevost as early as September 1777 when he was stationed with Malcolm's regiment at the northern end of the Cove, which was located fifteen miles from her home in northern New Jersey. Burr's visit may have been arranged by Theodosia's cousin John Watkins, who was an officer in Burr's regiment. Giving credibility to the story is that there is record of a Captain John William Watkins serving in Malcolm's regiment from March to October 1777.[15]

The leisurely voyage of the sloop *Liberty* to New York City down the Hudson River must have given Colonel Burr the opportunity to converse with Mrs. Prevost. He was attracted to educated, cultured women throughout his life and Theodosia evidently suited his temperament. She had the advantage of a good education in an age when women were mostly trained in domestic chores. She owned her liberal education to her stepfather, Philip De Visme. Discouraging Burr's romantic advances was that Theodosia was married with three sons. Her husband was James Marcus Prevost a lieutenant colonel in the British 60th Regiment. At least, conveniently for Burr, Colonel Prevost was stationed at the time with his regiment in Georgia. Theodosia was also ten years older than Aaron. She was thirty-two years old when they first met. Burr's youth (he was twenty-two at the time) is illustrated in a story that took place while he was in command at West Point. A local farmer arrived at Burr's headquarters stating that he had some business to transact with the colonel. The orderly sergeant conducted the farmer into Colonel Burr's office. "Sir, said the countryman, I wish to see Colonel Burr. You may proceed. I am Colonel Burr. I suppose," replied the farmer, "you are Colonel Burr's son."[16]

As the wife of a British officer, Mrs. Prevost would have been considered a Loyalist. However, she was one of the exceptional individuals who managed to retain friendly relations with both the British and Americans during the war. Her home, called the Hermitage (still standing but with major Victorian period alterations), was situated in colonial Paramus (the house is now in the borough of Ho-Ho-Kus, New Jersey, which was incorporated as a borough in 1908). It was said that the Hermitage was spared by both sides as it was a refuge from the war-torn region where a person could find a gracious hostess and polite society.

General Washington was among the Hermitage's overnight guests. He used the house as his headquarters from July 11–14, 1778.[17] Theodosia's ability to keep her home from being ransacked and possibly burned can be attributed to her unique circumstances. Theodosia's marriage to a British officer protected her from reprisals by the Crown forces and their Loyalist allies. Her safety from the Continental Army and its adherents was due to the fact that she was American born and on friendly terms with many influential American officers including Colonel James Monroe (the future president of the United States). Colonel Monroe wrote Theodosia after visiting her, "I am too much attached ever to forget the Hermitage."[18] Burr was added to the list of American officers who visited the Hermitage. His visits became more frequent and people assumed that the young colonel was courting Catherine De Visme, Theodosia's younger half-sister. But Burr's infatuation was with Theodosia whose attributes included fluent French and quoting French and Latin poets. She was not a particularly beautiful woman, but it was said that Burr loved the inner woman. He described her as "having the ripest intellect, and the most winning and graceful manners of any woman I ever met."[19] What transpired between Aaron and Theodosia during his visits was veiled in propriety, but the two evidently became intimate lovers. Burr continued to command his regiment at West Point dispersed with escorting Loyalists to New York City and visits with Theodosia.

In January 1779, General Washington gave Colonel Burr what would be the most difficult and dangerous assignment of his career. His new command followed Washington's pattern of giving Burr tedious assignments that were distant from headquarters. But this time Burr's mission was serious. It was a post of honor (stationed close to enemy lines) in a lawless section of Westchester County, New York, called the Neutral Ground. It was a no-man's land that extended for twenty-five miles north of British-held Manhattan Island to the American lines on the north shore of the Croton River. The Neutral Ground was subjected to roving bands of freelance plunders and ill-disciplined soldiers the most famous of whom were the Cowboys and the Skinners. There is some ambiguity about which side the Cowboys and Skinners supported. The most compelling evidence is that they were both recruited among Americans who sided with the British during the Revolution. The term Skinners is derived from the Loyalist General (and former Royal Attorney General of New Jersey) Cortland Skinner.[20] They concentrated their foraging, raiding, and intelligence gathering across the Hudson from Westchester County in Rockland County, New York, and northern New Jersey. The Cowboys were a Provincial (Loyalist) brigade headquartered in the Morrisania section of Westchester County (now part of the Bronx). Their commander was Colonel James De Lancey, the prewar sheriff of Westchester County. De Lancey's Brigade was called the Cowboys because they stole cattle that they herded to New York City to sell to the British Army.[21] De Lancey's unit consisted of three battalions of 500 infantry and dragoons for an impressive total of 1,500 men. Burr opposed them with his regiment (Malcolm's) consisting of 173 officers and common soldiers and the remnants of John Patton's Additional Regiment consisting of 119 men.[22] However, they were reinforced informally by additional Continental troops and militia to help even the odds.

James Thacher, a Continental Army doctor, traveled through the Neutral Ground with a military escort on November 24, 1780. He described the region as being rich and fertile but many of the farms were deserted with thousands of bushels of apples and other fruit rotting in orchards. Dr. Thacher called the Cowboys and Skinners "shameless marauders; British banditti who have become the scourge and terror to the people."[23]

Burr's orders were to protect American lives and property and put an end to the daily robberies and murders. He also had to stay alert to guard against a surprise attack or ambush. Burr called his new assignment "the most fatiguing and most troublesome that could be contrived." He called the Neutral Ground "a disgraceful scene of plunder and sometimes of murder."[24]

A respected Westchester resident named Samuel Young was a keen observer of the changes that Colonel Burr made to defend the Neutral Ground. Young had good reason to be interested in Burr's reforms. He claimed to have witnessed "every species of rapine and lawless violence" in Westchester including British raiders burning his father's house. He told of people going to bed not knowing if they would be murdered in their sleep or their house ransacked and torched during the night. "These calamities," Young said, "continued undiminished until the arrival of Col. Burr." According to Samuel Young, Burr began to make changes on the day that he took charge. The changes that Burr implemented are a valuable lesson for combating insurgents today. They included inspecting all the guard posts nightly and ordering them to change their location from time to time. Burr also organized his own spy network "of discreet and faithful persons living near the enemy's lines to watch their motions, and give him immediate intelligence." He took the information from his spies seriously and discounted "frivolous and vexatious applications [claims]" from anyone else.

Burr made a map of the country noting creek beds and morasses "which might be used as hiding-places for marauding parties." He dismissed incompetent officers, instituted mounted patrols, and imposed rigorous discipline among his troops. Young mentioned other deterrents Burr took including "employing mounted videttes" (correct spelling is vedette; a sentinel on horseback) in pairs to watch for enemy movements. One of the two could report to Burr while the other continued to observe the enemy. Young said that Burr was soon admired for his hard work. It was known that Burr seldom slept for more than an hour or two at a time. He was up every night visiting his guard posts with a small escort. He changed his route periodically to prevent being ambushed.[25]

Major Richard Platt was another eyewitness to Colonel Burr's efforts. He admired Burr's ability to restore order to the region. "A country," Major Platt said, "which, for three years before had been a scene of robbery, cruelty and murder, became at once the abode of security and peace."[26] But despite his responsibilities, Burr found time to be ferried across the Hudson River at night to spend time with Theodosia at the Hermitage.

The heavy workload took a toll on Burr's health. He was still suffering from the exhaustion and heat stroke he incurred during the previous year's Monmouth campaign. By early March 1779, Burr believed he needed to resign his commission to concentrate on recovering his health. He wrote General Washington on March 10, 1779, explaining that "the undertaking [command of the Neutral Ground] has convinced me that my Constitution is no longer equal to the Severities of active Service." In the same letter Burr stated that he was resigning from the army. He concluded his letter with a gracious farewell to the commander in chief, "My Attachment to the Service and your Excellency's Person are unabated and will direct my Conduct in every Exigence."[27] Washington responded to Burr's request to resign with his customary diplomacy. Writing from the Middlebrook encampment in distant central New Jersey on April 3, 1779, Washington said that he could not withhold his consent due to Burr's illness, and "I am not only to regret the loss of a good officer, but the cause [illness] which makes his resignation necessary."[28]

The personal danger that Burr faced in defending the Neutral Ground is evident by the experiences of the several officers who took over command of the dangerous region. Burr was replaced in March 1777 by Lieutenant Colonel William Hull who described his defense of the Neutral Ground as "the most fatiguing, the most difficult and most troublesome that could have been contrived."[29] Hull survived the ordeal and was replaced by Colonel Joseph Thompson. He was captured by De Lancey's Brigade on February 3, 1780, and brought to New York City where he was held captive.[30]

General Washington next assigned Colonel Christopher Greene to command the troops guarding the Neutral Ground. It will be recalled that Greene was a senior officer on the ill-fated 1775 Arnold Expedition. His subsequent military exploits included the heroic defense of Fort Red Bank, New Jersey, in 1777 against a determined Hessian attack. Greene took command of the defense of the Neutral Ground in early 1781. He established his headquarters at the Davenport House (still standing) located on a strategic hilltop near the northern bank of the Croton River. The surrounding area was open farmland giving his detachment an unobstructed view of the nearby countryside. Colonel Greene had twenty-eight battle-hardened men from his 1st Rhode Island Regiment protecting his headquarters on the night of May 14, 1781. Additional Continentals were nearby at various guard posts. Despite their vigilance, three hundred mounted troops from De Lancey's Brigade stealthily crossed the Croton River at a remote ford and attacked Greene's headquarters. The colonel and his bodyguard fought back. With most of his men dead or wounded, Greene retreated into the Davenport House and continued to fight. Even when cornered inside the building, he refused to surrender. De Lancey's men brutally stabled him with bayonets and swords. Then they put him on a horse and rode him three-quarters of a mile before dumping him in the woods to bleed to death.[31] It was only through ingenious preparations and guile that Burr managed to avoid a similar fate. Westchester resident Samuel Young witnessed the efforts made by various officers who followed Burr to defend the Neutral Ground. Young said, "the highest eulogy on Colonel Burr is that no man could be found capable of executing his plans, though the example [Burr] was before them."[32]

Aaron spent the months following his resignation from the army convalescing and visiting family and friends. He spent time recuperating with Theodosia who was now calling Burr "my inestimable friend."[33] He also traveled to nearby Connecticut to visit his sister in Litchfield and his cousin Thaddeus in Fairfield. By early 1780, Burr regained his health and could have returned to active service, but he probably realized that his chances for promotion or a prestigious command were slim. General Washington was the obstacle to his advancement in the army. While Washington believed that Burr was a good officer, he disliked Burr personally dating from his short tenure at headquarters in 1776. Burr's admission that he was friendly with General Charles Lee and Horatio Gates did not help his situation. In Matthew Davis's lengthy interviews with Burr, the colonel remarked that he was critical of Washington's "military movements."[34] However, in publishing Burr's *Memoirs*, Davis deleted any derogatory comments about Washington while emphasizing the commander in chief's good opinion of Burr's military abilities. There is a good example in *Memoirs* where Davis at least acknowledged his subject's peculiar relationship with the commander in chief. The entry reads,

> As a man and a citizen, he [Burr] was exceedingly disliked by General Washington. Causes, unnecessary to examine at this later period of time, had created between these gentleman feelings of hostility that were unconquerable, and were never softened or mollified. Yet even General Washington, while he considered Burr destitute of morals and of principle, respected him as a soldier and gave repeated evidence of entire confidence in his gallantry, his persevering industry, his judgement and his discretion.[35]

Burr begin the adjustment to civilian life while the war continued. He resumed his law studies with Titus Hosmer of Middletown, Connecticut. When Hosmer died Burr continued his studies with Thomas Smith who lived in Haverstraw, New York. Thomas Smith's brother was William Smith who was one of the disaffected Loyalists that Burr had transported to the British lines in 1778. Burr was licensed to practice law in New York State on January 19, 1782, by the New York State Supreme Court of Judicature. Later that year he was approved as a counselor-at-law, which allowed him to represent clients in a courtroom.

Another important event occurred in 1782 when Theodosia's half-sister, Catherine deVisme, read a story in the New York City Loyalist newspaper the *Royal Gazette*. It reported that Colonel James Prevost had died of yellow fever on the Caribbean island of Jamaica two months earlier.[36] Colonel Prevost's death cleared the way for Burr to marry Theodosia. On July 2, 1782, Aaron and Theodosia were married at the Hermitage. The newlyweds immediately set off for Albany, where Burr was already practicing law. The town was a provincial backwater of three thousand inhabitants at the time living in picturesque gabled houses that lined unpaved streets. While they were living in Albany, Theodosia gave birth to a baby girl on June 21, 1783. The happy parents named the girl Theodosia after her mother. Burr's wife Theodosia bore three additional pregnancies, but they all ended with the infants dying or still births. Their daughter Theodosia was their only child that survived to adulthood.

Burr was carefully following the events following the October 1781 surrender of Cornwallis's army at Yorktown, Virginia. The defeat resulted in a new British ministry coming to power led by the Earl of Shelburne. He agreed to American independence as a condition for a peace treaty. Burr was living frugally in Albany while negotiations in Paris to end the war were underway. His plan was to move to New York City and open a law office as soon as the war ended. Burr reasoned that there would be plenty of high-priced legal work for him there as the commercial city recovered from its long British occupation. In anticipation of his move to New York City, Burr rented a house for his family on Maiden Lane near Wall Street, "the rent to begin at the British evacuation."[37]

12

ALEXANDER HAMILTON PREVAILS

Alexander Hamilton was living in Albany, New York, with his new wife and practicing law in late 1782. He was in all likelihood acquainted and socializing with his fellow retired Continental Army officer and attorney Aaron Burr in the small provincial town. However, Hamilton's path to Albany in the months just prior to the end of the Revolution was very different than Burr's.

Hamilton continued to toil on Washington's staff following the 1778 Battle of Monmouth. The workload was heavy, and the general was a demanding boss. Hamilton jealously saw Washington promote some of his fellow aides to coveted line commands while he continued to work at headquarters. Aide Stephen Moylan, for example, was promoted to commander of an elite mounted regiment. Aide Samuel Blatchley Webb was commissioned to raise and command the 9th Connecticut Regiment of the Continental Army. Aide William Grayson was also promoted and given command of a Continental regiment known as Colonel Grayson's Additional Regiment.[1] James McHenry left to become an aide to General Lafayette. Others resigned with Washington's approbation including Edmund Randolph, Richard Cary, and John Fitzgerald. Washington also granted Hamilton's close friend and fellow aide John Laurens an extended leave of absence. By 1780, only Robert Hanson Harrison and Tench Tilghman had served in Washington's military family longer than Hamilton. However, they seemed content to remain at the general's side. Harrison and Tilghman enjoyed a warm and cordial relationship with Washington while the general's involvement with Hamilton was more reserved and businesslike. But Washington wanted Hamilton at headquarters. The young colonel was brilliant, and Washington did not want to lose him.

Hamilton had some relief during the winter of 1779–1780 when the army was encamped in Morristown, New Jersey. Hamilton met Elizabeth (Betsy) Schuyler during that winter. She was the twenty-three-year-old daughter of General Philip Schuyler, the wealthy New York landowner, businessman, and major general in the Continental Army. Betsy was spending the winter with Dr. John Cochran and his wife Gertrude (General Schuyler's sister) who were living just down the road from Washington's headquarters at the Ford Mansion. Betsy started seeing Hamilton socially during early February 1780. Their romance moved quickly, and they were married on December 14, 1780, at General Schuyler's mansion in Albany. It was a huge upward social leap for Hamilton whose marriage made him a member of the powerful Schuyler family. The war was surely on everyone's mind at the time, especially the shocking treason of Major General Benedict Arnold, which had occurred just months before Alexander and Betsy's wedding day.

Hamilton was at Washington's side on September 24, 1780, when Arnold's plot to deliver West Point to the British was discovered. Hamilton witnessed Arnold's beautiful, young wife, Peggy, put on a convincing performance that day that cleared her of any complicity in her husband's treason. Hamilton described the scene in a letter to Betsy Schuyler who was his fiancée at the time. He wrote Betsy, "I saw an amiable woman frantic with distress for the loss of a husband she tenderly loved—a traitor to his country. . . . All the sweetness of beauty, all the loveliness of innocence, all the tenderness of a wife and all the fondness of a mother showed themselves in her appearance and conduct."[2] Washington allowed Peggy Arnold to travel to Philadelphia to live with her family. On the way, she stopped at the Hermitage where she stayed one night. First reported in Burr's *Memoirs*, Mrs. Arnold believed that she could confide in Theodosia who was the wife of a British officer at the time. Peggy Arnold told Theodosia that she had encouraged and aided her husband's plot to deliver West Point to the British.[3] To enliven the story, it was said that Burr was visiting the Hermitage at the time and ravished Peggy during the night. According to the story, Burr made a crude sexual pass at Peggy "then moved in serpent circles, ever smaller around the intended victim."[4]

Long before Arnold's treason, Hamilton had become increasingly unhappy working at headquarters and wanted a field command. His request had been denied by Washington who said that he needed Hamilton's "*ready pen*." In a letter dated January 8, 1780, Hamilton told his confident and friend John Laurens that he wanted to go to the "Southward" (southern states) where the fighting had moved, "I have strongly solicited leave to go to the Southward. It could not be refused, but arguments have been used to dissuade me from it. . . . I have chagrined and unhappy but I submit."[5]

Hamilton's pent-up frustration finally vented in February 1781. Washington's headquarters at the time was at the home of William Ellison's two story house a few miles north of West Point. The episode was triggered by a minor incident. Hamilton wrote two accounts of what happened. One was to his father-in-law Philip Schuyler and the other to Washington's former aide James McHenry. From these two letters it is possible to piece together what transpired.

On that faithful day, February 16, 1781, headquarters was bustling as usual. Hamilton said that he was on his way downstairs from the second floor of the Ellison house as Washington was going upstairs to his office. His Excellency stopped Hamilton on the staircase and said that he wanted to see him immediately in his upstairs office. Hamilton acknowledged the order but continued downstairs to deliver a letter to Tench Tilghman. After handing Tilghman the letter, Hamilton turned around and started to go upstairs to Washington's office but was stopped on the stairway by Lafayette who conversed with him briefly concerning army business. When he reached the top of the stairs, Hamilton found his boss pacing on the landing. Washington told Hamilton in an unpleasant tone, "Col. Hamilton, you have kept me waiting at the head of the stairs these ten minutes. I must tell you, Sir you treat me with disrespect." Hamilton claimed he was calm but decisive when he replied, "I am not conscious of it Sir, but since you have thought it necessary to tell me so we must part." Washington, who insisted upon respect from his subordinates, fired back, "Very well Sir if it be your choice."[6]

Hamilton ran downstairs and poured out his outrage to his friend Lafayette. Hamilton believed that not more than a few minutes had elapsed from the time he passed Washington on the stairs until their confrontation.[7] Within an hour Washington sent Tilghman to talk to Hamilton. Tilghman said that His Excellency had great confidence in Hamilton's abilities, integrity, and usefulness and he would like to have a forthright conversation with him to reconcile their differences that had surfaced in a moment of passion. Hamilton told Tilghman that a conversation could serve no other purpose than to produce explanations mutually disagreeable. Hamilton would only agree to stay on until Washington could make other arrangements.

Despite what had passed between them, Hamilton admitted his genuine admiration for Washington in a letter to his father-in-law. Hamilton said, "The General is a very honest man. His competitors [Generals Charles

Lee, Horatio Gates, and Thomas Conway to name a few] have slender abilities and less integrity. His popularity has often been essential to the safety of America."[8]

In retrospect, Washington kept Hamilton on his staff longer than the young man wanted. What Hamilton longed for was the same regimental line command that Washington had arranged for several of his aides-de-camp in the past. But it seems that the general wanted Hamilton's energy and skills at headquarters and kept him chained to his writing desk beyond his time. It is to Washington's credit that his break with Hamilton was not permanent. Hamilton had been appointed Washington's aide as a young college student with few prospects, but he left as a man with a growing reputation and wide circle of influential friends including the Schuyler clan. But Washington could have ruined Hamilton's career at this point. His Excellency was the foremost American of the day and was well on the way to becoming a world figure. He could have destroyed Hamilton's future but instead decided to help him. When Hamilton subsequently wrote Washington a letter resigning his commission, the general arranged for his former aide to be given command instead in the army's elite Corps of Light Infantry. Hamilton's appointment appeared in the July 31, 1781, General Orders of the Army, "The Light Companies of the first and second regiments of New York with the two companies of York Levies . . . will form a Battalion under command of Lieutenant Colonel Hamilton."[9] Hamilton's newly formed battalion also included two experienced companies of Connecticut Continentals.[10] Hamilton and his new combat unit would soon be involved in a major campaign of the American Revolution: the Siege of Yorktown in Virginia.

The British strategy of conquering the southern states presented a unique opportunity for a major victory for the Patriots in Virginia in 1781. After fighting American forces in the Carolinas, General Cornwallis marched his army north to link up with a British force operating in Virginia. As the senior commander in the region, Cornwallis took command of all Crown troops in Virginia amounting to 7,500 men. Following some devastating raids in the state, Cornwallis moved his army to Virginia's Tidewater region to rendezvous with Royal Navy ships sailing from New York. Cornwallis arranged to meet the fleet at the small deep water port of Yorktown on the York River. There was a French Navy fleet operating in the Caribbean at the same time. If the Americans and their French allies could move quickly, they could trap Cornwallis's army at Yorktown. It was a near miracle, but the French fleet arrived in Virginia's waters in time to fight and chase off the Royal Navy fleet sent to relieve Cornwallis. The

American troops facing Cornwallis at Yorktown under Lafayette's command were reinforced by Washington's Grand Army and French troops under the command by the Viscount de Rochambeau. With the French Navy in control of Chesapeake Bay, a second French naval squadron arrived from Rhode Island with siege guns. These big cannons were necessary to smash the extensive earthworks and artillery batteries that Cornwallis had constructed to defend Yorktown. The allies had a combined force of 16,000 facing Cornwallis's 7,500 men, but Cornwallis had veteran troops who were well entrenched with artillery. They were prepared to stubbornly hold out when they learned that a second Royal Navy squadron was coming from New York to rescue them.

The allies used Williamsburg, a town thirteen miles from Yorktown, as a staging area for their siege. Hamilton and his light infantry battalion arrived in Williamsburg in late September 1781, where he was reunited with three old friends who were also fellow light infantry officers. One was General Lafayette who commanded the entire American Corps of Light Infantry. The other two were Lieutenant Colonel John Laurens and Lieutenant Colonel Francis Barber. It will be recalled that Barber was one of Hamilton's teachers at the Elizabethtown Academy. Hamilton and his companions stayed in Williamsburg for only a short time before joining the rest of the allied army on the road to Yorktown.

Across the open fields facing Yorktown, French engineers began work on a formal siege on September 29 to methodically reduce the enemy fortifications. The technique was to dig lines of trenches, called parallels, which would systematically draw closer to the town. The trenches, each 3.5 feet deep and 7 feet wide, were dug at night after which artillery protected by infantry occupied the completed trenches. Once a parallel was completed, a trench, called a sap, was dug at a right angle to where the next parallel trench was started. The encircling lines of trenches would eventually draw close enough to allow artillery to fire at close range into the enemy works. If Cornwallis, in this situation, still refused to surrender then infantry would charge into his shattered fortifications. At Yorktown, the work of digging the trenches was divided between the French and American armies. Each was assigned a section to dig.

The first parallel was completed on October 7 and Colonel Hamilton's light infantry was given the honor of being the first detachment to occupy the American section. At Hamilton's insistence, his battalion marched into the trench with colors flying and drums beating. Then, in a perilous act of bravado and defiance, Hamilton ordered his men to mount the top of the trench and go through the manual of arms with Hamilton pacing back and forth in plain sight of the British. They stopped firing at Hamilton and his men out of respect for their courage.

The popular legend is that General Washington fired the first cannon shot of the siege on the morning of October 9, 1781. It was immediately followed by a barrage of French and American artillery fire that continued around the clock as the allies slowly and systematically dug their trenches and moved their cannons closer to Yorktown.

By the night of October 11, the allied trenches were within three hundred yards of the besieged town. The new trenches, designated as the second parallel, were now close enough for six French mortars to lob shells into the town. But the British held two redoubts (a detached fortification forward of the main works), which had to be captured to complete the second parallel. The two redoubts were identified as Redoubts Nine and Ten. The latter fortification was just two hundred yards from the York River and three hundred yards from the main British defenses. It was decided that the French Army would attack Redoubt Number Nine and American light infantry would assault Number Ten. Everything was ready for simultaneous attacks on the night of October 14. As the Americans prepared for their assault, a conflict arose over who should lead the American attack. Lafayette gave the honor of leading them to Lieutenant Colonel Jean-Joseph Sourbader de Gimat. The Frenchman began his military career as a first lieutenant in the French Army. He accompanied Lafayette to America who secured a commission for him as a major in the Continental Army in June 1777. Gimat was promoted to lieutenant colonel in 1778 and given command of a light infantry battalion the following year. Lafayette assigned four hundred light infantrymen to Gimat for the mission. They consisted of Gimat's battalion along with the battalions led by Hamilton and Laurens plus a detachment from the Corps of Sappers and Miners (engineers). Lieutenant Colonel Barber would bring up the rear with a reserve battalion.[11] Colonel Hamilton protested the arrangement, claiming that he was the senior officer and should lead the attack. Lafayette was sympathetic but refused Hamilton's request. Still adamant, Hamilton took his claim to General Washington who settled the dispute in Hamilton's favor. Major Nicholas Fish, who was second in command of Hamilton's battalion, reported that Hamilton burst from Washington's tent and embraced Fish exclaiming, "we have it, we have it!"[12] As a result, the final disposition of the troops for the dangerous assignment was that Hamilton would personally lead a forlorn hope of twenty men quickly followed by Gimat's battalion.Rushing the redoubt behind Gimat's men would be the bulk of Hamilton's battalion under the command of Major Fish. A detachment of sappers and miners armed with axes to clear enemy obstructions would accompany Gimat's battalion. A second forlorn hope of twenty men commanded by Lieutenant John Mansfield would attack the redoubt from the flank.[13] Laurens with eighty men would follow Mansfield.[14]

The assault commenced at 8:00 p.m. on the evening of October 14. Rockets flew screaming into the air from the allied camp to signal the start of the simultaneous attacks on the two separate, but closely placed enemy redoubts. The French and American artillery along the siege line increased their firing to distract the enemy's attention.[15] Moments later, Hamilton gave a whispered order and his forlorn hope emerged from the second parallel and began running across a quarter mile of open ground. At the same time, Mansfield's detachment ran toward the redoubt from the flank. Both groups were slowed down in the darkness by craters that littered the ground from exploded artillery shells. There were sixty British and Hessian soldiers defending the square shaped redoubt. They frantically fired down on Hamilton's and Mansfield's men as they approached the abatis (sharpened tree branches laid in a row) protecting the redoubt. Fortunately, the abatis had been previously damaged by allied artillery fire allowing Hamilton's men to squeeze past the sharpened branches and scramble up and over the redoubt's earthen parapet. Hamilton was believed to be the first into the enemy works, yelling for his men to follow. Mansfield's men quickly joined the fight. Within moments, Laruen's eighty troops entered the redoubt followed by Gimat's battalion. The Americans overwhelmed the outpost's defenders and took Redoubt Number Ten at the point of the bayonet. It was said that from the instant Hamilton mounted Redoubt Number Ten at Yorktown, he became a hero and America never lost sight of him.[16]

The French had similar success in capturing Redoubt Number Nine. Allied cannons and mortars were quickly mounted in the captured redoubts adding to the pressure on Cornwallis to surrender. He made a sortie against the allied trenches the following night (October 15) but it only temporarily stopped the almost point blank shelling of his remaining defenses.

At about 10:00 a.m. on the morning of October 17, a British drummer appeared on the parapet of the Yorktown fortifications and beat a parley (from the French word *parler*, to speak). He went unheard in the din of the shelling until he was seen by allied infantrymen and then by the artillerists. As they became aware of the enemy drummer, one by one the allied batteries fell silent until all that could be heard was the sound of the drum. Next, a British officer came out of Yorktown holding a white handkerchief over his head. He passed a letter to the allies from General Cornwallis requesting a meeting to discuss terms of surrender. The French and Americans agreed and negotiations took place the following day. Cornwallis tried to use the negotiations to stall for time to at least learn of the location of the Royal Navy squadron sent to relieve him. However, the allies demanded his immediate and unconditional capitulation, or they would resume the siege. Fearing a vicious allied infantry assault on his starving, exhausted troops, Cornwallis submitted and the next day, October 19, 1781, the Crown troops marched out of Yorktown and surrendered. General Washington gave his aide Tench Tilghman the honor of delivering his dispatch announcing the surrender to Congress in Philadelphia. Sometime before dawn on October 24, Tilghman rode into the rebel capital. With the help of a night watchman, he aroused Thomas McKean, the president of Congress, at his home and handed him Washington's missive. After escorting Tilghman to McKean's home, the city's night watchman resumed his rounds, bellowing through the streets, "Past three o'clock—and Cornwallis is taken."

Colonel Hamilton's father-in-law, Philip Schuyler, had written him during the campaign, "Should Cornwallis and his Army fall into our hands, peace may and probably will be the consequence."[17] Schuyler's assessment was correct; the British public had grown wary of the war in America and the defeat of Cornwallis's army compelled King George and his ministers to negotiate an end to the fighting. Hamilton felt that he had done his part, and within a week of the British surrender at Yorktown he resigned from the army. Writing to his wife, Hamilton said, "if there should be another occasion [battle], it will not fall to my turn to execute it." He thought about how to earn money as a civilian and decided to resume his legal studies, which he had briefly started as a student at Kings College. Hamilton shared Colonel Burr's belief that practicing law in New York City when the war ended was particularly attractive. Hamilton was correct and there would be plenty of opportunities for a Patriot attorney in New York City as the state government had enacted the Disqualifying Act on November 20, 1781. Burr's *Memoirs* explained the act, which "*disqualified from practice, in the courts of the state, all attorneys, solicitors and counsellors at law who could not produce satisfactory certificates, showing their attachment and devotion to the Patriot cause.*"[18]

Hamilton and Burr chose to practice law because it had the pretensions of being a gentlemanly profession. While the term "gentleman" is a polite or formal way of referring to a man, it had a more specific meaning at the time. In the strict eighteenth-century definition, gentlemen were men who did not work for a living. Gentlemen earned money and acquired wealth by collecting rent from tenant farmers living on their large estates or through their investments. The gentlemanly lifestyle existed in England but was uncommon in America. In America, men like Hamilton and Burr

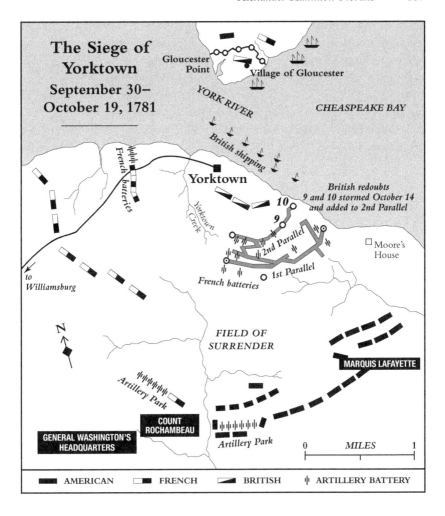

claimed that someone who did not work with their hands to earn a living was also a gentleman. Burr went further in his liberal explanation, saying that a gentleman is someone "who avoids being exposed to the scorn and ridicule of the less honorable part of mankind."[19] As a result of this broad definition, gentlemanly professions in America included merchants, doctors and lawyers. Burr and Hamilton also turned to practicing the gentlemanly profession of law to preserve the dignity and respect they had attained as senior officers in the Continental Army.

Hamilton rode for three weeks from Yorktown to Albany to be re-united with his wife and to begin a new life as a family man, celebrated war veteran, aide-de-camp to George Washington, and a member of the

Schuyler clan. Hamilton benefited from the New York State law that Burr had been instrumental in exacting in 1781 exempting veterans from serving as lawyer's apprentices for a minimum of three years before being eligible to practice law. Hamilton studied law on his own and was certified as an attorney in July 1782. On October 26, 1782, Hamilton added counsel to his legal credentials allowing him to practice law before the New York State Supreme Court. Hamilton had come a long way from his humble beginnings.

13

THE NEW MEN OF NEW YORK

Hamilton established a close friendship with several members of General Washington's military family during his four years at headquarters. With the end of the war in sight, several of them joined Hamilton in resigning from the army. James McHenry left in 1782 telling his wartime friend, "It appears to me, Hamilton, to be no longer either necessary or a duty, for you and I, to go on to sacrifice the small remnant of time that is left to us. We have already immolated [a sacrifice especially by burning] largely on the altar of liberty."[1]

Another of Hamilton's comrades who resigned was Robert Hanson Harrison. Calling his financial situation "embarrassing" and troubled with recurring illness, Harrison accepted a prestigious and well-paying position as the chief justice of the Maryland Court of Appeals (Maryland's highest court).[2] Harrison wrote Hamilton a poignant letter before leaving the army. Harrison said, "I am obliged to depart, and it is possible our separation may be forever. But be this as it may, it can only be with respect to our persons, for as to affection, mine for you will continue to my last breath."[3]

Colonel John Laurens, who was Hamilton's best friend at headquarters, chose to remain in the army after Yorktown to help defend his home state of South Carolina. A part of the state, including Charleston, was still occupied by the British following the defeat of Cornwallis's army at Yorktown. Even as negotiations to end the war were underway in Paris, the British continued to occupy Charleston. Major Alexander Garden, a fellow South Carolinian fought alongside Colonel Laurens during the prolonged British occupation. Garden spoke highly of Laurens during this period saying, "the warmth of his heart, gained the affection of his friends, his sincerity their confidence and esteem."[4] Laurens was an exceptional young man who seemed destined to become an important leader in postwar America. He was a strong advocate for ending slavery, and Hamilton supported his ideas that included the failed wartime proposal in the South Carolina legislature to grant freedom to slaves who agreed to serve in the army. Writing about their shared commitment to end slavery, author Ron Chernow said, "They were both unwavering abolitionists who saw emancipation of the slaves an inseparable part of the struggle for freedom."[5]

Hamilton was looking forward to being reunited with Laurens after the war ended when he received the shocking news in late 1782 that Laurens was killed in a skirmish with the British. His death occurred on August 27, 1782, when a British force of five hundred Loyalists and British troops were foraging near Charleston. Laurens was leading a party of fifty men and one cannon to reinforce an American force assembling in the British rear to cut off their return to Charleston. The British learned of Lauren's approach and ambushed his detachment in tall grass along his route. Two Americans were killed in the fighting, one of whom was Laurens.

Hamilton wrote to General Nathanael Greene, who commanded the American forces in the South, when he learned of Laurens' death, "The world will feel the loss of a man who has left few like him behind, and America of a citizen whose heart realized that patriotism of which others only talk."[6]

Just weeks after Laurens' death, the Treaty of Paris ending the American Revolution was signed on September 3, 1783. Benjamin Franklin, America's senior minister plenipotentiary (having full power to take independent action) to France led the American delegation, which included Henry Laurens, Colonel John Laurens father. The accord was a great victory for the Americans, as Article One of the treaty stated that the United States of America was a free and independent nation. The glorious news reached Congress on October 31, 1783. Elias Boudinot, president of Congress, wrote the American delegation in Paris on the following day, "I do most sincerely congratulate you, Gentlemen, on this most important and happy event, which has diffused the sincerest joy throughout these States."[7]

The last British Army troops evacuated New York City on November 25, 1783, taking with them shiploads of traumatized Loyalists, many of whom were resettled in Canada. Their acrimonious departure included one of the fabled stories of the American Revolution. What the British did was to have an agile sailor nail a Union Jack to the top of a flagpole at the Battery. The sailor greased the sturdy pole on his way down to prevent the rebels from climbing up and tearing down the flag. Then the British fleet sailed off with their flag still flying from the city. After futile attempts by a number of Patriots to reach the offensive flag, a soldier named John Van Arsdale is reported to have ascended the pole using a ladder and cleats attached to his shoes. He tore down the Union Jack and replaced it with an American flag. It was said that General Washington waited at the outskirts of the city until the British flag had been removed before entering.

Hamilton and Burr returned to newly liberated New York City after years of British occupation. Burr moved into his rented house on Maiden Lane on November 23, 1783, as the last British troops were preparing to leave. General Washington bid farewell to his officers a short time later (December 4, 1783) at Fraunces Tavern in lower Manhattan. Both Hamilton and Burr were living in New York City at the time. Hamilton was among the officers who attended the poignant celebration. Burr, however, was not invited to the event. The snub was further evidence of Washington's aversion to the young colonel.

New York City had suffered terribly during the war. To recap, at the start of the Revolution the island of Manhattan's population was divided in their sympathies between supporting the Patriots and remaining loyal to Britain. The arrival of Washington's Grand Army in March 1776 provoked many Loyalists to leave the city. The American military occupation prompted more residents to depart for safer places when it became evident that the British were going to attack the metropolis. The Americans commandeered buildings for barracks and erected barricades in anticipation of the British invasion. But New York City's defenses were never tested. Instead, the Americans hastily abandoned lower Manhattan on September 15, 1776, following the British landing at Kips Bay. The Crown forces fanned out from Kips Bay and occupied the city without a fight. Within a week of their occupation, on September 21, New York City erupted in flames. The fire destroyed one-third of the city, which remained a charred ruin throughout the war. Despite the damage, the British Army and Royal Navy made New York City their headquarters until the end of the war. Their resolve to hold the port city encouraged thousands of Loyalists to seek protection there, cramming into abandoned homes and shops. The military and civilians destroyed fences, cut down trees, and ripped apart derelict wooden buildings for firewood. The devastation of the city continued as the war dragged on with the metropolis' prewar thriving commerce reduced to a trickle.

The British left the city in ruins with the ownership of valuable real estate in dispute. There were many other complex legal issues to be settled as New York City began to rebuild and renew its prewar competition with Philadelphia as the leading city in America.

Both Hamilton and Burr began to practice law in the liberated city. Their services were in high demand as there was a shortage of attorneys in the city and the state. The scarcity was due in great measure to the New York State law that disbarred any attorneys who sided with the British during the war.

At no point in their lives were Hamilton and Burr more alike as when they were practicing law in the years following the American Revolution. They quickly established themselves as two of the best lawyers in New York. They sometimes worked together representing a client. They even traveled together to upstate New York to try cases, sleeping in crowded taverns in beds that "stunk intolerably," and eating coarse meals with back-woodsmen and teamsters. But these discomforts were trivial in comparison to their experiences in the war. Their distinguished wartime service was helping them to attract, as new clients, patriotic citizens and former Continental Army soldiers in need of a lawyer. Their practices were flourishing, and they were growing rich from their legal fees.

Hamilton and Burr's approach to the law reflected their personalities. Hamilton was erudite and dry with carefully researched and lengthy court dissertations while Burr was charismatic and easygoing with short but convincing arguments. But whatever their approach, both Hamilton and Burr were skilled and in high demand.

Up-and-coming postwar merchants, lawyers, and doctors were being called New York's "New Men" and their ranks included Hamilton and Burr. These professions might give a man sufficient income to live comfortably but not in the style of an English gentleman with a grand manor house, expensive coaches, fine art and furnishings, and elegant clothing. The get-rich-scheme to afford such luxuries in postwar America was land speculation. Buying thousands of acres of undeveloped land and selling it off in parcels was already popular during the colonial period that proceeded the Revolutionary War. However, it reached a frenzy after the war when vast tracts of land confiscated from Loyalists and Indians was offered for sale. Vast acreage in upstate New York was particularly attractive. The region was inhabited by the Iroquois nation who sided with Britain (except for the Oneida tribe) during the Revolution. Their land was confiscated by the New York State government after the war and the Indians were forced to move to British-held Canada. New York State sold their land to speculators to raise money. But land speculation was risky despite its great attraction. Burr in particular was involved in land deals in his efforts to live the life of a wealthy gentleman. He was among those who borrowed heavily to buy land and was constantly in debt. While wealth in America at the time was often measured by how much land an individual owned, vast land holding did not provide immediate hard cash to pay off loans and provide money for living expenses. Compounding the problem was that there were more sellers than buyers resulting in land often being sold to new immigrants at bargain prices with extended terms at low interest. Like many other speculators, for Burr, making a quick fortune from buying and selling undeveloped land was an elusive dream.

It was inevitable for New York City's "New Men" to build on their professional success by running for public office. Burr enjoyed politics and thought of it as a game. Hamilton approached the subject more seriously. National politics at the time offered little attraction under the weak Articles of Confederation, which were adopted by the thirteen states in 1777. As a result, many men, including Hamilton and Burr, became involved in state politics.

Hamilton's political ideas were already well-known from his extensive writings and brief tenure at the age of twenty-seven as a New York congressman under the Articles of Confederation. He was acknowledged as favoring a strong federal government and an urban, industrialized nation. Hamilton also advocated a large army and denying newly arrived immigrants the rights of citizenship, an ironic position since he was an immigrant.

In comparison to Hamilton, Burr's political ideas were purposely vague when he entered New York State politics in 1784. Instead, he relied on his impressive military record, success as a lawyer, and charismatic personality to win votes. He began his political career by serving for a single term (1784–1785) in the New York State Assembly. Little is known about Burr's underlying political philosophies throughout his political career because he avoided expressing them. He purposely evaded articulating any strong political opinion in an effort to win the support of a broad range of voters, from the poor working man to affluent merchants and property owners. Generally, Burr was liberal-minded with progressive ideas including supporting internal improvements, such as roads and bridges; an advocate for criminal justice reform; a champion of freedom of the press; proposed legislation to abolish slavery; educating women; and the protecting the rights of new immigrants. He even introduced a bill into the New York legislature that would grant women the right to vote. Burr was also an enthusiastic supporter throughout his political career of legislation that would benefit the people living in what was then the American West.

Very little remains in print about Burr's political ideas. However, there is an account of a speech he made before the New York Assembly in 1799 in which he spoke out against depriving the privileges of citizenship to newly arrived immigrants. Burr said, "America stood with open arms and presented an asylum to the oppressed of every nation: we invited them with the promise of enjoying equal rights with ourselves."[8]

Historian Nancy Isenberg wrote of Burr's liberal ideas in her biography of Burr. She said, "He consistently embraced an inclusive definition of democracy, defending freedom of speech, promoting the expansion of suffrage and economic rights to the middling class and battling prejudice against aliens, free blacks, petty criminals, and women."[9]

There was one aspect of their political careers where Burr and Hamilton were in accord. It was that they both understood that the appearance of wealth mattered in politics. Voters wanted to feel that their elected officials were indifferent to bribes or sponsoring legislation for financial gain. It was therefore important to their political careers to entertain lavishly and show all the trappings of success. In his bid to build his reputation as a wealthy person, Burr purchased Richmond Hill in 1791. It was an opulent mansion surrounded by gardens with a magnificent view of the Hudson River. The estate was on the west side of Manhattan Island about a mile and a half north of the then populated city. Washington used Richmond Hill as his headquarters after arriving in New York. Ironically, Burr's brief employment on Washington's staff took place there. Hamilton made an equally impressive show of wealth when he built a mansion bordered by expensive transplanted trees in northern Manhattan, which he called the Grange. Their desire to live like wealthy gentlemen required both men to turn to borrowing money to maintain their charades.

In 1788, Burr declined to serve as a delegate to the New York convention that decided if the state should adopt the federal Constitution. Burr's refusal to serve highlights his apathy toward public service. His interest was focused on anything that would help him or his loyal constituents. However, Hamilton took an active role in the convention and fought for New York's joining the new federal union. After a bitter debate, New York State was the eleventh state to ratify the Constitution on July 26, 1788. Its assent, along with Virginia's a month earlier, assured the success of the new federal government. George Washington was sworn in as the first president of the United States under the Constitution on April 30, 1789. The ceremony marked the shift in American politics from the individual states power over a weak central government (the Articles of Confederation) to the new much stronger central government.

Burr saw great opportunities for higher office in the new federal government. Never a laggard in making friends and helping his constituents, Burr devoted his time and energy to expand his political base to take an active role in the new offices created in the Constitution. But Burr's supporters paled in comparison to those of Hamilton who included President Washington. The president had supported the adoption of the Constitution from the outset and he appreciated Hamilton's impassioned efforts to secure its adoption. Hamilton's efforts included an active role in the Constitutional Convention, the New York Ratification Convention, and coauthored the *Federalist Papers*. Hamilton's contributions to the *Federalist Papers* include some of its most enduring prose in the series of essays, including "If men were angels, no government would be necessary" and "The fabric of American Empire ought to rest on the solid basis of the consent of the people." Hamilton had also become a vocal supporter of greater federal powers in the financial sector.

Many war veterans petitioned newly elected President Washington for a position in the new federal government. At one point Washington wrote that every "Tom, Dick and Harry" was asking him for a government job.[10] He rewarded many men whom he believed had made sacrifices during the war by appointing them to lucrative and important positions in the federal government. He was especially generous to his wartime aides. Washington rewarded his former aide Hamilton by naming him secretary of the Treasury in September 1789.

As Revolutionary War veterans, both Washington and Hamilton realized France's key role in winning the war. They had firsthand knowledge that the Patriots had depended on French armaments. As president, Washington wanted the new nation to be able to manufacture weapons for its own defense. He made this point in his first annual message to Congress on January 8, 1790, stating that "safety and interest require that they should promote manufactories as tend to rend them independent of others for essential, particularly for military supplies."[11] Hamilton voiced his agreement in his *Report on the Subject of Manufactures* (1791), "the extreme embarrassments of the United States during the late war, from an incapacity of supplying themselves, are still matters of keen recollection" and proposed the domestic manufacturing of weapons.[12] Congress agreed and authorized construction of a federal arsenal at Springfield, Massachusetts in 1794 to manufacture muskets for the US Army. Based on their experience during the Revolution, the Americans believed that French Army muskets were superior to the British Army patterns. Therefore, the first US military musket, known as the model 1795, was patterned after the French design.[13]

Washington and Hamilton's likeminded interest in mass produced American made weapons can be traced to their soldiering in the Revolutionary War.

President Washington supported Hamilton's other economic policies including the federal government's assumption of the Revolutionary War debts of the states; establishing the First Bank of the United States; the United States Mint, and the United States Customs Service.

President Washington's high regard for Hamilton was largely responsible for the general's wartime aide to survive America's first sex scandal. The episode began in 1791 when Hamilton was Washington's secretary of the treasury. Hamilton was thirty-four years old at the time and living in Philadelphia, which was the temporary capital of the newly established United States. He was visited in his office by a beautiful twenty-three-year-old woman named Maria Reynolds. She needed money and protection from her abusive husband who had abandoned her. Hamilton agreed to help her and arranged to meet Maria at her lodging that same night. Their nighttime meeting moved into her bedroom where Hamilton gave her money and made it clear that, "other than pecuniary consolation would be acceptable." Hamilton's wife and children were conveniently away at the time on an extended visit to her parents in Albany. Hamilton's nocturnal visit to Mrs. Reynold's bedroom was the start of a long affair that was eventually exposed. Hamilton managed to survive the widely publicized sex scandal due largely to his harmonious relationship with President Washington.

Colonel Burr, in comparison, was spurned by President Washington. His bid to be appointed the US minister to France was rejected by the president. Washington also refused to appoint Burr a brigadier general when the United States was threatened by war with France.

It was during Washington's first term as president that political parties were organized to support specific agendas. The men who wrote the Constitution didn't anticipate the rise of political parties, in fact they were anxious to avoid them as divisive and self-interested. However, two political parties quickly emerged. Thomas Jefferson led the Democratic-Republican Party (better known at the time as the Democratic Party).[14] The Democrats advocated a weak central government and an agrarian society of rural farmers who could not be controlled by urban moneyed interests. Jefferson had the backing of the small farmers throughout the United States. Hamilton became the leader of the opposing Federalist Party. His support was strongest in the northern states. The Federalists favored a powerful central government, banks, a strong army, and revenue-producing tariffs.[15] Burr saw the growing popularity of Jefferson's party and aligned himself with it.

But unlike Jefferson, Burr reached out to both upstate New York farmers as well as the laborers and wealthy merchants of New York City.

Jefferson aggressively sought the office of president following Washington's decision not to seek a third term. Jefferson ran for president in 1796 but the electors chose John Adams, a leading Federalist, instead. Jefferson finished second in the number of electoral votes and became vice president. Hamilton was also eligible to campaign for president under the terms of the Constitution despite his foreign birth.[16] However, he was a blunt and conceited man with superior airs despite his illegitimate birth and threadbare youth. His aloof and pompous personality kept him on the sidelines, and he was never a candidate for any office in the federal government. Author Thomas Fleming said that Hamilton's failure as a politician was due to his "fundamental lack of faith in the ability of the average citizen to participate in government."[17] But Hamilton was still the leading spokesman for Federalist ideas. He was also a monarchist who admired the elitist political and social system that existed in America when it was a British colony. Burr, in comparison, embraced the ordinary voter. He was warm, intelligent, charming, genteel, and approachable. Burr was a dazzling vote getter who alienated few people in part by being purposely vague about expressing his political ideas. He was perfect for the times; a Revolutionary War hero, optimistic, young man who eloquently spoke of the prodigious future of the new United States. After serving as the attorney general of New York State, Burr ran for a New York State seat in the US Senate. He defeated his opponent Philip Schuyler, Hamilton's father-in-law and political ally. Burr was swept into office and Hamilton was alarmed. He viewed Burr as a serious rival for political control of New York State and began his crusade to undermine Burr's popularity.

Burr was seated as a member of the Senate on October 24, 1791, and served in that body from 1791–1797. As a freshman senator, Burr was mostly involved with routine business. He was opposed to Hamilton's financial policies, which won him the friendship of like-minded members of Congress.

Philadelphia was the capital during the time that Burr served in the Senate. He boarded at the Philadelphia home Mrs. John Payne when the Senate was in session. While residing there he was introduced to Mrs. Payne's twenty-three-year-old daughter, Dorothea (who was called Dolly), whose husband John Todd had died in the yellow fever epidemic that had swept through Philadelphia in 1793. Dorothea had a two-year-old son from her marriage whom she wanted to have a good education. She became aware of Burr's supervision of his daughter Theodosia's outstanding education and asked him to be her son's guardian and mentor. Burr agreed and also decided to introduce his fellow senator and Princeton graduate James Madison to Dorothea. Burr acted as chaperone at their first meeting. The happy couple were married on September 15, 1794, after which the bride assumed her new married name, Dolly Madison.

A melancholy event occurred during Burr's time in the Senate. His beloved wife Theodosia died from stomach cancer on May 18, 1794. She was forty-eight years old at the time and had been in poor health for years. Senator Burr's precocious teenage daughter, Theodosia, became his confidant following his wife's death. She became the charming hostess of Richmond Hill often entertaining on her own while her father was in Philadelphia. From afar, Burr supervised his daughter's liberal and extensive education. It was the same classical education that he would have given a son. It included grammar, astronomy, mathematics, and Latin. These were in addition to the study of French, music, and dancing, the typical curriculum for wealthy young women. Burr created a clone of his late wife; his daughter was his radiant partner at Richmond Hill, the elegant mansion filled with fine furniture, paintings, and books. His guests included a talented young American artist named John Vanderlyn (1775–1852). Burr became Vanderlyn's patron and paid for his art training for six years at the École des Beaux-Arts in Paris. Burr's generosity toward Vanderlyn had the blathers speculating that the young artist was Burr's illegitimate son, along with unfounded stories that young Theodosia was Burr's lover. For good measure, Martin Van Buren (1782–1862), the eighth US president, was also erroneously mentioned as Burr's illegitimate offspring.

While serving in the Senate, Burr was being considered as the Democratic Party candidate for vice president. When he lost the bid, he realized that he needed a stronger political following if he was going to run again in the 1800 election. He retired from the senate in 1797, at the end of his term, and returned to New York City to expand his political organization. Burr then served as a New York State assemblyman where he was able to increase his political base by obtaining jobs for his constituents and helping to enact favorable legislation on their behalf. Hamilton was quick to accuse Burr of being involved in unrelenting patronage. However, Hamilton took the same tack when he was Secretary of the Treasury in Washington's administration. Hamilton used patronage to strengthen the new central government under the Constitution. He admitted that he achieved allegiance by "increasing the number of ligaments [connections] between the Government and the interests of Individuals."[18]

Burr's success as a politician was based on patronage and empathy for his constituents. He built a grassroots political organization in New York City, one which modern politicians would envy. Burr organized his followers based on his military experience, including the then novel ideas of having a campaign headquarters, making lists of voters and donors, rallies, personal appearances and speeches, and appointing lieutenants who canvassed their districts to get out to the electorates and persuade them to vote for Burr. Noah Webster, who was the editor at the time of the New York City newspaper *American Minerva*, criticized Burr's lack of political propriety with his direct appeals to the voters. "A certain little Senator, Webster wrote in his newspaper, "is running about the streets, whispering soft things in people's ears and making large entertainments."[19] Some people scoffed at Burr's methods, but his ideas worked and New York City in particular became a stronghold for Jefferson's Democratic Party.

It was during the time that Burr was building his political organization that he scored a financial coup. It happened in1799 when he was able to secure a state charter for a new legal entity to provide clean water to New York City. Burr and his partners established the Manhattan Company for the project. However, buried in the company's charter was a clause allowing it to use any surplus capital to engage in other ventures. Burr raised $2 million to finance the Manhattan Company. He used $100,000 toward building the water supply system and the rest to start a bank. Burr's Manhattan Bank went into competition with the Bank of New York, which Hamilton and his Federalist friends started in 1784. In 1808, the Manhattan Company sold its waterworks and turned completely to banking. Following a series of acquisitions and mergers, including a union with Chase National Bank in 1955, Burr's Manhattan Bank continues today as JPMorgan Chase & Company. It is widely believed that the bank's present-day octagon logo is a cut-away view of a wooden water pipe to commemorate its origins. It's a great story but the octagon logo is just a coincidence. As for Hamilton's Bank of New York, it evolved to become today's BNY Mellon Bank. The bank continues to proudly acknowledge Alexander Hamilton as its founder.

With his expanded and powerful New York State-based political organization, Burr reentered national politics in the presidential election of 1800. It was the first time that political parties selected their candidates. Burr success in building a strong political base for himself in New York made him a national figure in Jefferson's Democratic Party. Jefferson was the unanimous choice of the Democrats for president. The party wanted a New Yorker on the ballot as Jefferson's vice presidential candidate.

Winning the Empire State was important, and the Democrats picked Burr who was popular in the state to run as Jefferson's vice presidential candidate. Their opponents were the incumbent president and Massachusetts Federalist Party stalwart John Adams. His vice presidential candidate was Charles C. Pinckney of South Carolina.

The Framers of the Constitution did not have confidence in the general public to elect the president. To solve the problem, the Constitution stated that the people's popular vote was delegated to an electoral college whose members actually elected the president.

The number of electors from each state was specified in Article II of the Constitution; "Each State shall appoint . . . a Number of Electors, equal to the whole Number of Senators and Representatives to which the State may be entitled in the Congress." New York State, for example, had twelve electoral votes in the election of 1800 based on two Senators and ten members of the House of the Representatives. Finally, each member of the electoral college had two votes according to Article II, Section 2 of the Constitution.

There was no requirement at the time for the members of the electoral college to cast a separate vote for the president and vice president. Each state could also choose its own election day, and the popular voting lasted from April to October 1800. When the prescribed electoral votes were finally counted on February 11, 1801, Jefferson and Burr won the election but each of them received an equal number (73) of electoral votes. Jefferson's was the Democratic Party's clear choice for president, but Burr did not aggressively endorse Jefferson and accept the vice presidency. The Constitution stated that in case of a tie in the electoral college, the House of Representatives would decide the winner. There were sixteen states at the time and the Constitution stated that each state had one vote in the House of Representatives run-off election. Nine states voting for either Jefferson or Burr would decide which of them would be the next president. Theodore Sedgwick, a Federalist senator from Massachusetts, cynically encouraged the Federalist Party members of the House of Representatives to support Burr. Sedgwick reasoned that Burr was just an ordinary selfish politician who promoted whatever would benefit him and get him re-elected. Senator Sedgwick decided that Burr's indifference would keep him from changing the Federalists policies. It was therefore better for Federalist congressmen to vote for Burr for president instead of Jefferson.[20] Enough Federalist members of Congress agreed with Sedgwick and voted for Burr to prevent Jefferson from becoming president. The members of the House voted thirty-five times with no change; eight states voted for Jefferson and eight states voted for Burr. On February 17, on the thirty-sixth ballot, Jefferson was elected president with ten states voting for him.[21] Hamilton was responsible for breaking the tie. He orchestrated a complicated deal with the Federalist members of the House to allow Jefferson to win. Hamilton despised Jefferson's politics but felt he was at least truthful and honest, qualities, he said, that Burr lacked.

Jefferson's win made Burr his vice president. Burr took the oath of office as vice president in Washington, DC, on March 4, 1801.[22] He was forty-five years old at the time and described as "still youthfully spare and strikingly handsome and militarily erect."[23] No doubt he anticipated that like Adams and Jefferson before him, the vice presidency was a stepping stone to the presidency. Burr was optimistic and encouraged his daughter to attend his inauguration accompanied by her new husband Joseph Alston. The couple had married the month before in Albany, New York. Alston (1779–1816) was a wealthy and educated rice plantation owner. His ancestral home, called the Oaks, was along the banks of the Waccamaw River near Georgetown, South Carolina. Theodosia departed the capital following her father's inauguration to become a member of the Southern gentry. She wrote to her father frequently with news about her husband and plantation life. In 1802, she shared the happy news with her father of the birth of a son who was named Aaron Burr Alston.

Despite the joyous news that he was a grandfather, things were not going well for Burr. President Jefferson was convinced that Burr had secretly tried to steal the presidency from him. Despite their alliance, Jefferson also saw Burr as a dangerous threat to his own political future. The president rallied his Virginia dynasty (James Madison and James Monroe) to destroy Burr's political future.

Among the tactics that Jefferson adopted to injure Burr was withholding patronage. Burr was aggressive in recommending lucrative government jobs for his loyal constituents. The president was empowered to appoint thousands of executive and judicial positions in the federal government and Burr wanted some of the best ones for his supporters. But Jefferson grudgingly cooperated saying that Burr "was always at market" and warning his friend James Madison "against trusting him too much."[24]

Jefferson treated Burr as a pariah during his presidential administration. He dropped him from the ticket in favor of George Clinton, another New Yorker, when he ran for reelection in 1804. In that same year, Burr was defeated in a run for governor of New York by his opponent Morgan

Lewis. Burr was trounced in the election, winning only 41 percent of the vote. He blamed his defeat in the election on a smear campaign orchestrated by his rivals. Jefferson's enmity and losing the New York governor's race doomed Burr's political career. He would have faded from the scene as another lackluster politician if it were not for his accusing Hamilton for his defeat in the 1804 New York gubernatorial election. Hamilton's derision of Burr during the 1804 campaign led directly to their duel and Burr's conspicuous place in American history.

14

THE FATAL CONVERSATION
IN ALBANY

Aaron Burr challenged Alexander Hamilton to a duel as a result of a newspaper article that appeared in the April 24, 1804, issue of the *Albany Register*. The story began by describing a dinner party at the Albany home of Judge John Tayler. Attending the dinner were Judge Tayler, Hamilton, Hamilton's father-in-law Philip Schuyler, and Judge Tayler's son-in-law Dr. Charles D. Cooper. Dr. Cooper wrote a personal letter to New York judge James Kent describing a conversation during the dinner where Hamilton called Burr "a dangerous man, and one who ought not to be trusted with the reins of government." The *Albany Register* got hold of the letter and published it. The same newspaper reported that on another occasion Hamilton said that he had a "despicable opinion of Burr." Burr saw the article, which was the insult that finally provoked him to confront Hamilton. Burr told his friend William P. Van Ness "that it had of late been frequently stated to him that Genl Hamilton had at different times and at various occasions used language and expressed opinions high injurious to his [Burr's] reputation." Burr asked Van Ness to deliver a letter to Hamilton demanding "a prompt and unqualified acknowledgement or denial" of the April 24 Albany newspaper story.[1] Hamilton failed to give Burr a definitive answer, which led to their affair of honor (duel) on the morning of July 11, 1804.

Hamilton had a long history of criticizing Burr. It began in 1792 following Burr's defeat of Hamilton's father-in-law, Philip Schuyler, for US senator from New York. Burr's election to the Senate and growing popularity resulted in Hamilton's first known letter attacking Burr's character. In the letter, Hamilton described Burr as "unprincipled both as a public and private man. . . . He is for or against nothing, but as it suits his interest or ambition . . . and I feel it a religious duty to oppose his career."[2] During the presidential election of 1800, Hamilton wrote that Burr "is bankrupt beyond redemption, except by the plunder of his country. His public principles have no other spring or aim than his own aggrandizement. . . . He is truly the Catiline of America."[3] (Catiline was a Roman senator who conspired to overthrow the Roman Republic during the first century BC.)

Describing the details of the Hamilton-Burr duel is beyond the scope of this book. There are several excellent accounts of the incident including *Duel* by Thomas Fleming and Joanne Freeman's *Affairs of Honor*. Of interest is that both Hamilton and Burr were involved in duels prior to their facing one another with loaded pistols. Their involvement can be traced to their experience during the Revolutionary War. British officers were regularly fighting duels during the war to defend their honor. Dueling was reserved for officers and gentlemen. Common soldiers and working-class civilians settled their differences with fistfights, clubs, and knives. The American officers copied dueling from their British counterparts. This accounts for numerous challenges by Continental Army officers during the war, including a widely publicized duel fought in 1778 between General Charles Lee and Washington's aide John Laurens. Hamilton was Lauren's second in this "affair of honor." Hamilton challenged the gossipy Dr. William Gordon later in the war. He accused Gordon, who was a clergyman, of making impertinent comments about his political views. Gordon never responded to the challenge.

Dueling in America continued long after the Revolution ended. In 1792, for example, John Mercer accused Hamilton of corruption and called him a "mushroom excrescence." Hamilton challenged him but Mercer apologized averting a duel. Burr fought a duel in 1799 with John Baker Church who was Hamilton's brother-in-law. Church insulted Burr by accusing him of bribery. They fought a duel in which Church's bullet hit a metal button on Burr's jacket. Burr's shot barely missed hitting Church. There was no second round of gunplay; the two men left the dueling field feeling that their honor had been defended.

Both Hamilton and Burr had suffered serious setbacks by 1804 when they fought their duel. Neither man had much of a political future.[4] Nine months remained in Burr's term as vice president. He was shunned by President Jefferson and there was no chance that he would be considered as Jefferson's running mate for his second bid to be president. Burr had also been trounced in his bid to be elected the governor of New York. Hamilton's much publicized affair with Maria Reynolds, the death of his mentor George Washington, and his elitist demeanor eliminated any chance of his being elected to high office.[5] In addition, his Federalist Party was waning in power. Commenting on the diminishing influence of the Federalists, author John Ferling remarked, "Hamilton . . . feared that time was running against him, and he was exactly correct. The U.S. that emerged in the 19th Century was not a Federalist America, but a Jeffersonian Republican."[6] In addition to their political demise, both Hamilton and Burr were also heavily in debt from their lavish lifestyles and land speculation. Perhaps flirting with death in a duel was a way to resolve their problems.

An interesting aspect of the duel between Hamilton and Burr was that both men had experience with firearms. As combat veterans it can also be assumed that they were also able to stay calm in a tense situation, such as a loaded pistol being pointed at them. This was not always the case in a duel. A good example is the "affair of honor" fought in 1786 between Eleazer Oswald and Matthew Carey. Both men were Philadelphia newspaper publishers with strongly opposing views. They antagonized each other to the point that Oswald challenged Carey to a duel. However, they were not equally matched. Oswald served as a colonel of artillery in the American Revolution and had fought in several major battles including Monmouth. He also had the distinction of being one of the two known Americans to have fought in both the American Revolution and the French Revolution. (The other Patriot officer who fought in both wars was Colonel John Skey Eustace.) In comparison, Carey had no experience with firearms or military service.

Carey had a deformed leg and walked with a limp. The two antagonists faced off at ten paces near Camden, New Jersey, on January 18, 1786. Carey's shot predictably went wild while Colonel Oswald calmly took careful aim and shot Carey in the thigh just above the knee of his crippled leg.[7] In comparison, Hamilton and Burr were equally matched in their experience with guns and ready to settle their years of hostility with a single pistol shot.

The duel between Hamilton and Burr was conducted according to all the "rules of engagement." It was not the duel but the accusation that Burr had taken unfair advantage of Hamilton that created the uproar. Hamilton's admirers accused Burr of cheating. They claimed he knew that the triggers of the dueling pistols could be secretly set to fire with a slight squeeze. The problem with this notion was that Hamilton supplied the pistols. In another even more fabricated story, Burr was accused of wearing silk clothing which would defect a bullet. Another legend is that Burr engaged in the devious practice of firing at targets to prepare for the duel. It was also claimed that Burr shot Hamilton after Hamilton deliberately fired his pistol into the air. This is also incorrect as the men present on the dueling ground distinctly heard both pistols fired within split seconds of one another. Another assertion is that Burr hid behind a shrub during the duel. This preposterous story was even chronicled in the following poem,

> O Burr, O Burr, what hast thou done
> Thou hast shooted dead great Hamilton
> You hid behind a bunch of thistle
> And shooted him dead with a great hoss pistol.[8]

Hamilton's hatred of Burr was too deep for him to have thrown away his shot. Burr was the target of two grand jury indictments resulting from the duel. New York State indicated him for defying its laws against dueling. The New Jersey indictment was far more serious; Burr was accused of murder.

Hostile public opinion, the threat of being tried for murder, and hounded by creditors drove Burr to escape from New York. A July 27, 1804, New York newspaper reported that "He has for the present, and we trust forever, fled from the city and the state."[9] Burr traveled to South Carolina where he was welcomed by his daughter and her wealthy and politically prominent husband. Helping to protect Burr was that Hamilton's financial policies that favored the moneyed interests of the northern states were unpopular in the South.

Writing about Burr's life following his duel with Hamilton is particularly challenging. One reason is that the documentation is limited and often bias. In addition, Burr was circumspect about his activities. He was able to return to Washington after the furor over Hamilton's death subsided and served out the balance of his term as vice president.

Burr spent the years following Hamilton's demise and the death of his career in politics promoting various ideas to regain his influence and wealth. The highpoint of his intrigues was his so called western conspiracy. Historians have debated Burr's objectives for recruiting men beginning in 1805 for a voyage down the Mississippi River. It was rumored that he was raising a ten thousand-man army to create a new nation in the American west. President Jefferson believed the stories, which he saw as an opportunity to finally eliminate his once formidable political rival. The president ordered Burr arrested and brought to Richmond, Virginia, where a grand jury indicted him for treason.[10]

Burr's much publicized trial took place in 1807. It attracted national attention and newspapers sent reporters to cover the proceedings. They included twenty-four-year-old Washington Irving who was sent to Richmond by the *New York Evening Post*. Sympathetic toward Burr, Irving described him as "fallen, proscribed, pre-judged, the cup of bitterness has been administered to him with an unsparing hand [a reference to Jefferson]."[11] He was acquitted of the charge largely because of the narrow constitutional interpretation of treason set forth by Chief Justice John Marshall, sitting on the federal circuit court in Richmond. During the trial it was revealed that Burr only raised a force of around one hundred men, and very little actually happened. As a result, Marshall dismissed the charges of treason and conspiracy on the grounds that preparations with no treasonable acts did not qualify as a crime.

Burr never clearly explained his western expedition. Even his extensive *Memoirs*, written years later, included very little about his plans. Adding to the confusion is that Burr told people whatever they wanted to hear in order to raise money for his foray into the west. He was able to recruit a motley crew of about one hundred young men who were desperate or romantic enough to believe his vague stories of wealth and conquest. The possible key to unraveling Burr's intentions was his purchase (on credit) in July 1806 of the Bastrop Lands, a four hundred thousand acre tract bordering modern Arkansas and Louisiana.[12] Named after Felip Neri, the Baron de Bastrop, the tract was within a few days march of land along the Texas border claimed by both the United States and Spain. War between the two nations seemed likely to many people in 1806. Burr's plan may have been to settle the Bastrop Tract with his followers, who he would lead on a filibustering expedition into Spanish held Texas or Mexico itself once war was declared. Or he could start a war with Spain to claim Texas if all else failed. A good appraisal of Burr's foray into the American West was made by historian R. Kent Newmyer who said, "As to what Burr had in mind, it may be exactly what the convoluted and voluminous records show: a vague set of contingency plans, laced with a large dose of desperation-tinged romanticism, all calculated to benefit Aaron Burr."[13]

Burr lived to see Texas gain its independence in 1836 aided by thousands of American citizens who joined the Texas rebellion. The story is told that a gentleman called on the aged Burr one morning to find him engrossed in a newspaper account of Texas proclaiming itself an independent republic. "There, exclaimed the old man, [Burr] pointing to the news from Texas. I was thirty years too soon! What was treason thirty years ago, is patriotism today![14]

Among the fascinating people involved in Burr's so-called western conspiracy were two that stand out. They were General James Wilkinson and Harman Blennerhassett.

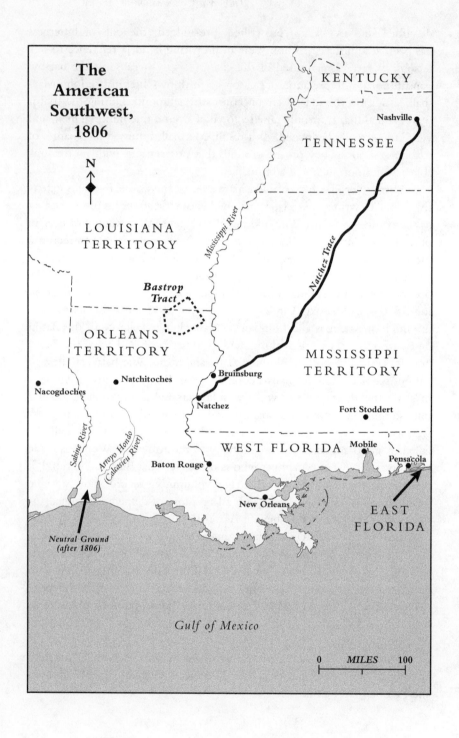

The
American
Southwest,
1806

N

KENTUCKY

Nashville

TENNESSEE

LOUISIANA
TERRITORY

Mississippi River

*Bastrop
Tract*

Natchez Trace

ORLEANS
TERRITORY

MISSISSIPPI
TERRITORY

Nacogdoches

Natchitoches

Bruinsburg

Natchez

Fort Stoddert

Sabine River

*Arroyo Hondo
(Calcasieu River)*

WEST FLORIDA

Mobile

Pensacola

Baton Rouge

New Orleans

EAST
FLORIDA

*Neutral Ground
(after 1806)*

Gulf of Mexico

0   *MILES*   100

Wilkinson is the better known of the two. He was a Revolutionary War veteran and the senior officer of the US Army during Thomas Jefferson's administration. Historian Robert Leckie describes him as "a general who never won a battle or lost a court martial." Wilkinson gave false and damaging testimony at Burr's trial. It was discovered years after his death in 1825 that he was a spy for the Spanish government.

Harman Blennerhassett, who helped finance Burr's enterprise, was born in 1767 in England to wealthy parents who provided him with an excellent education. He mysteriously immigrated to the United States in 1796 after marrying a beautiful young woman named Margaret Agnew. After arriving in America, the couple purchased the upper half of an isolated island on the Ohio River in 1798. The explanation for their strange behavior was uncovered in 1903 by a descendant who discovered that Harman was Margaret's uncle. The self-exiled couple built a palatial country estate on their wilderness island complete with a wine cellar, servants, and beautiful landscaped gardens. Burr stopped at Blennerhassett Island in 1805 during his fact-finding trip down the Ohio River. Some said that he drifted into this idyllic setting like the serpent into the Garden of Eden. The Blennerhassetts had spent most of their money on their island paradise and they were strapped for cash. Burr enchanted them with his get-rich schemes and besides giving him money, they made the fatal mistake of allowing him to use their island as the staging ground for his expedition. The Blennerhassett's lost everything in the hysteria resulting from the stories that Burr was plotting to take over the Louisiana Territory with an army. Their mansion was vandalized and wrecked by the local militia. After years of trying to rebuild their lives, Harman died penniless in England in 1831. His wife died in 1842 in a poor house in New York City. Blennerhassett Island is now part of West Virginia. It is a state park that includes a reconstruction of the seven thousand square foot mansion on its original foundations. In 1996, the bodies of Margaret and Harman were reburied on their island paradise.

Narrowly avoiding being hanged as a traitor did not end Burr's problems. He was being hounded by his creditors and he slipped away to Europe to avoid going to debtor's prison. Burr spent four years in Europe, often living in cheap rented rooms and nearly starving. He scraped together enough money to pay his return passage to America in early 1812. He arrived in Boston under the alias Adolphus Arnot. To further hide his identity, Burr disguised himself in a wig and heavy whiskers.[15] Several weeks hiding in Boston convinced him that he was a forgotten man and he returned to New York a penniless relic from the past.

During his absence in Europe his creditors seized his New York assets, the most valuable of which was Richmond Hill. The mansion and property were eventually sold to a shrewd businessman named John Jacob Aster. He moved into the mansion, which later become a theater, and divided the estate into four hundred small building lots, built and sold a house on each lot, and made a fortune. The mansion's furnishings were also auctioned off with the money going to Burr's creditors.

Burr managed to resume his law practice in New York and earn some badly needed money. His great joy were letters from his daughter with news of his grandson. Meanwhile, Alston wrote his father-in-law that Theodosia's health was failing. She suffered a further setback when ten-year-old Aaron Burr Alston died on June 30, 1812, from malaria. The little family was grief stricken by the boy's death. Burr encouraged his sick and heartbroken daughter to join him in New York and Alston agreed. Alston's reasoning was that the United States was at war with Britain (the War of 1812, which began in June 1812) and he was preoccupied in his responsibilities as the newly elected governor of South Carolina and commander of the state's militia. Theodosia would also be safer in heavily fortified New York City than in South Carolina.

Everything was arranged for Theodoisa's safe passage to New York. Burr sent his friend Timothy Green to South Carolina to escort her to New York. Green was chosen for the mission because he had some medical training. They boarded a fast, armed schooner named the *Patriot*, which sailed from Georgetown, South Carolina, on December 31, 1812. The passage to New York was expected to take five or six days. The ship had an experienced captain named William Overstocks and his crew included an expert New York pilot who could safely guide the *Patriot* into New York Harbor. Aware of the ship's schedule, Burr waited at his law office at 9 Nassau Street for news of the *Patriot*'s arrival. He became alarmed when the ship failed to appear in early January 1813. Burr thought that it was delayed by bad weather or some minor mishap and he began patrolling the waterfront every day in the hope that he would see the *Patriot* sailing into the harbor. But weeks went by with no sign of the ship. Burr's few remaining friends tried to calm him with the idea that the *Patriot* had run aground, perhaps in the dangerous waters off North Carolina's Outer Banks. Hopefully, they told the colonel, that his beloved daughter had made it to safety. But the *Patriot*, its crew, and passengers were never seen again and romantic accounts about twenty-nine year old Theodosia's fate became part of the folklore of Aaron Burr. The stories about Theodosia included that the crew of the *Patriot* had mutinied and killed its passengers. There were deathbed confessions by sailors who swore they seized the schooner and made Theodosia walk the plank. Another was that the beautiful Theodosia was captured by one of the pirate ships known to troll the Outer Banks and forcibly taken to Bermuda where she lived out her life as the concubine of a pirate despot.

Theodosia's mysterious disappearance in 1813 was another tragic event in the life of Aaron Burr. But the story does not end with Burr's grief for his daughter. Tragedy struck again for it was said that Theodosia's husband, the fabulously wealthy Joseph Alston, never recovered from the disappearance of his loving wife. Unable to recover from the shock of her loss, the legend is that Alston died in 1816 from a broken heart. Burr lived on, but he was a lonely and broken man who managed to earn a modest living as a lawyer.

Burr was unwelcomed by many Manhattan organizations and homes following his duel with Hamilton and notorious intrigues. There are several accounts of how the snubbed colonel ran into his follow Arnold Expedition veteran Samuel Spring on a New York City street. Spring, who was the chaplain on the Arnold Expedition, was walking with his son when he ran into Burr. As Chaplain Spring and Colonel Burr stood chatting on the street, the minister's son found an opportune moment to whisper to his father not to associate with Burr, who was regarded as a scoundrel by many genteel people in the city. The old clergyman replied that his image of young Burr during the march to Quebec was too vivid in his mind for him to heed his son's advice. The two old veterans met later that day in a restaurant where they talked amicably for hours, sharing their memories of their trek to Canada and Montgomery's desperate attack on Quebec.[16]

There is another story from the same period involving artist Charles Willson Peale. He owned a museum in Philadelphia where he exhibited artwork and "curiosities." Peale met an acquaintance named Rebecca Blodget while he was passing through Trenton, New Jersey. She was an attractive widow who was reputed to be one of Burr's lovers. Rebecca told Peale that she was on her way to New York to see the colonel, joking to Peale that he should put her on display in his museum "as a curiosity" because of her infatuation with Colonel Burr and complete disregard for public opinion.[17]

There is no doubt that Burr loved the company of women and that he was a notorious adulterer. His confident Matthew L. Davis inherited all of the colonel's surviving correspondence including his intimate love letters. Davis decided that the licentious letters reflected badly on Burr and he burned the lot. One result of the loss of the letters is that it makes it more complicated to unravel how many illegitimate children Burr fathered during his lifetime. The ridiculous stories are fairly easy to identify. It's entertaining the repeat the most preposterous legend about his offspring. The alleged love child was a girl named Chestnutiana, who Burr fathered with the Indian princess Jacataqua during the 1775 Arnold Expedition. The story goes that Jacataqua became infatuated with the youthful Burr and accompanied him as his mistress on the trek to Canada. The smitten Indian princess remained with Burr during the siege of Quebec and had his love child, a daughter named Chestnutiana. Their daughter Chestnutiana grew up to be a beautiful woman who came to New York to nurse her sickly father during the last years of his life.

There are other children attributed to Burr, whose stories are more plausible than Chestnutiana's. Burr acknowledged being the biological father of two girls by different mothers. The girls were identified in Burr's will only as Francis Anne and Elizabeth. He adopted a boy named Aaron Columbus Burr who he was believed to have fathered while living in Paris. Recent evidence has verified that his illegitimate offspring included two black children that he had with an East Indian woman named Mary Emmons who worked in his home as a servant. The black children are identified as Louisa Charlotte Burr (born 1788) and John Pierre Burr who was born in 1792. As adults, they married and lived in Philadelphia as free blacks.

Among Burr's most memorable liaisons was his marriage at the age of seventy-seven to the fifty-eight-year-old infamous Eliza Jumel. She was alleged to be a former prostitute and the richest woman in New York City. Better known as Madame Jumel, she inherited her wealth from her first husband Stephen Jumel who died in 1832 from pneumonia. Eliza married Burr four months later. Their marriage so soon after Stephen Jumel's death was the source of another invented story about Burr; that he conspired with Eliza to murder Stephen Jumel. A year later Madame Jumel sued Burr for divorce, charging the septuagenarian of adultery and stealing her money.[18] Ironically, Alexander Hamilton's second son Alexander Hamilton Jr. was Madame Jumel's divorce attorney. Madame Jumel died years later, a flamboyant relic of a bygone age. Upon reading her one line obituary in *The New York Times* of July 18, 1865, an adherent wrote, "A single sentence in this morning's Times serves to awaken many memories of the past and revives remembrances of men and parties long since crumbled or forgotten. Thus it reads, "Died on Sunday morning, July 16, Madame Eliza B. Jumel in the 92nd year of her age."[19]

It would seem that Madame Jumel's death in 1865 would mark the end of the people who knew Aaron Burr during his lifetime. Looking back, among the first of his contemporaries to die was his boyhood friend Matthias Ogden. General Ogden died in his New Jersey home in 1791. William P. Van Ness, Burr's law student and second in his duel with Hamilton died in 1826 and the colonel's political crony and biographer Matthew L. Davis died in 1850. But there was an article in the *New York Times* issue of May 31, 1878, written by a doctor who treated Burr and described him in vivid detail. The doctor was Ephraim Clark, who, as a young physician, visited the aged Burr in 1836. Dr. Clark recalled, "the first time I took his hand . . . thin, weak, wasted away, it was like the claw of a bird and I could not help thinking of the deed that hand had done." Clark said that Burr was, "a mere shadow of the glorious man he once was, but the fire of genius still blazed in him."

15

MY MOST IMPORTANT AIDE

In a lengthy letter dated September 25, 1798, George Washington wrote to President John Adams concerning arrangements for a pending war with France. In his letter Washington called Alexander Hamilton his "principal & most confidential aide." This line has been used by Hamilton's admirers to substantiate his importance to Washington during the Revolutionary War. This leads to the assumption that Hamilton was Washington's chief of staff or "right hand man" during the conflict.

An understanding of what prompted Washington's letter to Adams is essential to appreciate why Washington called Hamilton his most important aide. It began when Adams asked Washington to come out of retirement to lead a provisional (temporary) American army in a possible war with France. Washington agreed telling Adams, of his "sorrow at being drawn from my retirement; where I had fondly hope to have spent the few remaining years which might be dispensed to me."[1]

Washington had previously listed the three major generals he wanted for the provisional army in order of their ranking: Alexander Hamilton, Charles Cotesworth Pinckney, and Henry Knox. Adams changed the order to Knox, Pinckney, and Hamilton. He made the change without consulting Washington. Washington wrote his letter to give a stirring endorsement of Hamilton's abilities in an effort have Adams reinstate his former aide as the senior major general of the provisional army.

Adam's made the change in the ranking of the provisional army's major generals to assert his authority and pent-up resentment of Washington's immense popularity. Adam's had supported Washington's nomination to command the army but never really liked him. His jealously of His Excellency can be traced to a letter he wrote his wife, Abigail, on June 23,

1775. It was early in the Revolutionary War and Washington had just been named commander in chief of the Continental Army. In his letter Adams described how Washington was escorted from Philadelphia with "Musick playing &c.&c.," bitterly adding, "Such is the pomp of War." Then Adams grumbled, "I poor Creature, worn out with scribbling, for my Bread and my Liberty, low in Spirits and weak in Health, must leave others to wear the Lawrells [laurels] which I have sown; others, to eat the Bread which I have earned."[2]

Adam's bitterness toward Washington was mild in relation to his seething hostility toward Hamilton. And Adams had good reason to detest Hamilton and put him at the bottom of Washington's list of senior officers for the provisional army. Adams resentment dated from Washington's presidency during which Adam's served as vice president. During this time Adams despised Hamilton's influence over Washington as well as his assertiveness at cabinet meetings and attempts to dictate foreign policy. He resented Hamilton's clout as Washington's secretary of the treasury berating Hamilton as "an insolent coxcomb who rarely dined in good company, where there was good wine, without getting silly and vaporing about his administration."[3] Mixing no words, Adams called Hamilton "a man devoid of every moral principle."[4] But Adams best known temper tantrum aimed at Hamilton was when he called him " the bastard brat of a Scotch peddler."[5]

Adams had a strict sense of virtue concerning woman and was shocked by Hamilton's "audacious and unblushing attempts upon ladies of the highest rank and purest virtue" and his "debaucheries in New York and Philadelphia."[6] He said that Hamilton wanted "prostitutions [referring to prostitution] of power for the purposes of sensual gratification." An even cruder Adams reference to Hamilton's alleged womanizing was a comment he made to Dr. Benjamin Rush. Adams told Rush that Hamilton suffered from excess semen, "which turned into choler [in early medicine one of the bodily humors] and ascended to the brain—making Hamilton's military and economic policies the product of a superabundance of secretions which he could not find whores enough to draw off."[7] Adams's belief in Hamilton's promiscuous lifestyle was confirmed when Hamilton admitted to adultery with twenty-three-year-old Mrs. Maria Reynolds that began in the summer of 1791. There were also rumors that Hamilton had an affair with his attractive married sister-in-law Angelica Church.

Not surprisingly, Adams was furious when he learned that Washington wanted Hamilton to have the honor of being second in command of the provisional army. He exploded, calling Hamilton "the most restless, impatient, indefatigable and unprincipled intriguer in the United States, if not in the world."[8] It is no wonder that Washington had to contrive a compelling argument to get Adams to agree to make Hamilton the senior major general if "we entered into a serious contest with France."

Washington dredged up everything he could think of to enhance Hamilton's qualifications. He mentioned Hamilton's services in the "Old Congress" (under the Articles of Confederation), the "General Convention" (Constitutional Convention) "and having filled one of the most important departments of Government [Secretary of the Treasury] with acknowledged abilities and integrity."

Washington needed an explanation to address the blatant fact that Hamilton's Revolutionary War record hardly qualified him to be appointed a major general. The prestigious rank was traditionally awarded to officers with long experience commanding thousands of men in battle. Hamilton's highest rank during the war was lieutenant colonel. He saw extensive combat early in the war, but it was as an artillery captain who never commanded more than one hundred men. The light infantry battalion he commanded during the 1781 Siege of Yorktown was listed as consisting of 265 officers and common soldiers.[9] Other than these small commands, the bulk of Hamilton's military service was working in an office, behind the lines, as an aide-de-camp. Washington pumped up his credentials by telling Adams that Hamilton was his "principal & most confidential aide." The statement was included in Washington's letter to Adams in an effort to overcome Hamilton's lack of command experience. The relevant text in the letter reads,

> Although Colo. Hamilton has never acted in the character of a General Officer [senior field commander], yet his opportunities, as the principal & most confidential aide of the Commander in Chief, afford him the means of viewing everything on a larger scale than those whose attentions were confined to Divisions or Brigades.[10]

Understanding the overwrought circumstances in which Washington called Hamilton his principal wartime aide raises the question, was Hamilton actually Washington's most important wartime aide? Before addressing this issue, it is important to remember that none of Washington's thirty-two Revolutionary War aides-de-camp were military advisors to him. Nor were any of them his chief of staff. Their significant contributions to winning the war was their working with Washington on the organization and supervision of the day-to-day operations of the Continental Army.

Who was Washington's most important aide-de-camp based on their role as administrator and personal representative of the commander in chief? The distinction of being the most important member of Washington's military family can be narrowed down to four men based on their length of service at headquarters and Washington's favorable comments about them: Robert Hanson Harrison, Tench Tilghman, Alexander Hamilton, and David Humphreys.

Any decision made as to whom was the most important has to consider their length of service. Hamilton served as an aide for four of the eight years of the war:1777–1781. Therefore, he could not be considered as Washington's most important aide before or after these years. Prior to Hamilton's appointment, Washington's most important aide was either Robert Hanson Harrison or Tench Tilghman. Harrison, for example, was often left in charge of headquarters in Washington's absence. Washington said of Harrison, "his whole conduct . . . .has been marked by the strictest integrity and the most attentive and faithful services, while by personal bravery he has been distinguished on several occasions."[11] That Harrison was an intelligent person of great abilities is proven by the fact that he left his behind-the-scenes post at headquarters to accept an invitation to become the chief justice of Maryland. When he was president, Washington nominated Harrison as an associate justice of the Supreme Court. His nomination was approved by the Senate, but Harrison died on April 2, 1790, before he could take office.

Tench Tilghman was Washington's longest-serving aide-de-camp. He joined the commander in chief's military family as a volunteer aide in August 1776 and stayed on the job until December 1782. Writing about Tilghman in 1781 Washington said, "He has been in every action in which the Main Army was concerned. He has been a zealous servant and slave to the public, and a faithful assistant to me for nearly five years, a great part of which time he refused to receive pay."[12] Tilghman married after returning to civilian life and resumed his merchant business. But he did not live long after the war. He died at the age of forty-two on April 18, 1786. It was said that he never recovered his health following his long and demanding hours of work on Washington's staff. Following Tighman's death, his father James wrote Washington with a proposed inscription for his son's grave. Washington replied that "the inscription intended for the tomb of my deceased friend meets my entire approbation for I can assure you Sir, with much truth, that . . . no man enjoyed a greater share of my esteem, affection and confidence than Col. Tilghman."[13] The inscription approved by Washington reads,

In Memory of
Col. Tench Tilghman
He took an early and active part
In the great contest that secured
The Independence of The United States of America
He was an Aide-de-Camp to
His Excellency General Washington
Commander in Chief of the American Armies
And was honored with his friendship and confidence
But still more to his Praise
He was a good man[14]

Jumping ahead to Hamilton's resignation in 1780 along with Harrison's in 1781 and Tilghman's in 1782 arguably made David Humphreys Washington's most important aide during the final years of the war. It is debatable who was Washington's most important aide, but there is no doubt that Humphreys was his favorite.

It will be recalled that Washington used his influence to secure Humpreys a plum job as Jefferson's secretary in France. The year was 1784 and Washington wrote Humphreys a letter just prior to his former aide's departure for France. His demonstrative letter showed his friendship and high esteem of Colonel Humphreys,

> My dear Humphreys. I very sincerely congratulate you on your late appointment. It is honorable, and I dare say must be agreeable. . . . It only remains for me now to wish you a pleasant passage, and that you may realize all the pleasures which you have in expectations. It is not necessary to add how happy I shall be at all times to hear from you. . . . Mrs. Washington adds her best wishes for you, and you may rest assured that few friendships are warmer, or professions more sincere than mine for you.[15]

Turning to Hamilton, he was Washington's most important aide-de-camp during the four years (1777–1781) that he served in the position. He was serious and methodical, and Washington regularly assigned him to draft his most important letters. Remarking on Hamilton's importance, William M. Ferraro, senior associate editor of *The Papers of George Washington* said,

> Hamilton generally was Washington's choice to draft discrete or confidential communications that involved complex details or individual's feelings. These letters required more ability and skill than one on routine army matters, which Hamilton also wrote, abet with less frequency

than the other aides. There is no doubt that Washington reviewed Hamilton's drafts as he did his other aides, but he quite arguably thought Hamilton most likely to prepare a draft requiring the least revision.[16]

It is no wonder that Washington kept Hamilton working at headquarters long after he should have been rewarded for his dedicated service with a prestigious field command. Historian James Thomas Flexner agrees that that Washington "kept his hold on the brilliant youth even if unfairly." Referring to Hamilton, Flexner said that "Washington realized almost instantly that he had found a jewel." But Flexner also made another significant observation when he said, "when Hamilton departed, there was no significant change in the command." Headquarters continued to operate the same as before Hamilton arrived on the scene.[17]

If this author was pressed to state who was the most important of Washington's thirty-two Revolutionary War aides-de-camp it would be Hamilton. The reason is that the position gave Washington the opportunity to work closely with him for four years during the war and appreciate his outstanding intellect. Washington was impressed with Hamilton's rigid determination and scholarly style. It led to one of the most important associations in American history when Washington was president and asked Hamilton to become secretary of the treasury.

Whatever else one could say about Aaron Burr was that he was never dull. He was a complex and fascinating individual. An ambitious self-promoter who engaged in intrigue and secrecy dating from his days as a student at Princeton. He never attempted to justify or explain his actions to his friends or to his enemies. His furtive style led to hostility and distrust among his political opponents that resulted in misunderstandings and accusations. Burr was an eccentric who simply wanted to coast through life and have a good time. He expressed his approach to politics in an 1832 letter to his friend New York congressman Adam Ward. Burr wrote Ward, who was running for reelection at the time, "wishing you a great deal of fun and honor & profit during the campaign."[18] The sadness of Aaron Burr was that he was capable of being one of the important contributors to the drafting of the Constitution and a progressive leader in the early republic. He had enlightened ideas about abolishing slavery, selling low-cost land to new immigrants, the development of the American West and woman's rights. Burr was accused of treason in 1807 but his real duplicity was his failure to apply his genius to the benefit of the nation. Both Hamilton and Burr, for example, were opposed to slavery, but Hamilton's austere personality, publicized affair with Maria Reynolds, and controversial financial program made him a weak candidate for high office. Hamilton made the mistake of believing that political control was a matter of appealing to the influential and wealthy upper class.[19] Burr, on the other hand, embraced the common man. He was charismatic and persuasive and could have been a leading voice in the manumission of slaves, but he seemed too interested in pursuing the life of a New York aristocrat who viewed politics as an amusement and public service boring. Perhaps Burr's legendary quote sums up his attitude about politics, "the rule of my life is to make business a pleasure, and pleasure my business."[20]

Burr could have also played a greater part in our War for Independence. He was intelligent, courageous, organized, and a great motivator. There is no known evidence that Washington ever made a disparaging comment about Burr during the American Revolution, but his lackluster assignments to Burr during the war exhibited a pattern of frustrating his military career. His Excellency's wartime relation with Burr shows that Washington was not malicious, however, he typically disliked and shunned anyone who was not respectful to him or criticized him behind his back. Historian Stephen Brumwell concludes that the highborn Burr was "temperamentally ill suited to show the status-conscious Washington the deference he expected."[21]

Burr and Hamilton lived through a tremulous time in American history. They were both ardent patriots who fought for American independence. Their relationship with Washington was the key to their success. Hamilton benefited from his association with Washington while Burr suffered. Hamilton devoted his energies to the nation while Burr dabbled in politics.

Burr died in 1836 at the age of eighty. In his final days he was living in the Port Richard Hotel on Staten Island, New York, to be near his cousin Ogden Edwards.

On June 17, 1836, the Tompkins Guards, a fashionable Staten Island militia company, was holding its annual banquet in the downstairs dining room of the Port Richmond Hotel to celebrate the anniversary of the Battle of Bunker Hill.[22] During their festivities they learned that Colonel Burr, a combat veteran from the American Revolution, was residing in an upstairs room. A young lieutenant named D. V. N. Mersereau was sent upstairs to invite the colonel to join the celebration. After knocking on the door, Lieutenant Mersereau opened it to find a frail old man lying in bed. The young lieutenant tendered his invitation to this relic of the Revolutionary War to join the festivities below. Burr whispered that he was too feeble to attend, but he would be grateful if the company's officers would visit him. Mersereau returned downstairs and reported what had happened. Led by their commander, Captain John Laforge, the company's officers went upstairs where they talked for a long time with Colonel Burr and listened to his reminiscences from the Revolution. The militiamen were undoubtedly in awe in the presence of Colonel Burr who had participated in many of the great events of the American Revolution. The aged veteran may have described how he had marched with Arnold in Canada in 1775, charged the blockhouse at Quebec alongside the fearless General Mont-gomery, fought in the 1776 Battle of Long Island, wintered with General Washington at Valley Forge in 1777, led his Continental regiment into battle at Monmouth in 1778, and fought the sadistic Cowboys and Skinners in the no-man's land of Westchester County, New York.

After returning downstairs to the hotel's banquet room, Laforge as-sembled his company outside, below Burr's window, where they serenaded the old solider with patriotic songs and honored him with toasts and cheers.[23] Burr died a few months later on September 14, 1836. He deserves to be remembered as he was by the Thompkins Guards who serenaded him with patriotic songs and admiration: a courageous and devoted American officer in our War of Independence.

NOTES

INTRODUCTION

1. Jefferson originally went to France in 1784 to join an American delegation already there to negotiate trade agreements with various European nations. The commission was headed by Benjamin Franklin who was also the American minister to France at the time. Note that Franklin was a minister, which is a lower diplomatic rank than ambassador. The explanation is that the 1778 Treaty of Amity and Commerce Between the United States and the Court of Versailles specified that the senior American representative to France was to have the title of minister. The complete title to the position was Minister Plenipotentiary [having full power to take independent action] from the United States of America at the Court of Versailles. Franklin resigned as minister in May 1785 and was replaced by Jefferson later that month. Thus, it is incorrect to identify Jefferson as the American ambassador to France. The first person to hold the title of United States ambassador to France was James B. Eustis, who was appointed to the post in 1893.

2. Nancy Isenberg, *Fallen Founder* (New York: Viking Penguin, 2007), 211.

3. Captain George Smith, *An Universal Military Dictionary* (London: J. Millan, 1779), 66, 22.

4. Milton Lomask, *Aaron Burr: The Years from Princeton to Vice President 1756–1805* (New York: Farrar, Straus & Giroux, 1979), 112.

CHAPTER ONE: YOUTH

1. John Adams to James Lloyd. Letter dated February 17, 1815. Founders Online, National Archives. See founders.archives.gov/documents/Adams/99-02-02-6143.

2. Princeton University was the fourth college established in America. It was proceeded by Harvard, founded in 1636, the College of William & Mary in 1693, and Yale in 1701.

3. Milton Lomask, *Aaron Burr, The Years from Princeton to Vice President 1756–1805* (New York: Farrar, Straus & Giroux, 1979), 9.

4. Peter Kalm. *Travels into North America* (Barre, MA: The Imprint Society, 1972), 123.

5. The practice of naming children with their mother's surname explains some of the unusual names that are associated with colonial America. Tapping, for example, was an Anglo-Saxon family name dating from the early thirteenth century. It is believed to derive from the word "taeppere," which describes a person who taps casks, an inn keeper. Besides Tapping Reeve, the custom resulted in names including Button Gwinnett and Tench Tilghman. My favorite among people in American history whose given name was their mother's surname is Schuyler Colfax, an Indiana businessman and 17th vice president of the United States (1869–1873).

6. Tapping Reeve and Sarah Burr had one child named Aaron Burr Reeve (1780–1809) who attending his father's law school in Litchfield, Connecticut. Young Reeve met his future wife, Annabella Shedden, who was teaching music at the nearby Litchfield Female Academy. Annabella was the illegitimate daughter of Loyalist William Shedden, a prominent pre-Revolutionary War merchant in New York City. Sarah, Aaron Burr's sister, originally opposed her son's marriage because of Annabella's illegitimate birth. However, Sarah eventually consented, and the couple were married in 1808 and moved to the boomtown of Troy, New York, where young Reeve practiced law for a short time. He died in 1809. They had one child, a son named Tapping Burr Reeve. He died in 1829 at the age of twenty while attending today's Yale University. Annabella Shedden Reeve remarried in 1812 to David Judson Burr (no relation to Aaron Burr) of Richmond, Virginia. They had one son, also named David Judson Burr, who lived in Richmond and was a staunch Southern supporter during the Civil War. He had the distinction of being a member of the committee who surrendered Richmond to US troops on April 3, 1865.

7. Matthias Ogden (1754–1791) became a general in the American Revolution. He attended Princeton but apparently did not graduate. He died from yellow fever on March 31, 1791, at the age of thirty-six. Matthias's greatest wartime exploit was the plot he proposed to General Washington in 1782 to kidnap Prince William Henry, the seventeen-year-old son of King George III and third in line to the British throne. The prince was a midshipman in the Royal Navy at the time. He was living ashore when his ship, the HMS *Prince George*, visited British-held New York City. Ogden planned to snatch the prince from his city quarters during the night. Part of his plan was to set fire to buildings on the outskirts of the city to create a distraction while Ogden crossed the Hudson River with several boatloads of troops disguised as sailors. Washington approved the daring scheme and Ogden

began to move men and boats into position. However, the British noticed the unusual American activity around the city. Concerned for Prince William Henry's safety, the British substantially increased the number of soldiers guarding him. American spies in the city reported the increased security forcing Ogden to cancel his operation.

8. Matthew L. Davis, *Memoirs of Aaron Burr*, 2 vols. (New York: Harper & Brothers, 1836–1837). Vol. 1, 66. Matthew Davis (1773–1850) published the first biography of Colonel Burr. He was the colonel's intimate friend and political ally. Every subsequent biographer of Burr has relied heavily on Davis's work because Burr dictated much of the text. Davis said that he began to work with Burr in 1830 and continued to visit with his friend for six years until Burr's death in 1836. He said, "I frequently visited him, and made notes under his dictation." The collaboration did not always go smoothly as Davis opposed Burr's criticism of George Washington. Burr was particularly critical of Washington's military abilities, but Davis agreed with Burr's assessment that his political undoing was orchestrated by Thomas Jefferson and his spiteful "Virginia junto."

Davis also was the recipient of what remained of Burr's correspondence. Burr's important papers have an interesting history of their own. In 1808, the colonel packed all his correspondence in a trunk, which he left with his married daughter, Theodosia Alston, prior to departing for Europe. Mrs. Alston lived in South Carolina at the time. Burr remained in Europe until 1812 to avoid his creditors, attempting to drum up support for his so-called Western Adventure, and letting the criticism die down following his duel with Hamilton and acquittal in his 1807 trial for treason. Burr returned to New York City in 1812 shortly after which he invited his daughter to join him for a reunion. She agreed and sailed for New York in 1813 with her father's trunk. Her ship never reached New York. It was lost at sea with Theodosia and the trunk aboard. Burr bequeathed what remained of his early correspondence and routine papers from his law practice to Davis. Historians are quick to accuse Burr of leaving virtually no written account of his political career, including his position on the vital issues of the day such as immigration and public works projects. An example is author Ron Chernow's scathing criticism of Burr in his Hamilton biography published in 2004, "Washington, Jefferson, Madison, Adams, Franklin, and Hamilton all left behind papers that run to dozens of thick volumes, packed with profound ruminations. They fought for high ideals. By contrast, Burr editors have been able to eke out just two volumes of his letters, may full of gossip, title-tattle, hilarious anecdotes, and racy asides about his sexual escapades," Ron Chernow (New York: Penguin, 2004), 192. Perhaps Burr's legacy would be different if the trunk with his papers was not lying on the bottom of the Atlantic Ocean.

9. Davis, *Memoirs of Aaron Burr*. vol. 1, 28–29.

10. Davis, *Memoirs of Aaron Burr*, vol. 1, 43–44.

11. It is estimated that Burr inherited the equivalent of $300,000 in today's purchasing power. See *An Aaron Burr Chronology* in the website of the Aaron Burr Society, www.aaronburrassociation.org/chronology.htm.

12. Obituary of Eliza B. (Madame) Jumel in the *New York Times* of July 18, 1865. See www.nytimes.com/archives/obituary-madame-eliza- b-Jumel. Ms. Jumel was born Elizabeth Bowen on April 2, 1775, in Providence, Rhode Island. She died in New York City on July 16, 1865, at the age of ninety.

13. The Loyalists were as patriotic as the rebels, they just happened to be on the losing side. A popular rebel definition of a Loyalist was "a thing whose head is in England, and its body in America and its neck ought to be stretched." Washington denounced them as "unhappy wretches" and "deluded mortals." It is difficult to determine the percentage of the American population who remained loyal to Britain during the American Revolution. Estimates vary with claims that up to one-third of the colonists were Loyalists. Their numbers were substantial enough to make the American Revolution as much of a civil war as it was a Revolution. About fifty thousand Loyalists bore arms for the king during the war in Loyalist militia companies, Provincial regiments, or in the regular British Army and Royal Navy. The British were unable, or unwilling, to take full advantage of Loyalist sentiment. One reason was that the Crown forces lacked the manpower to protect them.

14. Text in a handbill circulated in Farmington, Connecticut, on May 15, 1774, in Peter Force, ed., *American Archives, Fourth Series*. Six volumes (Washington, DC: M. St. Clair Clarke and Peter Force, 1837–1846), vol. 1, 336. The complete text reads, "That those pimps and parasites who dared to advise their master to such detestable measures, be held in utter abhorrence by us and every Americans, and their names loaded with the curses of all succeeding generations." An additional paragraph in the handbill reads, "That we scorn the chains of slavery; we despise every attempt to rivet them upon us; we are the sons of freedom, and resolved that, bill time shall be no more that god-like virtue shall blazon our hemisphere."

15. Burr used the phrase "not a moment to spare" describing his desire to join the army in a letter to his brother-in-law Tapping Reeve. See manuscript letter from Aaron Burr to Tapping Reeve dated "Cambridge, August 2nd 1775" in Reeve Family Papers, Box One. Yale University Library, Manuscripts and Archives Division, Sterling Memorial Library.

16. Letter from John Adams to Benjamin Rush dated January 25, 1806, in Founders Online. National Archives.

17. James Thomas Flexner, *The Young Hamilton* (New York: Little Brown and Company, 1978), 16–18.

18. Harold C. Syrett, ed., *Papers of Alexander Hamilton* (New York: Columbia University Press, 1961–1987) vol. 25, 88

19. The name of this company sometimes appears as Beekman and Cruger. However, David Beekman sold his share of the business to Cornelius Kortright in 1769.

20. The money for Hamilton's schooling and living expenses in America were paid for by the New York office of Kortright and Cruger. Both Kortright and Cruger were major contributors toward Hamilton's education. Other subscribers mentioned are Hamilton's cousin Ann Venton, David Beekman (Cruger's former partner), the St. Croix merchant Thomas Stevens whose son Edward was Hamilton's friend, Cruger's father-in-law whose name was De Nully, and Governor Van Rospstorff, the chief magistrate of St. Croix.

21. Hercules Mulligan's father was named Hugh Mulligan Sr. While Hugh Sr. apparently was not wealthy, he was able to pay for his family's voyage to America and start his wig business. His name appears in a 1747 list of Freemen of the City of New York. A Freeman in colonial America was a man who was not a slave or indentured servant and had the right to hold public office and vote in town meetings. See Paul R. Misencik, *The Original American Spies* (Jefferson, NC: McFarland and Company, 2014), 92–93.

22. A haberdashery shop sells men's clothing. A millinery shop sells woman's clothing. The origin of the word "haberdashery" seems to come from the Old English word "haporas," which was a type of cloth. The origin of "millinery" is much clearer. It comes from the city of Milan, Italy. Milan was an early and important source for textiles.

23. Francis Barber was born in Longford County, Ireland, in 1751. He earned an undergraduate degree from Princeton in 1769 and a master's degree from the college in 1770. Barber served as the headmaster of the Elizabethtown Academy until 1776 when he resigned from his position to join the Continental Army. Barber was appointed major in the 3rd Regiment of New Jersey Artillery on January 18, 1776, and promoted to Lieutenant Colonel on November 28, 1776. He fought in several battles during the war including serving under his former student Hamilton during the 1781 Siege of Yorktown. Sadly however, Colonel Barber is best remembered for being killed accidently by a falling tree that was being cut by the army on February 11, 1783, in New Windsor, New York, . Barber was riding his horse at the time on his way to dine with General Washington.

24. Alexander McDougall was a successful New York City merchant. He was the leader of the city's Sons of Liberty. His military service during the French and Indian War helped him secure a commission as a lieutenant colonel and commander of the 1st New York Regiment when the war started. McDougall was subsequently appointed a Continental Army brigadier general in 1776 and a major general the following year.

25. Nathan Schachner, "The Narratives of Robert Troup and Hercules Mulligan," and delete "Robert Troup, "Narrative," *William and Mary Quarterly*, 3rd ser., VI (1947): 218. Robert Troup was Hamilton's roommate at King's College and a lifelong friend. He was commissioned as a second lieutenant in the Hearts of Oak militia company. Troup served as an aide-de-camp to General Horatio Gates during the 1777 Saratoga campaign. Troup was active in land speculation in upstate New York, and the town of Troupsburg, New York, is named after him. The

town of Charlotte, New York, near Rochester, was named by Troup in honor of his daughter.

26. The Hudson River was also called the North River in colonial America. The name North River originated with the Dutch who claimed all the land between the Delaware River and the Hudson River. The Dutch referred to the Delaware River as the South River and the Hudson as the North River.

CHAPTER TWO: YOUNG SOLDIERS IN THE AMERICAN REVOLUTION

1. Manuscript letter from Aaron Burr his brother-in-law Tapping Reeve dated "Cambridge, August 2nd, 1775," in Reeve Family Papers, Box One, Manuscript and Archives Division, Yale University, Sterling Memorial Library.

2. Matthew L. Davis, *Memoirs of Aaron Burr*, 2 vols. (New York: Harper & Brothers, 1836–1837), vol. 1, 61–62.

3. Milton Lomask, *Aaron Burr: The Years from Princeton to Vice President 1756–1805* (New York: Farrar, Straus & Giroux, 1979), 35.

4. W. W. Abbot et al., eds., *The Papers of George Washington, Revolutionary War Series*, 24 vols. to date (Charlottesville, VA: University Press of Virginia, 1985–). vol. 1, 132–33.

5. Abbot, *The Papers of George Washington, Revolutionary War Series*, vol. 1, 241. Apparently, Lewis Morris was a friend of the Ogden family. In a letter to Burr dated "Elizabethtown, August 9th, 1774," Matthias Ogden described a visit to New York as, "I stayed at Mr. Willett's three days, and then went to Colonel Morris's, and spent two days there very agreeably" see Davis, *Memoirs of Aaron Burr*, vol. 1, 47. Lewis Morris was an officer in the prewar New York militia. He was also a signer of the Declaration of Independence for New York. Lewis's brother was Staats Morris, who sided with the British during the war. The story is that Lewis was reminded that his brother Staats had warned him not to sign the Declaration of Independence to which Lewis replied, "Damn the consequences. Give me the pen."

6. Abbot, *The Papers of George Washington, Revolutionary War Series*, vol. 1, 240–41. Washington's August 4, 1775, letter to Morris establishes that Ogden and Burr were in Cambridge in early August.

7. The modern military term to describe the role of the Arnold expedition is "deep attack." Arnold's mission was to penetrate behind enemy lines into Canada, seize Quebec, and hold it until Montgomery could link up with him. The mission was Washington's idea who selected Arnold to lead it. In modern warfare, airborne (parachute or helicopter) forces are frequently used to hold a key position, such as a transportation hub or bridge behind enemy lines until stronger ground forces arrive. Modern examples of deep attacks include the Allies' attempt in World War

II to get across the Rhine River by seizing the bridge at Arnhem or paratroopers behind the beaches at Normandy on D–Day.

8. The phrase appears in a May 1776 letter written by a gentleman volunteer named John Howard. See Holly A. Mayer, *Belonging to the Army: Camp Followers and Community During the American Revolution* (Columbia, SC: University of South Carolina Press, 1996), 183.

9. Don H. Hagist, *British Soldiers in the American War* (Yardley, PA: Westholme Publishing, 2012). There is a propensity for modern writers to identify volunteers as gentleman volunteers. There is justification to identify men like young Ogden and Burr, willing to serve without pay as gentlemen volunteers. For example, in *Military Journal of the American Revolution*, James Thacher, wrote, "A gentleman volunteer, by name Requaw, received a dangerous wound." James Thacher, *Military Journal of the American Revolution*, (Hartford, CT: Hurlbut, Williams & Company, 1862), 255.

10. Simon Fobes's "Narrative of Arnold's Expedition to Quebec" in Kenneth Roberts, *March to Quebec* (Garden City, NY: Doubleday & Company, 1938), 581.

11. Manuscript letter from Arron Burr to Sally Burr Reeve dated "Newburyport Sept. 18, 1775" in Reeve Family Papers, Box One. Manuscript and Archives Division, Yale University Library, Sterling Memorial Library.

12. Reuben Colburn built an additional twenty bateaux when Arnold arrived at Colburn's boatyard. Some historians have accused Colburn of cheating the Continental Army by building poorly constructed boats made out of green lumber. However, Colburn had only a few weeks to build the boats and work with the available lumber. The boats were only meant to be used for a few weeks on a one-way trip to Quebec. The irony of Colburn's story is that he was never paid for the 220 boats. At first, the members of the Continental Congress disputed his invoices. Colburn pursued his unpaid bill for years without success. He finally decided to make a personal appeal to General Washington to help him get paid. Colburn traveled to Washington's home at Mount Vernon in Virginia, arriving unannounced on the morning of December 15, 1799. When he knocked on the front door of the retired general and former president, he was told that Washington had died during the previous night. Colburn petitioned the US Senate as late as 1824 for payment of his 1775 boat contract. His appeals were denied because he could not produce any records or receipts to support his claim. Colburn, years earlier, had turned over his documentation to the government, which had lost or misplaced his paperwork. Some additional records pertaining to his contract were destroyed when the British burned Washington, DC, during the War of 1812. The story of Colburn's efforts to collect his money can be found in *The Debates and Proceedings of the Congress of the United States*. (Washington, DC: Gates and Seaton, 1856), year 1824, vol. 2, 353.

13. There were six volunteers on the Arnold expedition. They were Aaron Burr, Matthias Ogden, Charles Porterfield, David Hopkins, John McGuire, and Mathew Duncan. Besides Burr and Ogden, the most famous volunteer on the

expedition was Charles Porterfield. He was a Virginian assigned to Daniel Morgan's Rifle Division. Porterfield rose to the rank of colonel later in the war. He was mortally wounded and captured leading his Virginia regiment at the Battle of Camden, South Carolina (August 16, 1780), and died from his wounds as a British prisoner of war.

14. Dr. Isaac Senter's journal in Roberts, *March to Quebec.* 200.

15. George Smith, *An Universal Military Dictionary* (London: J. Millan, 1779), 3.

16. Manuscript letter form Aaron Burr to Mrs. [Sally] Reeve. Dated "Fort Western, September 24, 1775," in Tapping Reeve Family Papers, Manuscript and Archives Division, Sterling Memorial Library.

17. Smith, *An Universal Military Dictionary*, 36.

18. A specific reference to Ogden being referred to as Major Ogden in a letter that Arnold wrote to the Continental Congress dated "Camp Before Quebeck, January 24, 1776." It reads in part, "Major Ogden, the bear of this [letter] . . . came out with me a volunteer proposes going down to Philadelphia." See Peter Force, ed., *American Archives, Fourth Series.* Six volumes (Washington, DC : M. St. Clair Clarke and Peter Force, 1837–1846), Vol. IV, 838.

19. Roberts, *March to Quebec,* 511. The quote is from the journal of the expedition kept by common solider George Morrison.

20. Justin H. Smith, *Arnold's March from Cambridge to Quebec* (New York: G. P. Putnam's Sons, 1903), 389.

21. Abbot, *The Papers of George Washington, Revolutionary War Series,* vol. 2, 245.

22. Davis, *Memoirs of Aaron Burr*, vol. 1, 66.

23. Davis, *Memoirs of Aaron Burr*, vol. 1, 66.

24. William Bell Clark, ed., *Naval Documents of the American Revolution.* 10 vols to date. (Washington, DC: U.S. Government Printing Office, 1964–), vol. 2, 1038–39.

25. John Joseph Henry, *An Accurate and Interesting Account of the Hardships and Sufferings of that Band of Heroes . . . in the Campaign Against Quebec* (Lancaster, PA: William Greer, 1812), 94–95.

26. Manuscript letter, Aaron Burr to Timothy Edwards dated "Point aux Tremble, November 22, 1775." Burr Papers, New York Historical Society. Reference CtFaiHi; 2876.

27. Davis, *Memoirs of Aaron Burr*, vol. 1, 68.

28. Colonel Arnold to General Montgomery dated "Point Aux Trembles, 30th Nov. 1775," in Roberts, *March to Quebec,* 101.

29. Macpherson was from Philadelphia where his family owned an estate along the eastern shore of the Schuylkill River. Called Mount Pleasant, the estate consisted of more than one hundred acres and a handsome mansion. Benedict Arnold took out a mortgage to buy Mount Pleasant in 1779.

30. General Montgomery to General Schuyler, dated "Holland House" [Montgomery's headquarters], "near the Heights of Abraham, December 5th, 1775," in Force, ed. *American Archives,* vol. IV, 189

31. Samuel H. Wandell and Meade Minnigerode, *Aaron Burr, A Biography Compiled from Rare, and in Many Cases, Unpublished Sources.* 2 vols. (New York: G. P. Putnam's Sons, 1925), vol. 1, 54.

32. George F. G. Stanley, *Canada Invaded, 1775-1776* (Toronto: A. M. Hakkert Ltd., 1973), 98.

33. Manuscript notes of an 1831 interview with Aaron Burr found inserted in *Arnold's Letter Book* (handwritten copies of Arnold's letter written during the Arnold expedition). The notes from the interview with Burr are signed *W. W.* Apparently, the interviewer was William Willis, the recording secretary of the Maine Historical Society at the time. Viewed by the author at the Library of The Maine Historical Society, Portland, Maine. Burr traveled to Maine to present the letters to the Maine Historical Society. How Burr acquired the letters is unknown.

34. Justin H Smith, *Our Struggle for the Fourteenth Colony, Canada and the American Revolution.* 2 vols. (New York: G. P. Putnam's Sons, 1907), vol. 2, 143.

35. Aaron Burr mentioned this story while visiting the Maine Historical Society where he presented them with Arnold's diary from the expedition.

36. Excerpt from a letter from Colonel Benedict Arnold to Hannah Arnold (his sister), "Camp before Quebeck, January 6, 1776. I received a wound by a ball through my left leg, at the time I had gained the first battery at the lower town, which, by the loss of blood, rendered me very weak. As soon as the main body came up, with some assistance I returned to the hospital, near a mile, on foot, being obliged to draw one lag after me, and in great part of the way under the continual fire of the enemy from the walls,"See Force, ed. *American Archives,* vol. 4, 589–90.

37. Letter from Janet Montgomery to Aaron Burr, March 7, 1779. See Worthington Chauncey Ford, *Some Papers of Aaron Burr* (Worcester, MA: Proceedings of the American Antiquarian Society, New Series, Vo. 29, 1919), 87.

38. A treatise is a scholarly detailed essay on a specific subject. Military treatises and books dealing with more general information of use to officers were widely read at the time of the American Revolution. There was no formal training for officers at the time (except for British Army artillery and engineer officers) and newly commissioned officers were expected to learn by reading books and on-the-job training. Washington was an avid reader of military treatises. His library at Mount Vernon included Humphrey Bland's *A Treatise of Military Discipline* (1762) and Roger Stevenson's *Military Instructions for Officers Detached in the Field.* The latter was a book about partisan warfare (today called guerilla warfare). It was published in London in 1770. It was popular reading among the Americans, which accounts for a second, Philadelphia edition published in 1775. Washington's library has the Philadelphia edition. For a detailed history of military books available during the Revolutionary War see, Ira D. Gruber, *Books and the British Army in the Age of the American Revolution* (Chapel Hill, NC: 2010).

39. Broadus Mitchell, *Alexander Hamilton, Youth to Maturity 1755–1788.* (New York: Macmillan,1957),79. Robert Harpur (1731–1825) was born in Ireland. He immigrated to America in 1761 where he eventually settled in New York City as

the mathematics professor at King's College. Hamilton was one of his prized students. Harpur sided with the Patriots and held various positions in the New York State government during the war. He was appointed the deputy secretary of the State of New York and the secretary of the State Land Board after the Revolutionary War. The latter position was important as the Iroquois Indians, who sided with Britain during the war, lost their upstate New York lands, which became known as the Military Tract. Harpur was responsible for apportioning the Military Tract into various counties. He is credited with giving the classical names to upstate cities and towns within the Military Tract including Utica, Troy, Syracuse, and Rome. Harpursville, New York, is named in his honor as well as Harpur College in Binghamton, New York. Originally an independent college, it is now the arts and sciences campus of Binghamton University.

40. Mitchell, *Alexander Hamilton Youth*, 79.

41. For information about Provincial troops (later called State troops) see Robert K. Wright, *The Continental Army* (Washington, DC: Center of Military History United States Army, 1989), 439. State troops sometimes were attached to the Continental Army for extended periods of time. All the troops under Washington's immediate command (Continentals, State Troops, and militia) were referred to during the Revolutionary War as the Main Army or the Grand Army.

42. Letter from Alexander Hamilton to Edward Stevens dated "St. Croix Novemr. 11th 1769" in Harold C. Syrett, ed., *Papers of Alexander Hamilton* (New York: Columbia University Press, 1961-1987), vol. 1, 4. Edward Stevens (1754–1834) was Hamilton's childhood friend in St. Croix. He was the son of Thomas Stevens, a St. Croix merchant. Stevens was in New York when Hamilton wrote him. He was sent to New York to study medicine with the expectation that he would return to fever-plagued St. Croix as a doctor. Stevens attended King's College from 1770–1774. He went to Scotland following his graduation to continue his medical studies at the prestigious University of Edinburgh. Stevens was awarded a doctorate from the university in 1777. He returned to St. Croix in 1783 where he practiced medicine. He also corresponded with Hamilton. Dr. Stevens moved to Philadelphia in 1793 where he successfully treated Hamilton and Hamilton's wife Elizabeth when they contracted yellow fever. Stevens was opposed to bloodletting, which was the accepted method for treating disease at the time. Instead, he prescribed Peruvian bark, wine, rest, and cold baths, a regimen that probably saved the lives of Hamilton and his wife.

43. Hal T. Shelton, *General Richard Montgomery and the American Revolution* (New York: New York University Press, 1994), 106.

44. Shelton, *General Richard Montgomery*, 98.

45. James Thomas Flexner, *The Young Hamilton* (New York: Little Brown and Company, 1978), 91. Flexner sites his source as the "Robert Troup Narrative," *William & Mary Quarterly*, 3rd Series, IV (1947), 212–25.

46. Abbot, *The papers of George Washington, Revolutionary War Series*, vol. 4, 93.

47. Abbot, *The papers of George Washington, Revolutionary War Series*, vol. 4, 229.

CHAPTER THREE: THE DEFENSE OF NEW YORK CITY

1. Henry Knox was a Boston bookseller prior to the start of the Revolution. He was one of the officers who was selected by Washington for promotion. One of Washington's strongest character traits was his skill in identifying talented men and giving them responsibilities. Other examples of Washington's talent were Nathanael Greene and Benedict Arnold.

2. Bernard Bailyn, *The Ideological Origins of the American Revolution*. (Cambridge, MA: Harvard University Press, 1967), 126.

3. It is generally believed that Knox used oxen to pull his sleds across Massachusetts. This idea is reinforced by a popular painting by Tom Lovell titled *The Noble Train of Artillery* (completed in 1946) in which the artists depicts teams of oxen pulling the sleds. However, Knox found the cost of contracting oxen from local farmers to be too expensive and he employed mostly horses for the journey. Lovell's painting is owned by the Dixon Ticonderoga Company (manufacturer of art supplies) and on permanent loan to the Fort Ticonderoga Museum.

4. Abbot et al., eds., *The Papers of George Washington, Revolutionary War Series*, vol. 3, p. 53.

5. Letter from Gen. Charles Lee to General Washington, dated New York, February *19th 1776 in The Lee Papers, 4 vols. (New York: The New York Historical Society, 1871-1874).* vol. 1, 309.

6. According to Henry P. Johnston, the first American troops arrived in New York on April 3rd, 1776 under the command of Gen. Israel Putnam. See Henry P. Johnston, *The Campaign of 1776 Around New York and Brooklyn* (Brooklyn, NY: The Long Island Historical Society, 1878), 63.

7. William S. Baker, *Itinerary of General Washington* (Philadelphia: J.B. Lippincott Company, 1892), 37

8. The Continental Army was the official name of the troops under the control of the Continental Congress. It did not include state troops or militia although they frequently operated with the Continental regiments. George Washington was Commander-in-Chief of the Continental Army. However, Continental troops sometimes operated far from his immediate control, such as in northern New York State, Canada, and the southern states. To clarify this confusing situation, the term Grand Army or Main Army was used during the American Revolution to identify all troops under Washington's immediate command, be they Continental regiments, state troops, or militia. Congress used the term Grand Army as early as June 16, 1775, when it resolved, *That there be one quartermaster general for the grand army, and a deputy under him, for the separate army.* See *Journals of Congress,* 34 vols. (Washington, D.C.: Library of Congress, 1904-1937), vol. 2, 94.

9. Peter Force, ed., *American Archives, Fourth Series* (Washington, D.C.: M. St. Clair Clarke and Peter Force, 1837-1946), vol. 6, 920.

10. All of New York City's docks were located along the East River side of Manhattan. The reason was that the East River was not a river but an estuary of

brackish New York harbor. Since salt water froze at a lower temperature than fresh water the East River was more likely to remain open to ships during the winter than the Hudson River.

11. Force, *American Archives, Fourth Series,* vol. 6, 920. This reference is a report (Return) submitted by Col. Knox on June 16, 1776. The title of Knox's report is interesting as it shows that Hamilton's was the only independent (Provincial) artillery company defending New York. The Return reads, *A Return of the Disposition of the Cannon, and of Ten Companies of the Continental Regiment of Artillery, and one Colony Company of Artillery, commanded by Captain Hamilton, in and about the City of New-York.*

CHAPTER FOUR: AARON BURR'S EPIC JOURNEY

1. Mathew Duncan was from Philadelphia and captured by the British while scouting Lower Town. He was eventually exchanged and appointed a captain in the 5th Pennsylvania Battle on January 5, 1776. He was captured again when Fort Washington (an American fort on upper Manhattan Island) surrendered to the British on November 16, 1776.

2. James Parton, *The Life and Times of Aaron Burr.* Two vols. (New York: Mason Brothers, 1864), vol. 1, 78–79.

3. Aaron Burr to his sister Sally Reeve in "The Papers of Aaron Burr," New York Historical Society, (microfilm) reel one.

4. Peter Force, ed., *American Archives, Fourth Series.* Six volumes (Washington, DC: M. St. Clair Clarke and Peter Force, 1837–1846), vol. 6, 590.

5. Parton, *The Life and Times.* Vol. 1, 78.

6. The phrase appeared in a letter Wooster wrote on February 11, 1776, lecturing his superior, General Philip Schuyler, on how to conduct the war in Canada. See Force, *American Archives,* vol. 4, 1218.

7. Samuel Chase and Charles Carroll of Carrollton, two of the commissioners to Canada, sent their fellow delegates to the Continental Congress a summary report of their mission. Dated May 27, 1776, their report included a scathing opinion of General Wooster. The Commissioners described Wooster as "unfit, totally unfit, to command your Army, and conduct the war. . . . His stay in this Colony is unnecessary, and even prejudicial to our affairs; we would therefore humbly advise his recall." See Force, *American Archives,* vol. 6, 589.

8. Extract of a letter from John Trumbull to his father, the governor of Connecticut, dated "Ticonderoga, July 12, 1776" in Henry Steele Commager and Richard B. Morris, ed., *The Spirit of Seventy-Six,* 2 vols. (New York: The Bobbs-Merrill Company, Inc., 1958), vol. 1, 221.

9. Matthew L. Davis, *Memoirs of Aaron Burr,* 2 vols. (New York: Harper & Brothers, 1836–1837), vol. 1, 78.

10. Three members of Congress were sent by that body to assess the situation in Canada. They were also given extraordinary authority that included "suspending of-

ficers for infractions of orders, make military appointments and take part in councils of war." The original commissioners were Benjamin Franklin, Charles Carroll, and Samuel Chase. The aged Franklin returned home after reaching Montreal following an arduous journey to arrive there. Charles Carroll (1737–1832) kept a journal of their mission. He was selected for the mission because he was a Catholic, which would appeal to the large Catholic population of Canada. Carroll was a Maryland plantation owner and reputed to be the wealthiest man in colonial America. He signed his name as Charles Carroll of Carrollton to distinguish himself from two similarly-named relatives. The legend is that he signed the Declaration of Independence as Charles Carroll of Carrollton to make sure that the British arrested the right person if therRevolution failed. Carroll was the last surviving signer of the Declaration of Independence and one of the founders of the Baltimore and Ohio Railroad.

11. Arnold's recommendation on behalf of Ogden appears in a letter Arnold wrote to Congress dated "Camp Before Quebeck, January 24, 1776." See Force, *American Archives*, vol. 4, 838.

12. Ogden's appointment was confirmed by John Hancock in a letter to Ogden dated "Philadelphia, March 7, 1776." The letter reads, "Sir, The Congress in consideration of my merit, and the services you have done you country, have thought proper to appoint you Lieutenant-Colonel in the first battalion of Jersey troops. I do myself the honor to enclose your commission . . . John Hancock, President." See Force, *American Archives*, vol. 5, 99.

13. W. W. Abbot et al., eds., *Papers of George Washington, Revolutionary War Series*, 24 vols. to date (Charlottesville, VA: University Press of Virginia, 1985–), vol. 2, 607.

14. Letter from George Washington to John Hancock dated New York, May 11, 1776 in Abbot et al., *The Papers of George Washington, Revolutionary War Series*, vol. 4, 276.

15. Letter from Matthias Ogden to Aaron Burr dated "Fort George [New York], 5th June 1776" in Davis, *Memoirs of Aaron Burr*, vol. 1, 80.

CHAPTER FIVE: AARON BURR'S
LOST OPPORTUNITY

1. W. W. Abbot et al., eds., *The Papers of George Washington, Revolutionary War Series*, 24 vols. to date (Charlottesville, VA: University Press of Virginia, 1985–), vol. 3, 282–83.

2. Dr. James McHenry quote. Dr. James McHenry was one of Washington's wartime aides. He described the writing process at headquarters as "the usual mode of writing a letter was to give an aide notes on what he wanted to be written. The aide prepared a letter from the instructions." See Bernard C. Steiner, *Life and Correspondence of James McHenry*. (Cleveland, OH: The Barrows Brothers Company, 1907), 27.

3. Abbot, *The Papers of George Washington, Revolutionary War Series*, vol. 12, 683.

4. Letter from Oliver Wolcott to Samuel Lyman dated "Philadelphia 3d Febry. 1776" in Paul H. Smith, ed., *Letters of Delegates to Congress, 1774-1789*. 27 vols. (Washington, DC: Library of Congress). vol. 3, 190

5. Richard Smith's Diary. Entry dated "18 Jany. 1776." In Smith, *Letters of Delegates*, vol. 3, 113.

6. Abbot, *The Papers of George Washington, Revolutionary War Series*, vol. 1, 58–59.

7. Abbot, *The Papers of George Washington, Revolutionary War Series*, vol. 3, 173.

8. Abbot, *The Papers of George Washington, Revolutionary War Series*, vol. 1, 365.

9. Francis B. Heitman, *Historical Register of Officers of the Continental Army* (Washington, DC: The Rare Book Shop Publishing Company, 1914), 585.

10. John C. Fitzpatrick, ed., *The Writings of George Washington,*39 vols (Washington, DC: U.S. Government Printing Office, 1931–1944), vol. 36, 431. For a detailed account of Anthony Walton White's brief tenure working at Washington's headquarters see Arthur Lefkowitz, *George Washington's Indispensable Men* (Mechanicsburg, PA: Stackpole Books, 2003), 13–14. There is a 2018 second edition of this book.

11. Milton Lomask, *Aaron Burr: The Years from Princeton to Vice President 1756–1805* (New York: Farrar, Straus & Giroux, 1979), 45.

12. Nathan Schachner, *Aaron Burr, A Biography* (New York: A. S. Barnes & Company, 1937), 45.

13. William Ferrand Livingston, *Israel Putnam, Pioneer, Ranger and Major-General*. (New York: G. P. Putnam's Sons, 1901), 280.

14. Matthew L. Davis, *Memoirs of Aaron Burr*, 2 vols. (New York: Harper & Brothers, 1836–1837), preface, 1.

15. Aaron Burr Declaration of Military Service, dated "City of New York, 15 April, 1834" in Mary-Jo Kline, ed. *Political Correspondence and Public Papers of Aaron Burr*. 2 vols (Princeton, NJ: Princeton University Press, 1983), vol. 2, 1224.

16. Lomask, *Aaron Burr*, 45.

17. James Parton, *The Life and Times of Aaron Burr*. Two vols. (New York: Mason Brothers, 1864), 83. Note that Parton said that Burr was "sinking into the condition of a clerk." Parton may have gotten this idea from Matthew Davis's *Memoirs* published in 1836. Davis gave the following sympathetic explanation for Burr's brief time at headquarters in which he describes him as being a clerk. What makes Davis's story unique is that it may have been told to him by his bitter and delusional friend Burr,

> During the short period that he remained in the family of General Washington, he was treated with respect and attention; but soon perceived, as he thought an unwillingness to afford that information, and those technical explanations of great historical military movements, which an inquiring and enlightened mind like Burr's, sought with avidity and perseverance. He therefore became apprehensive, if he remained with the commander-in-chief, that, instead of becoming a scientific soldiers, he should dwindle down into a practical clerk-a species of drudgery to which his pecuniary circumstances

did not render it necessary for him to submit, and for which neither his habits, his education, nor his temperament in any degree qualified him. He therefore determined promptly on a change, and was willing to enter the family of Major-general Putnam, because he would there enjoy the opportunities for study, and the duties which he would be required to perform would be strictly military.

See Davis, *Memoirs of Aaron Burr*, vol. 1, 82–83.

18. Nancy Isenberg, *Fallen Founder* (New York: Viking Penguin, 2007), 34.

19. Abbot, *The Papers of George Washington, Revolutionary War Series*, vol. 17, 120.

20. General Israel Putnam and his wife Hannah (1721–1765) had five sons and five daughters. Israel Putnam Jr. was the oldest son. He was born on January 28, 1740. Connecticut raised six regiments in May 1775 at the start of the American Revolution. Putnam Sr. was appointed the commander of the 3rd Connecticut Regiment and his son Israel Putnam Jr. was named a captain and commander of a company consisting of one hundred men in his father's regiment. Putnam Jr. only served as a company commander for a short time. When his father was appointed by Congress as a major general in the new Continental Army, Putnam Jr. became his aide-de-camp in July 1775. Putnam Jr. served as his father's aide until 1779 when he resigned. He was replaced by Daniel Putnam, the general's second oldest son.

21. Samuel P. Hildreth, *Biographical and Historical Memoirs of the Early Pioneer Settlers of Ohio* (Cincinnati, OH: H. W. Derby, 1852), 355.

22. Eben Putnam, *A History of the Putnam Family in England and America* (Salem, MA: The Salem Press and Publishing Company, 1891), 181. Eben is a man's name derived from Hebrew.

23. Samuel B. Webb was elected the commander of the Wethersfield militia at the start of the Revolution. He marched his company to Cambridge and fought in the Battle of Bunker Hill where he was wounded. Webb served as one of Washington's aides until early 1777 when he was given command of a line regiment.

24. John Adams to Abigail Adams. Letter dated "May 22 [1777]." In Smith, *Letters of Delegates to Congress*. Vol. 7, 103.

25. The General Orders of the Continental Army dated "Head Quarters, New York, June 21st 1776" establish the rank of the army's aides-de-camp. The relevant text reads, "The Honorable Continental Congress have been pleased to give the rank of Lieutenant Colonel, to the Aids-du-Camp of the Commander in Chief, and to his principal Secretary—Also the rank of Major to the Aids-du-Camp of the Majors General." See Abbot, *The Papers of George Washington, Revolutionary War Series*, , vol. 5, 61.

26. Letter from Lieutenant Colonel Aaron Burr to General George Washington, dated "Peekskill [N.Y.] 20th July 1777" in Abbot, *The Papers of George Washington, Revolutionary War Series*, vol. 10, 343–44.

27. Davis, *Memoirs of Aaron Burr*, vol. 1, 44.

28. Historian Milton Lomask wrote a laudable two volume biography of Burr. He concluded that "it was Burr's innate air of superiority, derived from his family

background" that accounted for his brief employment at Washington's headquarters and the general's "frequently ungracious treatment of Burr in the years to come." See Lomask, *Aaron Burr*, 44.

CHAPTER SIX: THE BATTLE FOR NEW YORK

1. W. W. Abbot et al., ed. *The Papers of George Washington, Revolutionary War Series* (Charlottesville: University of Virginia,1985), vol. 3, 217.

2. The legend is that Putnam introduced growing tobacco in the Connecticut River Valley near his home in the village of Pomfret in northeastern Connecticut. The tale begins with Putnam participating in the 1762 British expedition that captured Havana, Cuba, during the French and Indian War. He brought Cuban tobacco seeds to Connecticut where he successfully planted them in the Connecticut River Valley. The rich sandy soil of the valley and hot summers yielded an excellent tobacco crop. Tobacco growing continues in the area to this day with the leaves used as the two outside layers of premium cigars. The problem with the story is that the Indians were already growing tobacco in Connecticut when the first white settlers arrived there in 1633. Tobacco growing in the Connecticut River Valley was well established by 1700. The crop (actually a weed) continues to be cultivated today but in small quantities and known as a *Connecticut wrapper*.

3. David Humphreys, *An Essay on the Life of the Honourable Major-General Israel Putnam* (Hartford, CT: Hudson and Goodwin, 1788), 103.

4. Davis, *Memoirs of Aaron Burr* (New York: Harper & Brothers, 1836-1837), vol. 1, 82.

5. George Washington to John Hancock dated *New York, 23d April 1776* in Abbot, *The Papers of George Washington, Revolutionary War Series*, vol.4, 112.

6. Perhaps Putnam's greatest story was that he was captured by Indian allies of the French who tied him to a post to be burned alive. Just as the Indians were about to ritually burn him, a sudden rain storm smothered the flames. An astonished French officer intervened and saved Putnam's life. In another spellbinder, Putnam told how he survived a shipwreck in 1762 during a British Army campaign to capture Spanish held Havana, Cuba. Putnam brought back tobacco seeds from Cuba which he successfully cultivated on his Connecticut farm.

7. Davis, ed. *Memoirs of Aaron Burr*, vol. 1, 86-90.

8. The word strategy is derived from the Greek word *strategia* meaning generalship. The word existed at the time of the American Revolution but it was not widely used. However, the word tactics was in common use at the time of the war. The 1779 *An Universal Military Dictionary* defined tactics as *the art of ranging armies into forms proper for fighting and maneuvering*. The dictionary cites historical examples of tactics including the phalanx used by the Romans.

9. Edward H. Tatum, ed. *The American Journal of Ambrose Serle* (San Marino, CA: The Huntington Library, 1940), 30.

10. Charles H. Lesser, ed., *The Sinews of Independence, Monthly Strength Reports of the Continental Army* (Chicago: The University of Chicago Press, 1976), 26-27.

11. The British Admiralty divided the Royal Navy into rated and unrated vessels. Rated ships were those that were large enough to have a captain as its commanding officer. These larger ships were divided into six rates. The three largest rates were collectively called ships of the line, the equivalent of a modern battleship. They carried from 100 or more guns to 64 guns mounted on two or three decks. At 64 guns, the *HMS Eagle* was a Third Rate Ship of the Line. Warships carrying fewer guns were classified as Fourth, Fifth, and Six Rate. A Sixth Rate carried between 20 and 28 cannons. It was impractical to sail a First or Second Rate Ship of the Line into New York harbor at the time of the American Revolution because of shifting sandbars just outside the harbor. This accounts for Lord Howe using the Third Rate *HMS Eagle* as his flagship. Also, there is no such thing as the British Navy. It is always identified as the Royal Navy.

12. Edward Bangs, ed. *Journal of Lieutenant Isaac Bangs* (Cambridge, MA: John Wilson & Son, 1890), 59-60.

13. Caleb Clap, *Diary of Ensign Caleb Clap. The Historical Magazine.* Third Series, Vol. III. April 1875, 247.

14. John Stockton Littell, ed., *Memoirs of His Own Time . . . by Alexander Graydon.* (Philadelphia: Lindsay & Blakiston, 1846), 147-148.

15. Eric I. Manders. *The Battle of Long Island* (Monmouth Beach, NJ: Philip Freneau Press, 1978), 36.

16. William B. Reed, *Life and Correspondence of Joseph Reed.* 2 vols. (Philadelphia: Lindsay & Blakiston, 1847), vol. 1, 220.

17. Abbot, *The Papers of George Washington, Revolutionary War Series*, vol. 6, 126-127.

18. Parton, *The Life and Times of Aaron Burr.* vol. 1, 85.

19. The long delay between the time that the Crown forces first landed on Staten Island and launching their attack can to be attributed in part to their staggering logistical problems. Commenting on the problem at the outset of the New York campaign, author Rick Atkinson observed, "If Howe's host reached 35,000 troops and 4,000 horses later in the year [1776], as anticipated, thirty-seven tons of food and thirty-eight tons of hay and oats would be required every day, almost entirely from Britain. Since an army of that size would consume some four thousand tons of meat a year, ox-slaying Cork [England] would stay busy." See Rick Atkinson, *The British Are Coming* (New York: Henry Holt and Company, 2019), 246.

20. Abbot, *The Papers of George Washington, Revolutionary War Series*, vol. 1, 115.

21. Peter Force, ed. *American Archives.* Fifth Series (Washington, D.C.: M. St. Clair Clarke and Peter Force, 1837-1846), Vol. 1, 1259-1260.

22. Washington had no companies of mounted troops during the 1776 New York campaign. Historians have pointed out that a company of horsemen from Connecticut arrived in the American camp during the spring of 1776, but Washington turned them away. These same historians claimed that Washington refused

the services of these mounted troops because he had no experience in how to use them. But he actually sent them home because they were more trouble than they were worth. According to American Capt. Alexander Graydon, who saw the Connecticut horsemen, Washington had no real choice in the matter. "Among the military phenomena of this campaign," Graydon said, "the Connecticut light horse ought not to be forgotten. These consisted of a considerable number of old fashioned men, probably farmers and heads of families, as they were generally middle aged, and many of them apparently beyond the meridian of life. They were truly irregulars; and whether their clothing, their equipment or caparisons were regarded, it would have been difficult to have discovered any circumstance of uniformity. Instead of carbines and sabers, they generally carried fowling pieces; some of them very long, and such as in Pennsylvania, are used for shooting ducks. Here and there one, his youthful garments well saved, appeared in a dingy regimental of scarlet, with a triangular, tarnished laced hat." Graydon said that one of these horsemen was captured by the British, "and on being asked what had been his duty in the rebel army, he answered that it was to flank a little and carry tidings." Littell, ed., *Graydon . . . Memoirs of His Time*, 155–156.

23. Davis, *Memoirs of Aaron Burr*, vol. 1, 122.

24. Force, ed. *American Archives*. Fifth Series, Vol. 1, 1257–1258.

25. David Humphreys. *An Essay on the Life of the Honourable Major General Israel Putnam*. (Hartford, CT: Hudson & Goodwin, 1788), 82.

26. Edward H. Tatum, ed. *The American Journal of Ambrose Serle* (San Marino, CA: The Huntington Library, 1940), 95.

27. George F. Scheer, ed. *Private Yankee Doodle Being a Narrative of Some of the Adventures . . . of a Revolutionary Soldier by Joseph Plumb Martin* (Boston: Little, Brown and Company, 1962), 33. Martin was a 15-year-old private at the Battle of Kips Bay in a regiment of Connecticut state troops raised for short-term service with the Continental Army. He joined the Continental Army later in the war.

28. Michael Cohn. *Fortifications of New York During the Revolutionary War* (New York: New York City Archeological Group, 1962), 5.

29. Certificate from Isaac Jennings and Andre Wakeman in Davis, *Memoirs of Aaron Burr*, vol. 1, 104.

30. Humphreys, *Essay on the Life of Israel Putnam*, 92–94.

31. Newton, Michael. *Alexander Hamilton, the Formative Years* (Eleftheria Publishing, 2015), 165.

32. Letter from Nathaniel Judson to Commodore R. V. Morris dated *Albany, 10th February, 1814*, in Davis, *Memoirs of Aaron Burr*, vol. 1, 105.

33. Henry P Johnston, *The Campaign of 1776 around New York and Brooklyn* (Brooklyn, NY: The Long Island Historical Society, 1878), 245. The quote is attributed to a *Loyalist pastor* named Mr [Ewald] Shewkirk.

34. Besides not knowing if Hamilton's company had iron or brass six pounders, there is no known accurate reference if he had light six pounders. To explain, there is a six pound cannon and a light six pound cannon. The difference is the thickness

of the barrel. More metal in the barrel makes it heavier and allows it to shoot further. The cannon barrel is also less likely to break. The cannon barrel's bore is the same for a regular six pounder and a light six pounder; both fire the same size ball. Another consideration is where did Hamilton's two six pounders come from? The Americans in the Revolutionary War had cannons that they cast themselves as well as captured British cannons and imported French guns. The French were using a new system of artillery based on four, eight, and twelve pounders. The Americans sometimes drilled out the barrels of the French four pounders to make it a standard six pound cannon. Hamilton's company was probably equipped with captured British six pounders.

35. Harold L. Peterson, *Round Shot and Rammers* (New York: Bonanza Books, 1969), 66.

36. Washington Irving, *Life of George Washington*. Five-volume illustrated edition. (New York: G.P Putnam & Company, 1856-1859), vol. 2, 392. Unfortunately, Irving's *Life of George Washington* included no sources for his information and some historians question the authenticity of his work including his depiction of Hamilton at the Battle of White Plains. But Irving was a serious researcher and as well as an elegant writer. In researching his *Life of Washington*, Irving was known to have consulted 180 volumes, or sets of volumes as well as original documents and letters and interviewing Hamilton's wife Elizabeth (died 1854). The absence of sources in his *Life of Washington* does not mean that his information is incorrect.

37. Lesser, *The Sinews of Independence*, 36.

38. Stephen Kemble, *Journals of Lieutenant Colonel Stephen Kemble*, 2 vols. (New York: New York Historical Society, 1883), vol. 1, 97-98.

39. Davis, *Memoirs of Aaron Burr*, vol. 1, 99.

40. Isenberg. *Fallen Founder*, 36.

41. George Washington Parke Custis. *Recollections and Private Memoirs of Washington* (New York: Derby & Jackson, 1860), 343-344.

42. The officers attending the October 16, 1776, Council of War were listed in a report of their meeting. The report stated, "*Present*. His Excelly. General Washington, Major Generals Lee [*Charles Lee*], Putnam [*Israel Putnam*], Heath [*William Heath*], Spencer [*Joseph Spencer*], Sullivan [*John Sullivan*], Brigadier Generals Ld Sterling [*William Alexander, Lord Sterling*], Mifflin [*Thomas Mifflin*], McDougal [*Alexander McDougal*], Parsons [*Samuel Holden Parsons*], Nixon [*John Nixon*], Wadsworth [*Peleg Wadsworth*], Scott [*Charles Scott*], Fellows [*John Fellows*], Clinton [*James Clinton*], Lincoln [*Benjamin Lincoln*], Colo. Knox [*Henry Knox*], Commanr of Artilly." See Abbot, *The Papers of George Washington, Revolutionary War Series*, vol. 6, 576.

43. Newton, *Alexander Hamilton, The Formative Years*, 198.

44. Michael Cohn, *Fortifications of New York During the Revolutionary War* (New York: Privately printed by the Archeological Group, 1962), 2.

45. *Letter from George Washington to John Hancock dated New York, June 17th 1776*, in Abbot, *The Papers of George Washington, Revolutionary War Series*, vol. 5, 21.

46. Abbot, *The Papers of George Washington, Revolutionary War Series*, vol. 6, 249. For additional information about the term *war of posts* see John Ferling, *Almost a Miracle* (New York: Oxford University Press, 2007), 137.

47. Barnet Schecter. *The Battle for New York* (New York: Penguin Books, 2003), 131.

48. Letter from Silas Deane to his wife Elizabeth Deane dated *Philadelphia July 20ᵗʰ 1775*. Smith, ed., *Letters of Delegates to Congress*, vol. 1, 638.

CHAPTER SEVEN:
THE 1776 BRITISH INVASION OF NEW JERSEY

1. W. W. Abbot et al., eds., *The Papers of George Washington, Revolutionary War Series*, 24 vols. to date (Charlottesville, VA: University Press of Virginia, 1985–), vol. 1, 55. The General Orders from later in July 1775 included additional orders regarding deserters. Dated July 27, 1775, the orders made it clear that any deserters were to be brought to headquarters, "For the future when any Deserters come to any of the out Guards, they are with the least delay to be sent by a Corporals Guard, to the next Guard in the Lines, who is immediately to escort them in the same manner to the Major General commanding that division of the Army, who as soon as he has examined them with forth with send them under a proper Escort from his guard to the headquarters."

2. Abbot, *The Papers of George Washington, Revolutionary War Series*, vol. 7, 135.

3. Richard K. Showman et al., ed., *The Papers of General Nathanael Greene*. 13 volumes (Chapel Hill: The University of North Carolina Press, 1976- 2005), vol 1, 354, fn 2.

4. Andrew Jackson O'Shaughnessy, *The Men Who Lost America* (New Haven: Yale University Press, 2013), 249.

5. Frank Moore, *The Diary of the American Revolution from Newspapers and Original Documents*. 2 volumes (New York: Privately Printed in 100 copies, 1865), vol. 1, 350.

6. Edwin Nott Hopson, *Captain Daniel Neil* (Paterson, NJ: Braen Heusser Co., 1927), 11–14. New Jersey's other artillery company designated the Western Company, New Jersey State Artillery, joined Washington's army in December 1776. It was commanded by Captain Samuel Hugg. Its arrival added two additional cannons to Washington's arsenal.

7. Letter from George Washington to John Hancock dated "Brunswick. Novr. 30ᵗʰ 1776" in Abbot, *The Papers of George Washington, Revolutionary War Series*, vol. 7, 232.

8. Charles H. Lesser, ed., *The Sinews of Independence, Monthly Strength Reports of the Continental Army* (Chicago: The University of Chicago Press, 1976), 40.

9. The 1839 pension application of Robert L. English. National Archives and Records Administration, Washington, DC. Pension File R3354. Mr. English was a common soldier in Rawling's regiment.

10. Harry Miller Lydenberg, ed., *Archibald Robertson, His Diaries and Sketches in America* (New York: New York Public Library, 1930), 114.

11. Richard K. Showman et al., ed., *The Papers of General Nathanael Greene*. 13 volumes (Chapel Hill: The University of North Carolina Press, 1976- 2005), vol. 1, 362.

12. Samuel Steele Smith, *The Battle of Trenton* (Monmouth Beach, NJ: Philip Freneau Press, 1965), 5.

13. Abbot, *The Papers of George Washington, Revolutionary War Series*, vol. 7, 245.

14. John Church Hamilton, *The Life of Alexander Hamilton,* 2 vols. (New York: Halsted Et Voorhies, 1834–1841). vol. 1, 57.

15. Broadus Mitchell, *Alexander Hamilton, Youth to Maturity 1755–1788* (New York: Macmillan,1957), 96.

16. Douglas Southall Freeman, *George Washington*. 7 vols. (New York: Charles Scribner's Sons, 1948–1957). vol. 4, 196–97.

17. Washington, Greene, and Arnold were among the American senior officers who were known to be avid readers of European military treatises. Some of these books were published in America. For example, a treatise about partisan warfare titled *Military Instructions for Officers Detached in the Field*, was first published in London in 1770. A second edition was printed in Philadelphia in 1775.

18. John Stockton Littell, ed., *Memoirs of His Own Time . . . by Alexander Graydon* (Philadelphia: Lindsay & Blakiston, 1846), 179.

19. Abbot, *The Papers of George Washington, Revolutionary War Series*, vol. 7, 116.

20. William Farrand Livingston, *Israel Putnam, Pioneer, Ranger, and Major-General* (New York: G. P. Putnam's Son, 1901), 328.

21. David Humphreys, *An Essay on the Life of the Honourable Major-General Israel Putnam* (Hartford, CT: Hudson & Goodwin, 1788), 97.

22. Burr called Putnam "my good old general" in a letter to his friend Matthew Ogden dated "Princeton, 7th March, 1777." The pertinent text reads, "But, as I am at present happy in the esteem and entire confidence of my good old general, I shall be piqued at no neglect." See Matthew L. Davis, *Memoirs of Aaron Burr*, 2 vols. (New York: Harper & Brothers, 1836–1837), vol. 1, 109.

23. Hubbard, *Major General Israel Putnam*, 135.

24. General Putnam to General Washington, Philadelphia, dated "12 December, 1776" in Peter Force, ed., *American Archives,* Six volumes (Washington, DC: M. St. Clair Clarke and Peter Force, 1837–1846), Series Five, vol. 3, 1180.

25. Hubbard, *Major General*, 137.

26. Thomas Paine, *The American Crisis—Number One*. See Force, *American Archives*. Fifth Series, vol. 3, 1290–93.

27. Arthur Lefkowitz, *The Long Retreat, The Calamitous American Defense of New Jersey, 1776* (Metuchen, NJ: The Upland Press, 1998), 124.

28. Washington Irving, *Life of George Washington*. Five volume illustrated edition (New York; G. P Putnam & Company, 1856–1859), vol. 2, 446–47.

29. Irving, *Life of George Washington*, vol. 2, 471.

30. Samuel Steele Smith, *The Battle of Trenton* (Monmouth Beach, NJ: Philip Freneau Press, 1965), 14. Sam Smith founded the Philip Freneau Press primarily to publish books about the American Revolution. He owned a successful printing company before retiring to peruse his interest in the Revolutionary War. His Philip Freneau Press published thirteen excellent books about the war. He also authored several of them.

31. David Hackett Fischer, *Washington's Crossing* (New York: Oxford University Press, 2004), 392. The author lists the American artillery companies and number of cannons in each company who participated in the Battle of Trenton.

32. Accounts vary concerning the distance from McConkey's Ferry to the center of Trenton from nine to eleven miles. The differences are based on the fact that the rebel army split after arriving in New Jersey and followed two different roads to Trenton.

33. Fischer, *Washington's Crossing*, 405.

34. Letter from George Washington to John Hancock dated "head Quarters, Newtown {Pennsylvania] 27ᵗʰ Decemr 1776" in Abbot, *The Papers of George Washington, Revolutionary War Series*, vol. 7, 454.

35. William S. Stryker, *The Battles of Trenton and Princeton* (Boston and New York: Houghton, Mifflin and Company, 1898), 142.

36. "Thunder in New Jersey: Washington's Artillery during the Ten Crucial Days," American Battlefield Trust, https://www.battlefields.org/learn/articles/thunder-new-jersey-washingtons-artillery-during-ten-crucial-days, 2.

37. William Ferrand Livingston, *Israel Putnam, Pioneer, Ranger and Major-General*. (New York: G. P. Putnam's Sons, 1901), 335.

38. Livingston, *Israel Putnam*, 336.

39. Letter from General Nathanael Greene to Governor Nicholas Cooke of Rhode Island dated "Morristown [New Jersey] Jan.10.1777" inRichard K. Showman et al., ed., *The Papers of General Nathanael Greene*. 13 volumes (Chapel Hill: The University of North Carolina Press, 1976- 2005), vol. 2, 4.

40. William B Willcox, ed., *Sir Henry Clinton, The American Rebellion*. (New Haven, CT: Yale University Press, 1954),60, n4.

41. John C Miller, *Alexander Hamilton: Portrait in Paradox* (New York: Harper & Brothers, 1959), 2. There is conflict among historians whether Hamilton was accepted to Princeton. Legend has it that Hamilton held a grudge against Princeton because the trustees had turned down his application because they would not agree to let him study independently, advancing from class to class at his own pace. King's College was more flexible and allowed Hamilton greater independence in his course of study.

42. Letter from General Nathanael Greene to Thomas Paine dated "Morristown, N.J. 9 January 1777" in Showman, *Papers of General Nathanael Greene.*, vol. 2, 3.

43. Abbot, *The Papers of George Washington, Revolutionary War Series*, vol. 7, 535.

44. Abbot, *The Papers of George Washington, Revolutionary War Series*, vol. 7, 535.

45. Matthew L. Davis, *Memoirs of Aaron Burr*, 2 vols. (New York: Harper & Brothers, 1836–1837), 109.

46. Humphreys, *An Essay*, 102–3.

47. Dumas Malone, *Jefferson and the Ordeal of Liberty* (Boston: Little, Brown & Company, 1962), 56.

48. Dumas Malone, *Jefferson the President* (Boston: Little, Brown & Company, 1962), 629.

CHAPTER 8: HAMILTON JOINS WASHINGTON'S STAFF

1. Broadus Mitchell, *Alexander Hamilton, Youth to Maturity 1755–1788* (New York: Macmillan, 1957), p. 80.

2. James Thomas Flexner, *The Young Hamilton* (New York: Little Brown and Company, 1978), 114.

3. William Johnson, *Sketches of the Life and Correspondence of Nathanael Greene.* 2 vols. (Charleston, SC: A. E. Miller, 1822), vol. 1, 57.

4. George Washington Parke Custis, *Recollections and Private Memoirs of Washington* (New York: Derby & Jackson, 1860), 344–45.

5. W. W. Abbot et al., eds., *The Papers of George Washington, Revolutionary War Series*, 24 vols. to date (Charlottesville, VA: University Press of Virginia, 1985–), vol. 8, 116–17.

6. Flexner, *The Young Hamilton*, 133.

7. Harold C. Syrett, ed., *Papers of Alexander Hamilton* (New York: Columbia University Press, 1961–1987), vol.1, 196.

8. William S. Stryker, *The Battles of Trenton and Princeton* (Boston and New York: Houghton, Mifflin and Company, 1898), 158–59.

9. John Stockton Littell, ed., *Memoirs of His Own Time . . . by Alexander Graydon* (Philadelphia: Lindsay & Blakiston, 1846), 149.

10. Littell, *Memoirs of His Own Time*, 275–76.

11. Abbot, *The Papers of George Washington, Revolutionary War Series*, vol. 8, 468–69.

12. Abbot, *The Papers of George Washington, Revolutionary War Series*, vol. 8, 498.

13. Custis, *Reflections*, 345–46.

14. Syrett, *Papers of Alexander Hamilton*, vol. 2, 186. Duane included this comment in a letter he wrote to Hamilton on September 23, 1779.

15. The Provincial Convention of New York State established a Committee of Correspondence on September 17, 1776. It was empowered to "write letters to any correspondents, and take every other proper means to obtain intelligence." See Syrett, *Papers of Alexander Hamilton*, vol. 1, 208, n1.

16. Syrett, *Papers of Alexander Hamilton*, vol. 1, 209–10.

17. Harlow Giles Unger, *Lafayette* (New York: John Wiley & Sons, 2002), 28.

18. Alex Storozynski, "The Fiasco of July 4, 1777." *Huffington Post*, blog dated May 25, 2011. For example, in a letter to Henry Laurens dated August 31, 1778, Washington spelled Kosciuszko's name as Cosclusko. In the same sentence Washington spelled Duportail, another French officer in the Continental Army, as Portail. In another letter to Henry Laurens, dated November 10, 1777, Washington spelled Kosciusko as Cosieki.

19. General Washington to John Hancock. Letter dated "Head Quarters Morris town 20th Feby 1777" in Abbot, *Papers of George Washington*, vol. 8, 382.

20. Abbot, *The Papers of George Washington, Revolutionary War Series*, vol. 8, 378.

21. General Washington to Benjamin Harrison. Letter dated "Neshamony Bridge [Pennsylvania] August 19th, 1777" in Abbot, *The Papers of George Washington, Revolutionary War Series*, vol. 11, 4.

22. General Washington to Gouverneur Morris. Letter dated "White Plains July 24th 1778" in Abbot, *The Papers of George Washington, Revolutionary War Series*, vol. 16, 153–54.

23. General Washington to John Hancock. Letter dated "Head Qrs Heights of Harlem Octor the 7th 1776" in Abbot, *The Papers of George Washington, Revolutionary War Series*, vol. 6, 499.

24. General Washington to John Hancock. Letter dated "Head-Quarters Morris town 11th Feby 1777" in Abbot, *The Papers of George Washington, Revolutionary War Series*, vol. 8, 305.

25. Washington used this phrase in an order dated "Morristown, 4 February 1777" to Nathaniel Sackett to spy on the British. See Abbot, *The Papers of George Washington, Revolutionary War Series*, vol. 8, 242–43.

26. Hamilton's report is dated "Fredericksburg, New York, November 25, 1778" in Syrett, *Papers of Alexander Hamilton*. vol. 1, 588. Fredericksburg is in the lower Hudson River Valley. The Continental Army was camped there in November 1778.

27. Mrs. Mercy Otis Warren, "History of the Rise, Progress and Termination of the American Revolution," 3 vols. (Boston: E. Larkin, 1805), vol. 1, 370. Mrs. Warren wrote one of the first complete histories of the American Revolution. Her history was also one of the first books to be authored by an American woman. As an ardent patriot and the wife of the Revolutionary War governor of Massachusetts, she gained an introduction to many of the great American political and military leaders of the war. Early histories of the Revolution, like Mrs. Warren's, are neglected by modern historians. However, they are important sources because the authors were frequently passionate eyewitnesses to the rebellion. They are also surprisingly accurate because they substituted scholarly research with their own recollections and interviews with the men and woman who participated in the war.

28. Captain Friedrich von Muenchhausen, *At General Howe's Side 1776–1778* (Monmouth Beach, NJ: Philip Freneau Press, 1974), 21. Fort Ticonderoga was seized by Burgoyne's army on July 6, 1777.

29. Syrett, *Papers of Alexander Hamilton*, vol. 1, 321.

30. Major Samuel Shaw, *The Journals of Major Samuel Shaw* (Boston: Wm. Crosby and H.P. Nichols, 1847), 34–36. Samuel Shaw (1754–1794) is one of the obscure, but fascinating, people who make delving into history so interesting. He was born in Boston and was the son of a prominent merchant. Shaw was working in a counting house when the Revolution began. He was commissioned a lieutenant in Henry Knox's Continental Artillery Regiment in December 1775. Shaw fought in the Battles of Trenton, Princeton, Brandywine, Germantown, and Monmouth. He was appointed an aide to General Henry Knox in 1779 with the brevet rank of major. Major Shaw helped Knox organize the Society of the Cincinnati, a fraternal organization of officers who served in the war. Shaw was penniless when the Revolution ended and he signed on as the supercargo on the *Empress of China*, the first American ship to engage in trade with China. He returned home with a valuable cargo of tea, silk, and porcelain chinaware. Shaw was subsequently appointed the first American consul in Canton in 1786. As president, Washington renewed his appointment. Shaw contracted a liver disease while returning home from one of his voyages from China. He died on May 30, 1794, and was buried at sea. Shaw brought to China an original sketch of the eagle symbol of the Society of the Cincinnati from which sets of china dishes were made. Washington purchased a set from Shaw for $150. The dishes can be seen today at Mount Vernon. Shaw also had large beautiful punch bowls made in China with the eagle symbol of the Cincinnati. Two have survived: one is in the collection of the Morristown National Historical Park and the other is in the Metropolitan Museum of Art in New York City. The Chinese artist who created these bowls signed his name on the bottom, "Synchong."

31. Curtis Lewis led Howe's flanking column to the unguarded Jeffries Ford. In his postwar petition to the British Parliament asking for a pension, Lewis swore "on the arrival of the British Army at the head of Elk immediately joined them where from his knowledge of the County he rendered them essential Services by acting as a guide at the Battle of Brandywine." Captain Johann Ewald, a Hessian officer who was part of Howe's flanking column, noted in his diary that Lewis was a "veritable geographical chart . . . I was often amazed at the knowledge that this man possessed of the country." See Samuel S. Smith, *The Battle of Brandywine* (Monmouth Beach, NJ: Philip Freneau Press, 1976), 13.

32. Flexner, *The Young Hamilton*, 173.

33. Lieutenant Colonel Robert Hanson Harrison, technically Washington's military secretary, was not a well man. He frequently remained at headquarters during an arduous engagement with the enemy. Harrison wrote a report to John Hancock on the morning of the Battle of Brandywine. His letter is dated "Chads Ford, Sepr 11th 1777. ¾ after 8 OClock A.M." Its opening sentences read, "Sir, The Enemy are now advancing. Their present appearance indicates a disposition to pursue this Route (cross the Brandywine at Chad's Ford). If they do, I trust, they will meet with a suitable reception and such as will establish our Liberties." See Abbot, *The Papers of George Washington, Revolutionary War Series*, vol. 11, 195.

34. Smith, *The Battle of Brandywine*, 8.

35. Abbot, *The Papers of George Washington, Revolutionary War Series*, vol. 11,196.

36. Thomas J. McGuire, *The Philadelphia Campaign*, 2 vols. (Mechanicsburg, PA: Stackpole Books, 2006), vol. 1, 191–92. It turned out that Major Spear had scouted the Great Valley Road in the early morning and hours before Howe's flanking column would use it to reach Jefferis' Ford. Spear's report did not arrive at Washington's headquarters until later in the day.

37. Abbot, *The Papers of George Washington, Revolutionary War Series*, vol. 11, 197.

38. John Ferling, *Almost a Miracle* (New York: Oxford University Press, 2007), 247.

39. Flexner, *The Young Hamilton*, 175.

40. Philip M. Hamer et al., ed., *The Papers of Henry Laurens*, 16 vols. (Columbia: University of South Carolina Press, 1968–1990), Vol. 11, 428.

41. Syrett, *Papers of Alexander Hamilton*, vol. 1, 34.

42. Michael Harris, *Brandywine: A Military History of the Battle* (New York: Savis-Beatie, 2014), 434.

43. "Extract from a letter that accompanied a memoir sent from Philadelphia about the 12th of September 1777" by Charles-Francois Chevalier du Buysson in Stanley J Idzerda, ed., *Lafayette in the Age of the American Revolution*, 5 vols. (Ithaca, NY: Cornell University Press, 1977–1983), vol. 1, 84.

44. Syrett, *Papers of Alexander Hamilton*, vol. 3,192.

45. Smith, *Letters of Delegates to Congress*, vol. 7, 649.

46. Syrett., *Papers of Alexander Hamilton*, vol. 1, 326.

47. Worthington Chauncey Ford, ed. *Journals of the Continental Congress, 1774-1789*, 23 vols. (Washington, DC: Government Printing Office, 1904–1914), vol. 8, 754. The journal entry for Thursday, September 18, 1777, read, "Adjourned to 10 o' Clock to Morrow. During the adjournment, the president [John Hancock] received a letter from Colonel Hamilton, one of General Washington's aides, which intimated the necessity of Congress removing immediately from Philadelphia. Whereupon the members left the city, and agreeable to the resolve of the 14, repaired to Lancaster."

48. Smith, *Letters of Delegates to Congress*, vol. 8, 3.

49. Smith, *Letters of Delegates to Congress*, vol. 8, 8.

50. Robert Francis Seybolt, *A Contemporary British Account of General Sir William Howe's Military Operations in 1777* (Worcester, MA: Published by the American Antiquarian Society, 1931), 17.

51. Henry Lee, *Memoirs of the War in the Southern Department of the United States*, 2 vols. (Philadelphia: Bradford and Inskeep, 1812), vol. 1, 29. Henry Lee (1756–1818) is probably best known as the father of Civil War General Robert E. Lee. Henry Lee had a full and impressive life. He graduated from today's Princeton University in 1773. Nicknamed "Light Horse Harry," he served throughout the American Revolution as a light dragoon officer. Following the war Lee served as the ninth governor of Virginia and a Virginia delegate to the US House of Representatives. George Washington appointed him a major general in the US Army in 1798 in anticipation

for a war with France. Lee famously eulogized Washington at the president's funeral as "first in war, first in peace, and first in the hearts of his countrymen."

52. Flexner, *The Young Hamilton*, 187.

53. Abbot, *The Papers of George Washington, Revolutionary War Series*, vol. 11, 410. There is a scene in the movie *The Patriot* based on this incident.

54. Robert K Wright, *The Continental Army* (Washington, DC: U.S. Government Printing Office, 1983), 98–99. The same resolutions from Congress, dated December 27, 1776, also promoted Henry Knox to a brigadier general of the artillery.

55. Letter from William Livingston to George Washington dated "Haddonfield [New Jersey] 15ᵗʰ February 1777" in Abbot, *The Papers of George Washington, Revolutionary War Series* vol. 8, 344.

56. Abbot, *The Papers of George Washington, Revolutionary War Series*, vol. 10, 131.

57. Abbot, *The Papers of George Washington, Revolutionary War Series*, vol. 10, 343–44.

58. Matthew L. Davis, *Memoirs of Aaron Burr*, 2 vols. (New York: Harper & Brothers, 1836–1837), vol. 1, 112.

59. Charles Burdett, *The Beautiful Spy* (Philadelphia: John E. Potter, 1865), 410.

60. Davis, *Memoirs of Aaron Burr*, vol. 1, 113.

61. "Alexander Dow's Account of a 1777 Skirmish," John U. Rees, revar75.com/library/rees/dow.htm.

62. Howard H. Peckham, *The Toll of Independence* (Chicago: The University of Chicago Press, 1974), 40.

63. Parton, *The Life and Times of Aaron Burr*, 2 vols. (New York: Mason Brothers, 1864), vol. 1, 103.

CHAPTER NINE: VALLEY FORGE

1. General Johann Kalb quoted in Douglas Southall Freeman, *George Washington*, 7 vols. (New York: Charles Scribner's Sons, 1948–1957), vol. 4, 565. Kalb (1721–1780) is best known in American history as Baron de Kalb. He was a French officer who came to America with Lafayette and was appointed a major general in the Continental Army by Congress in September 1777. DeKalb was killed in the Battle of Camden (August 10, 1780). There are nine cities or town and six counties in the United States named in his honor.

2. Colonel Jeduthan Baldwin (1732–1788) was the chief engineer of Gates' Northern Army. Kosciuszko was Baldwin's assistant. Thaddeus Kosciuszko was born in 1746 in Poland. He attended Warsaw's Royal Military College where he graduated in 1769 with the rank of captain. Kosciuszko continued his military studies in France, Germany, and England. He came to America in 1776 where he joined the Patriot cause. He was appointed an engineer in the Continental Army with the rank of colonel by the Continental Congress on October 18, 1776.

3. Matthew L. Davis, *Memoirs of Aaron Burr*, 2 vols. (New York: Harper & Brothers, 1836–1837), vol. 1, 119–20.

4. The story of the attempt to kill Burr appears in Parton, *The Life and Times of Aaron Burr*, 2 vols. (New York: Mason Brothers, 1864), vol. 1, 105–7.

5. Joseph Lee Boyle, *Writings from the Valley Forge Encampment of the Continental Army* (Bowie, MD: Heritage Books, Inc., 2000), 42.

6. W. W. Abbot et al., eds., *The Papers of George Washington, Revolutionary War Series*, 24 vols. to date (Charlottesville, VA: University Press of Virginia, 1985–), vol. 12, 60–61.

7. Harold C. Syrett, ed., *Papers of Alexander Hamilton* (New York: Columbia University Press, 1961–1987), vol. 1, 351–52.

8. Syrett, *Papers of Alexander Hamilton*, 357–58.

9. Gates accused Hamilton of reading his confidential correspondence when Hamilton was left alone in Gates' office during Hamilton's mission to Albany. See Arthur Lefkowitz, *George Washington's Indispensable Men* (Mechanicsburg, PA: Stackpole Books, 2003), 151.

10. Abbot, *The Papers of George Washington, Revolutionary War Series*, vol. 12, 577.

11. Syrett, *Papers of Alexander Hamilton*, vol. 1, 426.

12. Letter from historian Lee Boyle to author dated April 22, 1997. Mr. Boyle was the historian at Valley Forge National Historical Park at the time. See Lefkowitz, George Washington's Indispensable Men, 152-153 for more information about Lee Boyle's comments regarding the so-called Conway Cabal.

13. There were freed blacks and black slaves serving in the American Army when Washington arrived in Cambridge, Massachusetts, in July 1775. At first, he prohibited their serving but later reversed his decision due to the urgent need for men to serve. The American Army was integrated during the American Revolution with blacks accounting for about 5 percent of the troops. The army was segregated following the war and for almost the next two hundred years. The United States Armed Forces were integrated by President Harry Truman. He signed Executive Order on July 26, 1948, which abolished discrimination in the armed forces "on the basis of race, color, religion or national origin."

14. Letter from Alexander Hamilton to John Laurens dated "September 11, 1779" in Syrett, *Papers of Alexander Hamilton*, vol. 2, 166–67. Demosthenes was an Athenian statesman recognized as the greatest of the ancient Greek orators. Although Hamilton's comments were written over a year after Laurens first made his proposal to raise black troops, they are inserted at this point because they are a clear statement of Hamilton's support for recruiting blacks as well as Hamilton's realistic appraisal of the opposition to the idea.

15. Syrett, *Papers of Alexander Hamilton*, vol. 1, 428.

16. Syrett, *Papers of Alexander Hamilton*, vol. 1, 445–46.

17. Elias Boudinot, *Journal of Historic Recollections during the Revolutionary War* (Philadelphia: Frederick Bourquin, 1894), 49.

18. Friedrich Knapp, *The Life of Frederick William Von Steuben* (New York: Mason Brothers, 1859), 124.

19. Account by Joseph Clark in Abbot, *The Papers of George Washington, Revolutionary War Series*, vol. 15, 41.

20. Nancy Isenberg, *Fallen Founder* (New York: Viking Penguin, 2007), 62–63.

CHAPTER TEN: THE BATTLE OF MONMOUTH

1. Letter from Alexander Hamilton to Elias Boudinot dated "5 July 1778" in www.founder.archives.gov/documents/Hamilton. The text of the letter reads, "When we came to Hopewell Township, The General unluckily called a council of war, the result of which would have done honor to the most honorable society of midwives, and to them only. The purport was, that we should keep at a comfortable distance from the enemy, and keep up a vain parade of annoying them by detachment."

2. Michael Newton, *Alexander Hamilton, the Formative Years* (Phoenix, AZ: Eleftheria Publishing, 2015), 199.

3. A "Flying Army" is defined as "a strong body of horse and foot, commanded for the most part by a lieutenant-general, which is always in motion, both to cover its own garrisons, and to keep the army in continual alarm." See Captain George Smith, *An Universal Military Dictionary* (London: J. Millan, 1779), 11–12

4. *The Lee Papers*, 4 vols. (New York: The New York Historical Society, 1871–1874), vol. 2, 424.

5. *The Lee Papers*, vol. 3, 79.

6. *The Lee Papers*, vol. 3, 72.

7. Matthew L. Davis, *Memoirs of Aaron Burr*, 2 vols. (New York: Harper & Brothers, 1836–1837), vol. 1, 128.

8. Davis, *Memoirs of Aaron Burr*, vol. 1, 126.

9. *The Lee Papers*, vol.3, 67.

10. Davis, *Memoirs of Aaron Burr*, vol 1, 135.

11. Robert A Hendrickson, *Hamilton* (New York: Mason/Charter, 1976), 208.

CHAPTER ELEVEN:
AARON BURR'S FINEST COMMAND

1. Report from Connecticut militia captan James Morgan to headquarters dated "South Amboy [New Jersey] Jun 29th 1778 four oclock." New York's outer harbor is visible from South Amboy. See W. W. Abbot et al., eds., *The Papers of George Washington, Revolutionary War Series*, 24 vols. to date (Charlottesville, VA: University Press of Virginia, 1985–), vol. 15, 588.

2. William S. Baker, *Itinerary of General Washington* (Philadelphia: J. B. Lippincott Company, 1892), 136.

3. Matthew L. Davis, *Memoirs of Aaron Burr*, 2 vols. (New York: Harper & Brothers, 1836–1837), vol. 1, 129. Burr's instructions to gather information about the enemy's movements in New York came from General Lord Sterling on July 2, 1778. However, in his memoirs Burr stated that "he was immediately ordered by General Washington, through Lord Sterling, to repair to Elizabethtown, on highly important and confidential business." See Davis, *Memoirs of Aaron Burr*, 128–29.

4. Davis, *Memoirs of Aaron Burr*, vol. 1, 129.

5. Elias Boudinot was a prewar lawyer and land speculator. As the American Commissary of Prisoners, Boudinot's responsibilities included seeing that British and Hessian prisoners of war were securely confined and provided with food and other necessities. In addition, he was in charge of helping American prisoners held by the British. Boudinot also served as a New Jersey delegate to the Continental Congress.

6. Nathan Schachner, *Aaron Burr, A Biography* (New York: A. S. Barnes & Company, 1937), 59.

7. Davis, *Memoirs of Aaron Burr*, vol. 1, 122–23.

8. Charles H. Lesser, ed., *The Sinews of Independence, Monthly Strength Reports of the Continental Army* (Chicago: The University of Chicago Press, 1976), 77. Interestingly, the same Return lists a Connecticut militia regiment also stationed at West Point. It was commanded by Roger Enos. He was second in command of the 1775 Arnold expedition. Enos turned back with his detachment during the campaign when he realized that they were far from Quebec and running out of food.

9. Davis, *Memoirs of Aaron Burr*, vol. 1, 131.

10. Burr's order to escort the Loyalists to New York City was written by General Washington's military secretary Robert Hanson Harrison on August 1, 1778. See Abbot, *The Papers of George Washington, Revolutionary War Series*, vol. 16, 349, n2.

11. Davis, *Memoirs of Aaron Burr*, vol. 1, 131.

12. Barnet Schecter, *The Battle for New York* (New York: Penguin Books, 2003), 318. Surprisingly, Schecter's otherwise authoritative account of this event incorrectly identifies Burr as an aide to Washington.

13. An example of Mrs. Prevost acting as an American spy is in Nancy Isenberg, *Fallen Founder* (New York: Viking Penguin, 2007), 67. The pertinent text reads, "Theodosia and her female relatives had proved that they could be extremely helpful in gathering intelligence in the British occupied city."

14. Worthington Chauncey Ford, "Some Papers of Aaron Burr." Proceedings of the American Antiquarian Society, New Series, vol. 29, April 9, 1919–October 15, 1919 (Worcester, MA: Published by the Society, 1919), 79.

15. Francis B. Heitman, *Historical Register of Officers of the Continental Army* (Washington, DC: The Rare Book Shop Publishing Company, 1914), 575.

16. Davis, *Memoirs of Aaron Burr*, vol. 1, 138.

17. General Washington resided in the Hermitage and used it as his headquarters at the invitation of Mrs. Prevost. Her invitation to the general is dated July 10, 1778, and reads, *"Mrs. Prevost Presents her best respects to his Excellency Genl Washington—requests the Honour of his Companyas She flatters herself the accommodations will be more Commodious than those to be procured in the Neighbourhood [sic]. Mrs. Prevost will be particularly happy to make her House Agreeable to His Excellent, and [military] family."* See Abbot, *The Papers of George Washington, Revolutionary War Series*, vol. 16, 47.

18. Worthington Chauncey Ford, "Some Papers of Aaron Burr." Proceedings of the American Antiquarian Society, New Series, vol. 29, April 9, 1919–October 15, 1919 (Worcester, MA: Published by the Society, 1919), 83.

19. Milton Lomask, *Aaron Burr: The Years from Princeton to Vice President 1756–1805* (New York: Farrar, Straus & Giroux, 1979), 68.

20. Part of the confusing regarding which side the Skinners and the Cowboys supported comes from James Fenimore Cooper's book *The Spy: a Tale of the Neutral Ground* (1821). Cooper has General Cortland Skinners regiment aligned with the Continental Army.

21. Charles M. Lefferts, *Uniforms of the American, British, French, and German Armies in the War of the American Revolution* (New York: The New York Historical Society, 1926), 216.

22. Lesser, *The Sinews of Independence*, 104.

23. James Thacher, *Military Journal of the American Revolution* (Hartford, CT: Hurlbut, Williams & Company, 1862), 238.

24. Davis, *Memoirs of Aaron Burr*, vol. 1, 139.

25. Samuel Young to Commodore Valentine Morris. Letter dated "Mount Pleasant [Westchester], 25th January, 1814" in Davis, *Memoirs of Aaron Burr*, vol. 1, 158–66.

26. Charles Burdett, *The Beautiful Spy* (Philadelphia: John E. Potter, 1865), 406–7.

27. Abbot, *The Papers of George Washington, Revolutionary War Series*, vol. 19, 429.

28. Davis, *Memoirs of Aaron Burr*, vol. 1, 168.

29. Arcadia Zahn, "Aaron Burr and William Hull." *Rye Record Newspaper*, July 12, 2018, edition.

30. Francis B. Heitman, *Historical Register of Officers of the Continental Army* (Washington, DC: The Rare Book Shop Publishing Company, 1914), 540–41.

31. Arthur Lefkowitz, *Benedict Arnold in the Company of Heroes* (Eldorado Hills, CA: Savas Beatie, 2012), 175.

32. Davis, *Memoirs of Aaron Burr*, vol. 1, 166.

33. Lomask, *Aaron Burr*, 71.

34. Joanne B. Freeman, *Affairs of Honor* (New Haven, CT: Yale University Press, 2001), 203.

35. Davis, *Memoirs of Aaron Burr*, vol. 1, 167.

36. Mary-Jo Kline, ed. *Political Correspondence and Public Papers of Aaron Burr*. 2 vols (Princeton, NJ: Princeton University Press, 1983), vol. 1, lxvi.

37. Kline, *Political Correspondence*, vol. 1, lxvi.

CHAPTER TWELVE:
ALEXANDER HAMILTON PREVAILS

1. Fred Anderson Berg, *Encyclopedia of Continental Army Units* (Harrisburg, PA: Stackpole Books, 1972), 48.

2. Harold C. Syrett, ed., *Papers of Alexander Hamilton* (New York: Columbia University Press, 1961–1987), vol. 2, 441.

3. Matthew L. Davis, *Memoirs of Aaron Burr*, 2 vols. (New York: Harper & Brothers, 1836–1837), vol. 1, 219–20.

4. Mark Jacob and Stephen H. Case, *Treacherous Beauty*. (Guilford, CT: Lyons Press, 2012), 170–71.

5. Syrett, *Papers of Alexander Hamilton*, vol. 2, 255.

6. Syrett,*Papers of Alexander Hamilton*, vol. 2. Hamilton's letter to Philip Schuyler is on pp. 563–68. His letter to James McHenry, who was an aide-de-camp to Lafayette at the time, is on p. 569.

7. Fitzpatrick, John C. *The Spirit of the Revolution* (Boston: Houghton Mifflin Company, 1924), 81.

8. Syrett, *Papers of Alexander Hamilton*, vol. 2, 567.

9. Syrett, *Papers of Alexander Hamilton*, vol. 2, 658.

10. Broadus Mitchell, *Alexander Hamilton, Youth to Maturity 1755–1788*. (New York: Macmillan, 1957), 250–51.

11. Henry B. Carrington, *Battles of the American Revolution* (New York: A. S. Barnes & Company, 1876), 638.

12. Mitchell, *Alexander Hamilton*, 257.

13. Lieutenant Colonel Hamilton's account of the attack on Redoubt Ten. Dated "Camp before Yorktown, Virginia, October 15, 1781" in Syrett, *Papers of Alexander Hamilton*, vol. 2, 679.

14. Brendan Morrissey, *Yorktown 1781* (Oxford: Osprey Publishing, 1997), 71.

15. James Thomas Flexner, *The Young Hamilton* (New York: Little Brown and Company, 1978), 363.

16. Mitchell, *Alexander Hamilton*, 249.

17. Syrett, *Papers of Alexander Hamilton*, vol. 2, 676.

18. Davis, *Memoirs of Aaron Burr*, vol. 1, 243.

19. Caroline Cox, *A Proper Sense of Honor, Service and Sacrifice in George Washington's Army* (Chapel Hill: The University of North Carolina Press, 2004), 28.

CHAPTER THIRTEEN:
THE NEW MEN OF NEW YORK

1. Harold C. Syrett, ed., *Papers of Alexander Hamilton* (New York: Columbia University Press, 1961–1987), vol. 3, 129.

2. The Maryland Constitution of 1776 specified that the state's highest court would be called the Court of Appeals instead of the customary State Supreme Court. Also, the jurists on the Maryland Court of Appeals are called judges not justices. Interestingly, unlike other American federal, state, and local courts, the judges on the Maryland Court of Appeals follow the British tradition of wearing red robes with white cross-collars instead of customary black robes. Harrison's high standing in Maryland is evident from his appointment, which specifies that the Court of Appeals "be composed of persons of integrity and sound judgement in the law, whose judgement shall be final and conclusive in all cases of appeal."

3. Syrett, *Papers of Alexander Hamilton*, vol. 2, 584.

4. Alexander Garden, *Anecdotes of the Revolutionary War* (Charleston, SC: A. B. Miller, 1822), 86. Alexander Garden is sometimes confused with his father who had the same name. His father was an eminent physician and botanist. The gardenia was named in his honor.

5. Ron Chernow, *Alexander Hamilton* (New York: Penguin, 2004), 121.

6. Syrett, *Papers of Alexander Hamilton*, vol. 3, 183–84.

7. Paul H. Smith, ed., *Letters of Delegates to Congress, 1774-1789*. 27 vols. (Washington, DC: Library of Congress), vol. 21, 135.

8. Speech by Aaron Burr during the debate on proposed amendments to the US Constitution in the Legislature of New York, House of Assembly, January 8, 1799, in Mary-Jo Kline, ed. *Political Correspondence and Public Papers of Aaron Burr*. 2 vols (Princeton, NJ: Princeton University Press, 1983), vol. 1, 367.

9. Nancy Isenberg, *Fallen Founder* (New York: Viking Penguin, 2007), 413.

10. John C. Fitzpatrick, ed. *The Writings of George Washington*. 39 vols. (Washington, DC: United States Government Printing Office, 1931–1944), vol. 28, 65.

11. Transcript of the First Annual Message to Congress, January 8, 1790, in www.millercenter.org/the presidency/presidential-speeches.

12. Syrett, *Papers of Alexander Hamilton*, vol. 10, 230.

13. James A. Huston, *Logistics of Liberty, American Services of Supply in the Revolutionary War and After* (Newark: University of Delaware Press, 1991), 298.

14. The correct name for Jefferson's political party is confusing. The noted historian and author John Ferling explained the history of the party as follows. In one of those essays that Jefferson got James Madison to write in the early 1790s, Madison used the term "Republican party." Party was in lower case but readers picked up on it and the faction that Jefferson and Madison had been trying to put together to oppose Hamilton's faction soon was called the Republican Party. Late in the decade, as the party unabashedly endorsed democracy, people began to call it the Democratic-Republican Party. After Jefferson's election, it just became the Democratic Party (email to the author).

15. There is a delightful poem that best describes the political differences between Jefferson and Hamilton. Titled "Penny for your Thoughts" it was written by Rosemary and Stephen Vincent Benet. The poem appeared in *A Book of Americans*,

which was published in 1933 with stories for children about important people in American history:

> Jefferson said, "The Many!"
> Hamilton said, "The Few!"
> Like opposite sides of a penny
> Were these exalted two.
> Hamilton liked the courtly,
> Jefferson liked the plain,
> They'd bow for a while, but shortly
> The fight would break out again.
> H. was the stripling colonel
> That Washington loved and knew,
> A man of mark with a burning spark
> Before he was twenty-two
> He came from the warm Antilles
> Where the love and the hate last long,
> And he thought most people sillies
> Who should be ruled by the strong.

16. Article II of the Constitution states "No person except a natural born Citizen, or a Citizen of the United States, at the time of the Adoption of this Constitution, shall be eligible to the Office of President." Hamilton was a citizen of the United States when the Constitution was adopted.

17. Thomas Fleming, *Duel* (New York: Basic Books, 2000), 317.

18. Alexander Hamilton to Robert Troup. Letter dated April 13, 1795, in Syrett, *Papers of Alexander Hamilton*, vol. 19, 329.

19. Isenberg, *Fallen Founder*, 144.

20. Theodore Sedgwick to Alexander Hamilton, January 10, 1801, in Syrett, *Papers of Alexander Hamilton*, vol. 25, 311–12.

21. This problem in the electoral college was corrected by the Twelfth Amendment to the Constitution. Adopted in 1804, the amendment requires each member of the electoral college to cast one of their votes for president and one for vice president.

22. Burr biographer James Parton eloquently describes this moment in Burr's political career, "We behalf our hero now upon the summit of his career....ten years after becoming known in national politics, he stands one step below the highest place to which by politics a man can rise."

23. Lomask, *Aaron Burr, The Conspiracy and Years of Exile* (New York: Farrar-Straus-Giroux, 1982), 297–98.

24. Julian Boyd et al., ed., "Notes on a Conversation with Aaron Burr," on January 26, 1804, in *The Papers of Thomas Jefferson. Original Series*, 44 vols (Princeton, NJ: Princeton University Press, 1950–2019), vol. 42, 346.

CHAPTER FOURTEEN:
THE FATAL CONVERSATION IN ALBANY

1. Mary-Jo Kline, ed. *Political Correspondence and Public Papers of Aaron Burr.* 2 vols (Princeton, NJ: Princeton University Press, 1983), vol. 2, 877.

2. Alexander Hamilton to unknown recipient. Letter dated "Philadelphia, September 21, 1792," in Founders Online website, www.founders.archives.gov/documents/Hamilton/01-12-02-0309. 3.

3. Joseph Ellis, *Founding Brothers* (New York: Vintage Books, 2002),. 42.

4. Michael J. Drexler and Ed White, *The Traumatic Colonel* (New York: New York University Press, 2014), 141.

5. Alexander Hamilton was eligible to become president of the United States although he was foreign born. The Constitution states that "No person except a natural born citizen, or citizen of the United Sates at the time of the adoption of this Constitution, shall be eligible to the office of President." Hamilton was a citizen of the United States when the Constitution was adopted. He wrote in a letter dated February 21, 1795, to New York senator Rufus King, "Am I then more of an American than those who drew their first breath on American ground?"

6. Email correspondence with the author.

7. James N. Green, *Mathew Carey, Publisher and Patriot* (Philadelphia: The Library Company of Philadelphia, 1985), 5–6.

8. James Parton, *The Life and Times of Aaron Burr.* Two vols. (New York: Mason Brothers, 1864), vol. 2, 265.

9. Tom Miller, "The Lost Aaron Burr House–11 Reade Street." Daytonian in Manhattan, blog, February 6, 2017, http://daytoninmanhattan.blogspot.com/2017/02/the-lost-aaron-burr-house-11-reade.html.

10. Richmond, Virginia, was chosen as the location for Burr's treason trial because Blennerhassett Island, then part of Virginia, was considered "the scene" of Burr's conspiracy. See David McCullough, *The Pioneers* (New York: Simon & Schuster, 2019), 162.

11. Samuel H. Wandell, *Aaron Burr in Literature* (Port Washington, NY: 1936), 130.

12. David O. Stewart, *American Emperor, Aaron Burr's Challenge to Jefferson's America,* (New York: Simon & Schuster, 2011), 135. The Bastrop Tract lied between the modern towns of El Dorado, Arkansas, and Bastrop, Louisiana. The streams and marshes of the region drain into the nearby Ouachita (Washita) River. The Ouachita joins the Red River downstream, which flows into the Mississippi River.

13. R. Kent Newmyer, *John Marshall and the Heroic Age of the Supreme Court* (Baton Rouge: Louisiana State University Press, 2001), 181.

14. Parton, *e*, vol. 2, 319.

15. John Sedgwick, *War of Two, Alexander Hamilton, Aaron Burr, and the Duel that Stunned the Nation* (New York: Berkley Books, 2015), 400.

16. Henry Childs Merwin, *Aaron Burr* (Boston: Small, Maynard & Company, 1899), 27. The story also appears in Charles Burr Todd, *Life of Colonel Aaron Burr* (New York: S.W. Green, 1879), 84.

17. Victoria Johnson, *American Eden* (New York: Liveright Publishing Corporation, 2018), 277.

18. Milton Lomask, *Aaron Burr, The Conspiracy and Years of Exile* (New York: Farrar-Straus-Giroux, 1982), 398–99

19. Wadell. *Aaron Burr* (London: Kegan Paul, Trench, Trubner & Co. Ltd, 1936), 147.

CHAPTER 15: MY MOST IMPORTANT AIDE

1. "To John Adams from George Washington, 25 September 1798, Founders Online," National Archives, last modified June 13, 2018, http/founders.archives .gov/documents/Adams/99-02-02-3028.

2. "John Adams to Abigail Adams, 23 June 1775, Founder Online," National Archives. http/founders.archives.gov/documents/Adams/04-01-02-0153.

3. Joanne B. Freeman, *Affairs of Honor* (New Haven, CT: Yale University Press, 2001),106.

4. Freeman, *Affairs of Honor*, 105.

5. Freeman, *Affairs of Honor*, 106.

6. James Parton, *The Life and Times of Aaron Burr*. Two vols. (New York: Mason Brothers, 1864), vol. 2, 298.

7. Victoria Johnson, *American Eden* (New York: Liveright Publishing Corporation, 2018), 104. The comment appears in a letter that Adams wrote to Rush on November 11, 1806.

8. Gordon S. Wood, *Revolutionary Characters* (New York: The Penguin Press, 2006), 138.

9. "Return of the Continental and Virginia State Troops under the Immediate Command of His Excellency General Washington, September 26, 1781" in Charles H. Lesser, ed., *The Sinews of Independence, Monthly Strength Reports of the Continental Army* (Chicago: The University of Chicago Press, 1976), 208.

10. George Washington to John Adams, September 25, 1798, in *Papers of George Washington*, Digital Edition (Charlottesville: University of Virginia Press, Rotunda 2008).

11. John C. Fitzpatrick, ed., *The Writings of George Washington,* 39 vols (Washington, DC: U.S. Government Printing Office, 1931–1944), vol. 21, 377.

12. William B. Reed, *Life and Correspondence of Joseph Reed*. 2 vols. (Philadelphia: Lindsay and Blakiston, 1847), vol. 1, 231.

13. Fitzpatrick, *Writings of George Washington*, vol. 29, 101–2.

14. L. G. Shreve, *Tench Tilghman* (Centerville, MD: Tidewater Publishers, 1982), 199–200.

15. Fitzpatrick, *Writings of George Washington*, vol 27, 414–15.

16. July 5, 2018, email to the author from William M. Ferraro, Research Associate Profession and Senior Associate Editor of *Papers of George Washington*.

17. James Thomas Flexner, *The Young Hamilton* (New York: Little Brown and Company, 1978), 146.

18. Mary-Jo Kline, ed. *Political Correspondence and Public Papers of Aaron Burr*. 2 vols (Princeton, NJ: Princeton University Press, 1983), vol. 2, 1211.

19. Gordon S. Wood, *Revolutionary Characters* (New York: The Penguin Press, 2006), 130.

20. Burr letter to Louis-Andre Pichon, Secretary of the French Legation at Washington. Reported in Marshall Brown, *Wit and Humor of Bench and Bar* (Chicago: J. H. Flood & Company, 1899), 67.

21. Email exchange with the author.

22. The hotel on Staten Island, New York, where Burr spent the final months of his life is often identified as the Port Richmond Hotel. It originally was the home of a wealthy Staten Islander named David Mesereau. It was considered one of the most beautiful homes on the island. Mersereau's large and ornate house was sold in 1820 and converted to the fashionable Port Richmond Hotel. However, when Burr resided there it was still a beautiful hotel but had been renamed the Continental Hotel.

23. Loring McMillian, *The Port Richmond Hotel. The Staten Island Historian*. Vol. VII, Number 1, Serial Number 28. October 1944-December 1945, 27.

BIBLIOGRAPHY

MANUSCRIPTS AND UNPUBLISHED SOURCES

Benedict Arnold's Letter Book (copies of his letters) from the 1775 Arnold Expedition, Collection of the Maine Historical Society.

Manuscript notes of 1831 interview with Aaron Burr found in Benedict Arnold's Letter Book. Collection of the Maine Historical Society. Burr visited Portland, Maine to gift Arnold's Letter Book to the Historical Society.

Revolutionary War Pension and Land Bounty Records, National Archives

Reeve Family Papers, Box One Tapping and Sally [Burr] Reeve. Manuscript and Archives Division, Yale University, Sterling Memorial Library.

The Aaron Burr Papers, New York Historical Society.

PRIMARY SOURCES

Bangs, Lt. Isaac Edward, ed. *Journal of Lieutenant Isaac Bangs.* Cambridge, MA: John Wilson & Son, 1890.

Baule, Steven M. *British Army Officers Who Served in the American Revolution 1775-1783.* Westminster, MD: Heritage Books, Inc., 2008.

Boudinot, Elias. *Journal of Historic Recollections of American Events During the Revolutionary War.* Philadelphia: Frederick Bouriquin, 1894.

Boyle, Joseph Lee. *Writings from the Valley Forge Encampment of the Continental Army.* Bowie, MD: Heritage Books, Inc., 2000.

Burr, Aaron. Mary-Jo Kline et al., eds. *Political Correspondence and Public Papers of Aaron Burr.* 2 vols. Princeton, NJ: Princeton University Press, 1983.

Clark, William Bell, ed. *Naval Documents of the American Revolution.* 11 vols to date. Washington, D.C.: U.S. Government Printing Office, 1964-1996.

Force, Peter. *American Archives: Consisting of A Collection of Authentic Records, State Papers, Debates, And Letters and Other Notices of Publick Affairs, The Whole Forming a Documentary History of The Origin and Progress of The North American Colonies, Of The Causes And Accomplishment Of the American Revolution, And of The Constitution of Government For The United States To The Final Ratification Thereof.* 4th series, 6 vols; 5th series, 3 vols. Washington, D.C.: M. St. Clair Clarke and Peter Force, 1837-1853.

Ford, Worthington C. et al., eds. *Journals of the Continental Congress 1774-1789.* 34 vols. Washington, D.C.: United States Government Printing Office, 1904-1937.

Graydon, Alexander. John Stockton Littell, ed. *Alexander Graydon, Memoirs of His Own Time.* Philadelphia: Lindsay and Blakston, 1846.

Greene, General Nathanael. Showman, Richard K. et al., eds. *The Papers of General Nathanael Greene.* 13 vols. Chapel Hill: The University of North Carolina Press, 1976-2005.

Hamilton, Alexander. Syrett, Harold C. and Jacob E. Cooke. *The Papers of Alexander Hamilton.* 27 vols. New York: Columbia University Press, 1964-1981.

Henry, John Joseph. *An Accurate and Interesting Account of the Hardships and Sufferings of that Band of Heroes . . . in the Campaign Against Quebec.* Lancaster, PA: William Greer, 1812.

Jefferson, Thomas. Boyd, Julian et al., eds. *The Papers of Thomas Jefferson,* 44 vols. to date. Princeton, NJ: Princeton University Press, 1950-2019.

Kalm, Peter. *Travels Into North America Containing its Natural History and A Circumstantial Account of its Plantations and Agriculture in General.* 2 vols. London: Printed for T. Lowndes, 1772.

Kemble, Stephen. *Journals of Lieutenant Colonel Stephen Kemble.* 2 vols. New York: New York Historical Society, 1883-1884.

Lafayette, Marquis. Idzerda, Stanley J. et al., eds. *Lafayette in the American Revolution.* 5 vols. Ithaca, NY: Cornell University Press, 1977-1983.

Laurens, John. Hamer, Philip M. et al., eds. *The Papers of Henry Laurens.* 16 vols. Columbia: University of South Carolina Press, 1968-2003.

Lee, General Charles. *The Lee Papers.* 4 vols. New York: The New York Historical Society, 1871-1874.

Lee, Lieutenant-Colonel Henry. *Memoirs of the War in the Southern Department of the United States.* 2 vols. Philadelphia: Bradford and Inskeep, 1812.

Lesser, Charles H., ed. *The Sinews of Independence; Monthly Strength Reports of the Continental Army.* Chicago: University of Chicago Press, 1976.

Martin, Joseph Plumb. *A Narrative of Some of the Adventures, Dangers and Sufferings of a Revolutionary War Soldier.* Hallowell, ME: Glazier, Masters and Company, 1830.

Moore, Frank. *Diary of the American Revolution from Newspapers and Original Documents.* 2 vols. New York: Privately Printed, 1865.

Muenchhausen, Captain Levin Frederick Ernst von. Ernst Kipping and Samuel Steele Smith, eds. *At General Howe's Side 1776-1778.* Monmouth Beach, NJ: Philip Freneau Press, 1974.

Reed, Joseph. Reed, William B. *Life and Correspondence of Joseph Reed.* 2 vols. Philadelphia: Lindsay and Blakiston, 1847.

Roberts, Kenneth. *March to Quebec, Journals of the Members of Arnold's Expedition Including the Lost Journal of John Pierce.* Garden City, NY: Doubleday & Company, Inc., 1940.

Robertson, Royal Engineer Archibald. Lydenberg, Harry Miller, ed. *Archibald Robertson, His Diaries and Sketches in America.* New York: New York Public Library, 1930.

Shaw, Major Samuel. *The Journals of Major Samuel Shaw.* Boston: Wm. Crosby and H.P. Nichols, 1847.

Smith, Paul H., ed. *Letters of Delegates to Congress 1774-1789.* 26 vols. Washington, D.C.: United States Government Printing Office, 1976-2000.

Tatum, Edward H., ed. *The American Journal of Ambrose Serle.* San Marino, CA. The Huntington Library, 1940.

Thacher, James. *Military Journal of the American Revolution.* Hartford, CT: Hurlbut, Williams & Company, 1862.

Washington, George. W.W. Abbot et al., eds. *The Papers of George Washington, Revolutionary War Series.* 27 vols. to date. Charlottesville: University of Virginia Press, 1985-2020.

Washington, George. Fitzpatrick, John C. et al., eds. *The Writings of George Washington.* 39 vols. Washington, D.C.: U.S. Government Printing Office, 1931-1944.

SECONDARY SOURCES

Bailyn, Bernard. *The Ideological Origins of the American Revolution.* Cambridge, MA: Harvard University Press, 1967.

Baker, William S. *Itinerary of General Washington.* Philadelphia: J.B. Lippincott Company, 1892.

Berg, Fred Anderson. *Encyclopedia of Continental Army Units.* Harrisburg, PA: Stackpole Books, 1972.

Blanco, Richard L., ed. *The American Revolution, 1775-1783.* 2 vols. New York: Garland Publishing, Inc. 1993.

Brown, Marshall. *Wit and Humor of Bench and Bar.* Chicago: J. H. Flood & Company, 1899.

Burdett, Charles. *Margaret Moncrieffe; The First Love of Aaron Burr.* New York: Derby & Jackson, 1860.

Burdett, Charles. *The Beautiful Spy.* Philadelphia: John E. Potter, 1865.

Carrington, Henry B. *Battles of the American Revolution.* New York: A.S. Barnes & Company, 1876.

Chernow, Ron. *Alexander Hamilton.* New York: The Penguin Press, 2004.

Commager, Henry Steele and Morris, Richard B. *The Spirit of Seventy-Six.* 2 vols. New York: The Bobbs-Merrill Company, Inc., 1958.

Cox, Caroline. *A Proper Sense of Honor, Service and Sacrifice in George Washington's Army*. Chapel Hill: The University of North Carolina Press, 2004.

Custis, George Washington Parke. *Recollections and Private Memoirs of Washington*. New York: Derby & Jackson, 1860.

Davis, Matthew L. *Memoirs of Aaron Burr with Miscellaneous Selections from his Correspondence.*2 vols. New York: Harper & Brothers, 1836-1837.

Drexler, Michael J. *The Traumatic Colonel: The Founding Fathers, Slavery, and the Phantasmatic Aaron Burr*. New York: New York University Press, 2014.

Ellis, Joseph. *Founding Brothers, The Revolutionary Generation*. New York: Vintage Books, 2002.

Ferling, John. *Almost a Miracle*. New York: Oxford University Press, 2007.

Fischer, David Hackett. *Washington's Crossing*. New York: Oxford University Press, 2003.

Fitzpatrick, John C. *The Spirit of the Revolution*. Boston: Houghton Mifflin Company, 1924.

Fleming, Thomas. *Duel, Alexander Hamilton, Aaron Burr and the Future of America*. New York: Basic Book, 1999.

Flexner, James Thomas. *The Young Hamilton: A Biography*. New York: Little, Brown and Company, 1978.

Freeman, Douglas Southall. *George Washington*. 7 vols. New York: Charles Scribner's Sons, 1948-1957.

Freeman, Joanne B. *Affairs of Honor: National Politics in the New Republic*. New Haven, CT: Yale University Press, 2001.

Garden, Alexander. *Anecdotes of the Revolutionary War*. Charleston, SC: A.B. Miller, 1822.

Green, James N. *Mathew Carey, Publisher and Patriot*. Philadelphia: The Library Company of Philadelphia, 1985.

Gruber, Ira D. *Books and the British Army in the Age of the American Revolution*. Chapel Hill: The University of North Carolina Press, 2010.

Hagist, Don H. *British Soldiers in the American War*. Yardley, PA: Westholme Publishing, 2012.

Harris, Michael. *Brandywine, A Military History of the Battle*. New York: Savas-Beatie, 2014.

Heitman, Francis B. *Historical Register of Officers of the Continental Army*. Washington, D.C.: The Rare Book Shop Publishing Company, 1914.

Hendrickson, Robert A. *Hamilton II (1789-1804)*. New York: Mason/Charter, 1976.

Hildreth, Samuel P. *Biographical and Historical Memoirs of the Early Pioneer Settles of Ohio*. Cincinnati, OH: H.W. Berby, 1852.

Hopson, Edwin Nott, Jr. *Captain Daniel Neil*. Paterson, NJ: Published by Braen Heuser Printing Company for the Captain Abraham Godwin Chapter, New Jersey Society, Sons of the American Revolution, 1927.

Hubbard, Robert Ernest. *Major General Israel Putnam Hero of the American Revolution.* Jefferson, NC: McFarland & Company, 2017.

Humphreys, David. *An Essay on the Life of the Honorable Major-General Israel Putnam.* Hartford, CT: Hudson and Goodwin, 1788.

Huston, James A. *Logistics of Liberty, American Services of Supply in the Revolutionary War and After.* Newark, Delaware: University of Delaware Press, 1991.

Irving, Washington. *Life of George Washington.* 5 vols. New York: G.P. Putnam & Co., 1856-1859.

Isenberg, Nancy. *Fallen Founder, The Life of Aaron Burr.* New York: Viking Penguin, 2007.

Jacob, Mark and Case, Stephen H. *Treacherous Beauty, Peggy Shippen, the Woman Behind Benedict Arnold's Plot.* Guilford, CT: Lyons Press, 2012.

Johnson, Henry P. *The Campaign of 1776 Around New York and Brooklyn.* Brooklyn, NY: The Long Island Historical Society, 1878.

Johnson, Victoria. *American Eden, David Hosack, Botany, and Medicine in the Garden of the Early Republic.* New York: Liveright Publishing Corporation, 2018.

Johnson, William. *Sketches of the Life and Correspondence of Nathanael Greene,* 2 vols. Charleston, SC: A.B. Miller, 1822.

Knapp, Friedrich. *The Life of Frederick William Von Steuben.* New York: Mason Brothers, 1859.

Knapp, Samuel L. *Life of Aaron Burr.* New York: Wiley & Long, 1835.

Lefferts, Charles M. *Uniforms of the American, British, French and German Armies in the War of the American Revolution.* New York: The New York Historical Society, 1926.

Lefkowitz, Arthur. *The Long Retreat: The Calamitous American Defense of New Jersey 1776.* Metuchen, NJ: The Upland Press, 1998.

Lefkowitz, Arthur. The *American Turtle Submarine: The Best Kept Secret of the American Revolution.* Gretna, LA: Pelican Publishing Company, 2012. Originally published as *Bushnell's Submarine,* 2006.

Lefkowitz, Arthur. *George Washington's Indispensable Men: The 32 Aides-de-Camp Who Helped Win American Independence.* Mechanicsburg, PA: Stackpole Books, 2003. Second edition, 2018.

Lefkowitz, Arthur. *Benedict Arnold's Army: The 1775 American Invasion of Canada During the American Revolution.* New York: Savas- Beatie, 2008. Second edition, 2017.

Lefkowitz, Arthur. *Benedict Arnold in the Company of Heroes.* California: Savas-Beatie, 2012.

Lender, Mark Edward and Stone, Garry Wheeler. *Fatal Sunday, George Washington, the Monmouth Campaign, and the Politics of Battle.* Norman, OK: University of Oklahoma Press, 2016.

Livingston, William Farrand, *Israel Putnam, Pioneer, Ranger, and Major-General.* New York: G. P. Putnam's Son, 1901.

Lomask, Milton. *Aaron Burr: The Years from Princeton to Vice President, 1756-1805.* New York: Farrar, Straus and Giroux, 1979.

Malone, Dumas. *Jefferson and the Ordeal of Liberty.* Boston: Little, Brown & Company, 1962.

Malone, Dumas. *Jefferson the President*, First Term. Boston: Little, Brown & Company, 1970.

Manders, Eric I. *The Battle of Long Island.* Monmouth Beach, NJ: Philip Freneau Press, 1978.

Mayer, Holly A. *Belonging to the Army: Camp Followers and Community During the American Revolution.* Charleston: University of South Carolina Press, 1996.

McCullough, David. *The Pioneers.* New York: Simon & Schuster, 2019.

McGuire, Thomas J. *The Philadelphia Campaign; Brandywine and the Fall of Philadelphia.* Mechanicsburg, PA: Stackpole Books, 2006.

McGuire, Thomas J. The Philadelphia Campaign; *Germantown and the Roads to Valley Forge.* Mechanicsburg, PA: Stackpole Books, 2007.

Merwin, Henry Childs. *Aaron Burr.* Boston: Small, Maynard & Company, 1899.

Miller, John C. *Alexander Hamilton: Portrait in Paradox.* New York: Harper & Brothers, 1959.

Misencik, Paul R. *The Original American Spies.* Jefferson, NC: McFarland and Company, Inc. 2014.

Mitchell, Broadus. *Alexander Hamilton, Youth to Maturity.* New York: Macmillan, 1957.

Newmyer, R. Kent. *John Marshall and the Heroic Age of the Supreme Court.* Baton Rouge: Louisiana State University Press, 2001.

Newton, Michael. *Alexander Hamilton, The Formative Years.* Phoenix, AZ: Eleftheria Publishing, 2015.

O'Shaughnessy, Andrew Jackson. *The Men Who Lost America.* New Haven, CT: Yale University Press, 2013.

Parmet, Herbert S., and Marie B. Hecht. *Aaron Burr: Portrait of an Ambitious Man.* New York: The Macmillan Company, 1967.

Parton, James. *The Life and Times of Aaron Burr, Lieutenant-Colonel in the Army of the Revolution, United States Senator, Vice-President of the United States, etc.* 2 vols. New York: Mason Brothers, 1860.

Peckham, Howard H. ed. *The Toll of Independence; Engagements & Battle Casualties of the American Revolution.* Chicago: The University of Chicago Press, 1974.

Peterson, Harold L. *Round Shot and Rammers.* New York: Bonanza Books, 1969.

Putnam, Eben. *A History of the Putnam Family in England and America.* Salem, MA: The Salem Press and Publishing Company, 1891.

Schachner, Nathan. *Aaron Burr, A Biography.* New York: A.S. Barnes & Company, 1937.

Schecter, Barnet. *The Battle for New York.* New York: Penguin Books, 2003.

Sedgwick, John. *War of Two, Alexander Hamilton, Aaron Burr and the Duel that Stunned the Nation.* New York: Berkley Books, 2015.

Seybolt, Robert Francis. *A Contemporary British Account of General Sir William Howe's Military Operations in 1777*. Worcester, MA: The American Antiquarian Society, 1931.

Shelton, Hal T. *General Richard Montgomery and the American Revolution*. New York: New York University Press, 1994.

Shreve, L.G. *Tench Tilghman*. Centerville, MD: Tidewater Publishers, 1982.

Smith, Captain George. *An Universal Military Dictionary*. London: Printed for J. Millan, 1779.

Smith, Justin H. *Our Struggle for the Fourteenth Colony: Canada in the American Revolution*. 2 vols. New York: G.P. Putnam's Sons, 1907.

Smith, Justin H. *Arnold's March from Cambridge to Quebec*. New York: G.P. Putnam's Sons, 1903.

Smith, Samuel Steele. *The Battle of Brandywine*. Monmouth Beach, NJ: Philip Freneau Press, 1976.

Stanley, George F.G. *Canada Invaded, 1775-1776*. Toronto: Samuel Stevens Hakkert Ltd., 1973.

Steiner, Bernard C. *Life and Correspondence of James McHenry*. Cleveland, OH: The Barrows Brothers Company, 1907.

Stevenson, Roger. *Military Instructions for Officers Detached in the Field*. Philadelphia: R. Aitken, 1775.

Stewart, David O. *American Emperor, Aaron Burr's Challenge to Jefferson's America*. New York: Simon & Shuster, 2011.

Stryker, William S. *The Battles of Trenton and Princeton*. Boston: Houghton, Mifflin and Company, 1898.

Todd, Charles Burr. *Life of Colonel Aaron Burr*. New York: S.W. Green, 1879.

Unger, Harlow Giles. *Lafayette*. New York: John Wiley & Sons, 2002.

Wandell, Samuel H. *Aaron Burr in Literature*. London: Kegan Paul, Trench, Trubner & Co. Ltd., 1936.

Wandell, Samuel H., and Meade Minnigerode. *Aaron Burr*. 2 vols. New York: G.P. Putnam's Sons, 1925.

Warren, Mrs. Mercy Otis. *History of the Rise, Progress and Termination of the American Revolution*. 3 vols. Boston: Printed by Manning and Loring, for E. Larkin, 1805.

Wood, Gordon S. *Revolutionary Characters: What Made the Founders Different*. New York: Penguin Publishing Group, 2006.

Wright, Robert K., Jr. *The Continental Army*. Washington, D.C.: Center of Military History, United States Army, 1980.

PERIODICALS, MONOGRAPHS AND WEBSITES

Clap, Caleb. *Diary of Ensign Caleb Clap*. The Historical Magazine, third series, vol. 111, August 1878.

Coln, Michael. *Report of Fortifications of New York During the Revolutionary War.* New York: New York City Archeological Group, 1962.

Ford, Worthington Chauncey. *Some Papers of Aaron Burr.* Proceedings of the American Antiquarian Society. New Series, vol. 29, April 1919—October 1919. Worcester, MA: Published by the American Antiquarian Society, 1919.

Burr, Aaron. Arron Burr Society website; www.aaronburrassociation.org.

Burr, Aaron. *Memories of Aaron Burr, The Miserable Old Age and Death of a Once Great Man.* Interview with Dr. Ephraim Clark. *New York Times*, Wednesday, May 31, 1878.

English, Robert L. *pension file R3354, Revolutionary War pension application*, 1839. Founders Online, National Archives and Record Administration, Washington, D.C., http://founders.archives.gov.

Houton, James A. *The Logistics of Arnold's March to Quebec.* Military Affairs, vol. 32, issue 3 (December 1968), pages 110-124.

Jumel, Eliza (Madame). *Obituary of Eliza B. (Madame) Jumel. New York Times*, July 18, 1865; www.nytimes.com/archives/obituary-madame-eliz-b-jumel.

Lapham, Lewis H. et al., eds. *Alexander Hamilton.* New York: *Lapham's Quarterly Magazine* Special Issue, undated.

McMillian, Loring. *The Port Richmond Hotel.* The Staten Island Historian. Vol. VII, Number 1, Serial Number 28. October 1944-December 1945.

Rees, John U. *Alexander Dow's Account of a 1777 Skirmish.* Revar75. Com/library/rees/dow.htm.

Storozynski, Alex. *The Fiasco of July 4, 1777: Misspelling of Kosciuszko's Name.* Huffington Post blog dated May 25, 2011.

Senter, Isaac. *The Journal of Isaac Senter, Physician and Surgeon to the Troops Detached from the American Army Encamped at Cambridge, Mass., on a Secret Expedition Against Quebec. Bulletin of the Historical Society of Pennsylvania*, vol. 1, no. 5 (1846).

The Lost Aaron Burr House. Article in www.daytoninmanhattanblogspot.com.

Thunder in New Jersey: Washington's Artillery During the Ten Crucial Days. American Battlefield Trust website. Battlefields.org/learn/articles/thunder-new-jersey.

Troup, Robert. *Robert Troup Narrative. William & Mary Quarterly*, 3rd Series, IV (1947).

Zahn, Arcadia. *Aaron Burr and William Hull. Rye* [New York] *Record* [newspaper]. July 12, 2018.

INDEX

splitting, 79–80. *See also* Patriot army
Continental Artillery Regiment, 70, 214n30
Continental Congress, xii, 16, 49; additional regiments authorized by, 120; Arnold, B., promoted by, 44; Baltimore move of, 86; Boudinot member of, 19; Canada situation assessed by, 204n10; Colburn, R., disputed by, 200n12; Continental Army controlled by, 18; French government contact with, 104–5; Hamilton, A., attack on, 128; Howe brothers meeting with, 67–68; Lafayette commissioned by, 113–14; officer commissions and, 104; Philadelphia fled by, 116, 216n47; powers given by, 46–47; Provincial, 36; Putnam, I., commissioned by, 55; surrender announcement delivered by, 158; Washington, G., writing to, 82–83
Conway, Thomas, 127
Conway Cabal, 127–28
Cooke, Nicholas, 83, 90
Cooper, Charles D., 175
Cooper, James Fenimore, 209n20, 220n20
Cornwallis, Earl, 81, 84, 131; British Army commanded by, 154–55; Patriot army escaping, 91; Philadelphia occupied by, 117; Yorktown surrender of, 149–50
Corps of Light Infantry, 154–56
Corps of Sappers and Miners, 156–57
Corsicans (Patriot militia company), 16
Coryell's Ferry, 134
council of war, 46, 75, 134–35
court-martial, of Lee, C., 139–40
covert techniques, 105–6
Cowboys (Loyalist), 145–46, 209n20
Crown forces. *See* British Army

Cruger, Nicholas, 13–14, 198n20
Custis, George Washington Parke, 74, 97, 138

Davis, Matthew L. ("Matthias"), x–xi, 66, 74, 183; Burr, A., and, 29, 206n17; Burr, A., biography by, x–xi, 54, 128, 138–39, 142, 148–49, 196n8, 206n17
Deane, Silas, 56, 78, 104–5, 113
Dearborn, Henry, 27
De Borre, Philippe-Hubert, Chevalier do Preudhomme, 114
deep attack, 200n9
De Lancey, James, 146–47
Democratic Party, 168, 170–72, 223n14
Demosthenes, 218n10
deserters, 210n1
De Visme, Catherine, 145, 149
discrimination, 218n9
Disqualifying Act, 158
docketed copy, 50
Dow, Alexander, 122
Duane, James, 102
Du Coudray, Philppe Tronson, 114
Duncan, Matthew, 42, 204n1

Eagle, HMS, 62, 66–67
economic policies, 168
education, 6, 14–15
Edwards, Jonathan, 7
Edwards, Ogden, 192
Edwards, Timothy ("uncle"), 7–8
electoral college, 224n21
Elizabeth (colonial town), 7–8, 15, 82, 141–42
Elizabethtown Academy, 8, 15, 155, 198n23
Ellison, William, 153
Emmons, Mary, 184
Empress of China (ship), 214n30
enemy drummer, 157